THE
DISCOURSES
OF EPICTETUS
and the
ENCHIRIDION

ROYAL

CLASSICS

Mailing address:
Royal Classics
PO BOX 4608
Main Station Terminal
349 West Georgia Street
Vancouver, BC
Canada, V6B 4A1

Cover design by: A.R. Roumanis

Text set in Minion Pro. Chapter headings
set in News Gothic Standard.

ISBN: 978-1-77437-853-3

FIRST EDITION / FIRST PRINTING

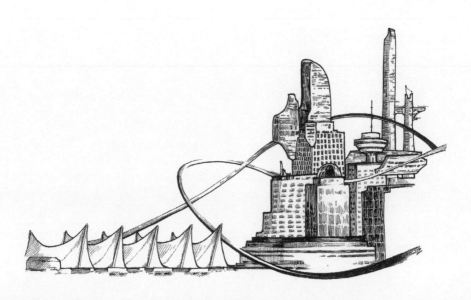

THE
DISCOURSES
OF EPICTETUS
and the
ENCHIRIDION

EPICTETUS

VANCOUVER:
ROYAL CLASSICS
2020

CONTENTS

Preface

I DID NOT WRITE down the Lectures of Epictetus in the form of a book, as one might do with such utterances as his, nor did I of my own will give them to the public, for, as I say, I did not write them down for publication. What I tried to do was to make notes of all that I used to hear him say word for word in the very language he used, so far as possible, and to preserve his sayings as reminders for myself hereafter of the nature of his mind and the directness of his speech. It follows then, as is natural, that the words are just such as a man might use to another on the impulse of the moment, not such as he would write for formal publication, with a view to a circle of readers hereafter. Moreover, such as they are, somehow or other they were put abroad among men without my consent and without my knowledge. Well, to me it is no great matter, if I appear in the world's eyes incapable of writing a book; and to Epictetus it will not matter in the least if men despise his lectures, for in the very act of giving them he made it plain that his one and only desire was to impel the minds of his hearers towards the noblest objects. If then these lectures should accomplish this result and no other, I take it they would be just what the lectures of philosophers ought to be; and if they fail, yet I would have those who read them understand that when Epictetus himself was speaking, his hearers were forced to feel just what he would have them feel. If the words read by themselves do not achieve this result, it may be that I am to blame, but it may be also that it could not be otherwise. Farewell.

Book One

CHAPTER ONE

On Things in our Power and Things not in our Power

OF OUR FACULTIES IN general you will find that none can take cognizance of itself; none therefore has the power to approve or disapprove its own action. Our grammatical faculty for instance: how far can that take cognizance? Only so far as to distinguish expression. Our musical faculty? Only so far as to distinguish tune. Does any one of these then take cognizance of itself? By no means. If you are writing to your friend, when you want to know what words to write grammar will tell you; but whether you should write to your friend or should not write grammar will not tell you. And in the same way music will tell you about tunes, but whether at this precise moment you should sing and play the lyre or should not sing nor play the lyre it will not tell you. What will tell you then? That faculty which takes cognizance of itself and of all things else. What is this? The reasoning faculty: for this alone of the faculties we have received is created to comprehend even its own nature; that is to say, what it is and what it can do, and with what precious qualities it has come to us, and to comprehend all other faculties as well. For what else is it that tells us that gold is a goodly thing? For the gold does not tell us. Clearly it is the faculty which can deal with our impressions. What else is it which distinguishes the faculties of music, grammar, and the rest, testing their uses and pointing out the due seasons for their use? It is reason and nothing else.

The gods then, as was but right, put in our hands the one blessing that is best of all and master of all, that and nothing else, the power to deal rightly with our impressions, but everything else they did not put in our hands. Was it that they would not? For my part I think that if they could have entrusted us with those other powers as well they would have done so, but they were quite unable. Prisoners on the earth and in an earthly body and among earthly companions, how was it possible that we should not be hindered from the attainment of these powers by these external fetters?

But what says Zeus? 'Epictetus, if it were possible I would have made your body and your possessions (those trifles that you prize) free and untrammelled. But as things are–never forget this–this body is not yours, it is but a clever mixture of clay. But since I could not make it free, I gave you a portion in our divinity, this faculty of impulse to act and not to act, of will to get and will to avoid, in a word the faculty which can turn impressions to right use. If you pay heed to this, and put your affairs in its keeping, you will never suffer let nor hindrance, you will not groan, you will blame no man, you will flatter none. What then? Does all this seem but little to you?'

Heaven forbid!

'Are you content then?'

So surely as I hope for the gods' favour.

But, as things are, though we have it in our power to pay heed to one thing and to devote ourselves to one, yet instead of this we prefer to pay heed to many things and to be bound fast to many–our body, our property, brother and friend, child and slave. Inasmuch then as we are bound fast to many things, we are burdened by them and dragged down. That is why, if the weather is bad for sailing, we sit distracted and keep looking continually and ask, 'What wind is blowing?' 'The north wind.' What have we to do with that? 'When will the west wind blow?' When it so chooses, good sir, or when Aeolus chooses. For God made Aeolus the master of the winds, not you. What follows? We must make the best of those things that are in our power, and take the rest as nature gives it. What do you mean by 'nature'? I mean, God's will.

'What? Am I to be beheaded now, and I alone?'

Why? Would you have had all beheaded, to give you consolation? Will you not stretch out your neck as Lateranus did in Rome when Nero ordered his beheadal? For he stretched out his neck and took the blow, and when the blow dealt him was too weak he shrank up a little and then stretched it out again. Nay more, on a previous occasion, when Nero's freedman Epaphroditus came to him and asked him the cause of his offence, he answered, 'If I want to say anything, I will say it to your master.'

What then must a man have ready to help him in such emergencies? Surely this: he must ask himself, 'What is mine, and what is not mine? What may I do, what may I not do?'

I must die. But must I die groaning? I must be imprisoned. But must I whine as well? I must suffer exile. Can any one then hinder me from going with a smile, and a good courage, and at peace?

'Tell the secret!'

I refuse to tell, for this is in my power.

'But I will chain you.'

What say you, fellow? Chain me? My leg you will chain–yes, but my will–no, not even Zeus can conquer that.

'I will imprison you.'

My bit of a body, you mean.

'I will behead you.'

Why? When did I ever tell you that I was the only man in the world that could not be beheaded?

These are the thoughts that those who pursue philosophy should ponder, these are the lessons they should write down day by day, in these they should exercise themselves.

Thrasea used to say 'I had rather be killed to-day than exiled to-morrow'. What then did Rufus say to him? 'If you choose it as the harder, what is the meaning of your foolish choice? If as the easier, who has given you the easier? Will you not study to be content with what is given you?'

It was in this spirit that Agrippinus used to say–do you know what? 'I will not stand in my own way!' News was brought him, 'Your trial is on in the Senate!' 'Good luck to it, but the fifth hour is come'–this was the hour when he used to take his exercise and have a cold bath–'let us go and take exercise.' When he had taken his exercise they came and told him, 'You are condemned.' 'Exile or death?' he asked. 'Exile.' 'And my property?' 'It is not confiscated.' 'Well then, let us go to Aricia and dine.'

Here you see the result of training as training should be, of the will to get and will to avoid, so disciplined that nothing can hinder or frustrate them. I must die, must I? If at once, then I am dying: if soon, I dine now, as it is time for dinner, and afterwards when the time comes I will die. And die how? As befits one who gives back what is not his own.

CHAPTER TWO

How One may be True to One's Character in Everything

To the rational creature that which is against reason is alone past bearing; the rational he can always bear. Blows are not by nature intolerable.

'What do you mean?'

Let me explain; the Lacedaemonians bear flogging, because they have learnt that it is in accord with reason.

'But is it not intolerable to hang oneself?'

At any rate, when a man comes to feel that it is rational, he goes and hangs himself at once. In a word, if we look to it we shall see that by nothing is the rational creature so distressed as by the irrational, and again to nothing so much attracted as to the rational.

But rational and irrational mean different things to different persons, just as good and evil, expedient and inexpedient, are different for different persons. That is the chief reason why we need education, that we may learn so to adjust our preconceptions of rational and irrational to particular conditions as to be in harmony with nature. But to decide what is rational and irrational we not only estimate the value of things external, but each one of us considers what is in keeping with his character. For one man thinks it reasonable to perform the meanest office for another; for he looks merely to this, that if he refuses he will be beaten and get no food, while if he does it nothing hard or painful will be done to him. To another it seems intolerable not only to do this service himself, but even to suffer another to do it. If then you ask me, 'Am I to do it or not?' I shall say to you, to get food is worth more than to go without it, and to be flogged is worth less than to escape flogging: therefore, if you measure your affairs by this standard, go and do it.

'But I shall be false to myself.'

That is for you to bring into the question, not for me. For it is you who know yourself; you know at how much you put your worth, and at what price you sell yourself. For different men sell at different prices.

That is why Agrippinus, when Florus was considering whether he should go down to Nero's shows, to perform some part in them himself, said to him, 'Go down.' And when he asked, 'Why do you not go down yourself?' said, 'Because I do not even consider the question.' For when a man once lowers himself to think about such matters, and to value external things and calculate about them he has almost forgotten his own character. What is it you ask me? 'Is death or life to be preferred?' I say 'life'. 'Pain or pleasure?' I say 'pleasure'.

'But, if I do not act in the tragedy, I shall be beheaded.'

Go then and act your tragedy, but I will not do so. You ask me, 'Why?' I answer, 'Because you count yourself to be but an ordinary thread in the tunic.' What follows then? You ought to think how you can be like other men, just as one thread does not wish to have something special to distinguish it from the rest: but I want to be the purple, that touch of brilliance which gives distinction and beauty to the rest. Why then do you say to me, 'Make yourself like unto the many?' If I do that, I shall no longer be the purple.

Priscus Helvidius too saw this, and acted on it. When Vespasian sent to him not to come into the Senate he answered, 'You can forbid me to be a senator; but as long as I am a senator I must come in.'

'Come in then,' he says, 'and be silent.'

'Question me not and I will be silent.'

'But I am bound to question you.'

'And I am bound to say what seems right to me.'

'But, if you say it, I shall kill you.'

'When did I tell you, that I was immortal? You will do your part, and I mine. It is yours to kill, mine to die without quailing: yours to banish, mine to go into exile without groaning.'

What good, you ask, did Priscus do, being but one? What good does the purple do to the garment? Just this, that being purple it gives distinction and stands out as a fine example to the rest. Another man, had Caesar in such circumstances told him not to come into the Senate, would have said, 'Thank you for sparing me.' Such a one he would never have forbidden to come in; he would know that he would either sit silent like a pipkin or if he spoke would say what he knew Caesar wished and pile on more besides.

This spirit too was shown by a certain athlete, who was threatened with death if he did not sacrifice his virility. When his brother, who was a philosopher, came to him and said, 'Brother, what will you do? Are we to let the knife do its work and still go into the gymnasium?' he would not consent, but endured to meet his death. (*Here some one asked*, 'How did he do so, as an athlete or as a philosopher?') He did so as a man, and a man who had wrestled at Olympia and been proclaimed victor, one who had passed his days in such a place as that, not one who anoints himself at Bato's. Another man would have consented to have even his head cut off, if he could have lived without it.

That is what I mean by keeping your character: such is its power with those who have acquired the habit of carrying it into every question that arises.

'Go to, Epictetus, have yourself shaved.'

If I am a philosopher I say, 'I will not be shaved.'

'I must behead you then.'

Behead me, if it is better for you so.

One asked, 'How then shall we discover, each of us, what suits his character?'

How does the bull, he answered, at the lion's approach, alone discover what powers he is endowed with, when he stands forth to protect the whole herd? It is plain that with the possession of his power the consciousness of it also is given him. So each of us, who has power of this sort, will not be unaware of its possession. Like the bull, the man of noble nature does not become noble of a sudden; he must train through the winter, and make ready, and not lightly leap to meet things that concern him not.

Of one thing beware, O man; see what is the price at which you sell your will. If you do nothing else, do not sell your will cheap. The great, heroic style, it may be, belongs to others, to Socrates and men like him.

'If then this is our true nature, why do not all men, or many, show it?'

What? Do all horses turn out swift, are all dogs good at the scent?

'What am I to do then? Since I have no natural gifts, am I to make no effort for that reason?'

Heaven forbid. Epictetus is not better than Socrates: if only he is as good as Socrates I am content. For I shall never be a Milo, yet I do not neglect my body; nor a Croesus, and yet I do not neglect my property; nor, in a word, do we abandon our effort in any field because we despair of the first place.

CHAPTER THREE

What Conclusions may be Drawn from the Fact that God is Father of Men

IF A MAN COULD only take to heart this judgement, as he ought, that we are all, before anything else, children of God and that God is the Father of gods and men, I think that he will never harbour a mean or ignoble thought about himself. Why, if Caesar adopts you, your arrogance will be past all bearing; but if you realize that you are a son of Zeus, will you feel no elation? We ought to be proud, but we are not; as there are these two elements mingled in our birth, the body which we share with the animals, and the reason and mind which we share with the gods, men in general decline upon that wretched and dead kinship with the beasts, and but few claim that which is divine and blessed.

And so, since every one, whoever he be, must needs deal with each person or thing according to the opinion that he holds about them, those few who think that they have been born to be faithful, born to be honourable, born to deal with their impressions without error, have no mean or ignoble thought about themselves. But the thoughts of most men are just the opposite to this. 'What am I? A miserable creature of a man'; and 'my wretched rags of flesh'. Wretched indeed, but you have too something better than your 'rags of flesh'. Why then do you discard the better and cling to your rags?

By reason of this lower kinship some of us fall away and become like wolves, faithless and treacherous and mischievous, others like lions, savage and brutal and untameable, but the greater part of us become foxes and the most god-forsaken creatures in the animal world. For a foul-mouthed and wicked man is no better than a fox or the meanest and most miserable of creatures. Look to it then and beware lest you turn out to be one of these god-forsaken creatures.

CHAPTER FOUR

On Progress, or Moral Advance

HOW SHALL WE DESCRIBE 'progress'? It is the state of him who having learnt from philosophers that man wills to get what is good, and wills to avoid what is evil, and having learnt also that peace and calm come to a man only if he fail not to get what he wills, and if he fall not into that which he avoids, has put away from him altogether the will to get anything and has postponed it to the future, and wills to avoid only such things as are dependent on his will. For if he tries to avoid anything beyond his will, he knows that, for all his avoidance, he will one day come to grief and be unhappy. And if this is the promise that virtue makes to us–the promise to produce happiness and peace and calm, surely progress toward virtue is progress toward each of these. For to whatever end the perfection of a thing leads, to that end is progress an approach.

How is it then that, though we admit that this is the nature of virtue, we search elsewhere for progress and display it elsewhere?

What does virtue produce?

Peace of mind.

Who then makes progress? Is it he who has read many treatises of Chrysippus? Can this be virtue–to have understood Chrysippus? For if this be so, we must admit that progress is nothing but to understand a lot of sayings of Chrysippus. But, the fact is, we admit that virtue tends to one result, and yet declare that progress, the approach to virtue, tends to another.

'Yonder man', he says, 'can already read Chrysippus by himself.'

Bravo, by the gods, you make progress, fellow. Progress indeed! Why do you mock him? Why do you draw him away from the sense of his own shortcomings? Will you not show him what virtue really means, that he may learn where to seek for progress? Miserable man, there is only one place to seek it–where your work lies. Where does it lie? It lies in the region of will; that you may not fail to get what you will to get, nor fall into what you will to avoid; it lies in avoiding error in the region of impulse, impulse to act and impulse not to act: it lies in assent and the withholding of assent, that in these you may never be deceived. But the first department I have named comes first and is most necessary. If you merely tremble and mourn and seek to escape misfortune, progress is of course impossible.

Show me your progress then in this field. You act as though when I was talking to an athlete and said, 'Show me your shoulders', he answered, 'Look at my leaping-weights.' That is for you and your leaping-weights to look to; I want to see the final result of your leaping-weights.

'Take the treatise on "Impulse" and learn how I have read it.'

Slave, that is not what I am looking for–I want to know what impulses you have, for action and against it, to know what you will to get and will to avoid; how you plan and purpose and prepare–whether in harmony with nature, or out of harmony with nature. Show me that you act in harmony with nature, and I will tell you that you are making progress; act out of harmony with nature, and I bid you begone and write books on such things and not merely expound them. What good, I ask, will they do you? Do not you know that the whole book is worth but five pence? Do you think then that the man who expounds it is worth more? Therefore never seek your work in one place and progress in another.

Where then is progress?

If any one of you, dismissing things without, has brought his mind to bear on his own will, to work out its full development, that he may bring it into perfect harmony with nature–lofty, free, unhindered, untrammelled, trustworthy, self-respecting; if he has learnt that he that wills to get or to avoid what is not in his power cannot be trustworthy nor free, but must needs himself change as they change, fitful as the winds, and must needs have made himself subservient to others, who can procure or hinder such things; and if, in a word, when he rises in the morning he guards and keeps these principles, washes as one that is trustworthy, eats as one that is self-respecting, and on each occasion that arises labours to achieve his main tasks, even as the runner makes running his one aim and the voice-trainer his training–he is the man who is indeed in the path of progress and who has not travelled to no purpose.

But if all his efforts are turned to the study of books, if on this he spends his labour, and for this has gone abroad, then I bid him go straight home and not neglect what he finds there; for this that he has gone abroad for is nothing; his true work is to study to remove from his life mourning and lamentation, the 'ah me' and 'alas for my misery', the talk of 'bad fortune' and 'misfortune'; and to learn, what is death, what is exile, what is imprisonment, what is the cup of hemlock; that he may be able to say in prison, 'My dear Crito, if it pleases the gods, so be it', and not such words as 'miserable old man that I am, is it for this I kept my grey hairs?' (Plato, *Crito*, 43d) Whose words are they? Do you think I shall name to you a mean man of no reputation? Are they not the words of Priam and of Oedipus? Are they not the words of all kings that are? For what else are tragedies but a portrayal in such metrical form of the sufferings of men who have set their admiration on outward things? If delusion after all were the only means for a man to learn this lesson– the lesson that not one of the things beyond the compass of our will concerns us, then I for my part would choose a delusion such as this, if it should procure me a life of undisturbed tranquillity; I leave it to you to see what you choose.

What then does Chrysippus offer us?

'That you may know', he says, 'that these truths from which tranquillity and peace of mind come to men are not false–take my books and you shall find that what gives me peace of mind is true and in harmony with nature.'

O great good fortune! O great benefactor, who shows us the way! And yet–though all men have raised temples and altars to Triptolemus, for teaching us the cultivation of the crops, yet what man of you ever set up an altar in honour of him who found the truth and brought it to light and published it among all men–not the truth of mere living, but the truth that leads to right living? Who ever dedicated a shrine or an image for this gift, or worships God for it? I say shall we, who offer sacrifices because the gods gave us wheat or the vine, never give thanks to God that they produced this manner of fruit in the mind of men, whereby they were to show us the true way of happiness?

CHAPTER FIVE

Against Followers of the Academy

IF A MAN, says Epictetus, objects to what is manifestly clear, it is not easy to find an argument against him, whereby one shall change his mind. And this is not because of his power, nor because of the weakness of him that is instructing him; but, when a man, worsted in argument, becomes hardened like a stone, how can one reason with him any more?

Now there are two ways in which a man may be thus hardened: one when his reasoning faculty is petrified, and the other when his moral sense is petrified, and he sets himself deliberately not to assent to manifest arguments, and not to abandon what conflicts with them. Now most of us fear the deadening of the body and would take all possible means to avoid such a calamity, yet we take no heed of the deadening of the mind and the spirit. When the mind itself is in such a state that a man can follow nothing and understand nothing, we do indeed think that he is in a bad condition; yet, if a man's sense of shame and self-respect is deadened, we even go so far as to call him 'a strong man'.

Do you comprehend that you are awake?

'No,' he says, 'no more than I comprehend it, when I seem to be awake in my dreams.'

Is there no difference then between the one sort of impression and the other?

'None.'

Can I argue with him any longer? What fire or sword, I say, am I to bring to bear on him, to prove that his mind is deadened? He has sensation and pretends that he has not; he is worse than the dead. One man does not see the battle; he is ill off. This other sees it but stirs not, nor advances; his state is still more wretched. His sense of shame and self-respect is cut out of him, and his reasoning faculty, though not cut away, is brutalized. Am I to call this 'strength'? Heaven forbid, unless I call it 'strength' in those who sin against nature, that makes them do and say in public whatever occurs to their fancy.

CHAPTER SIX

On Providence

EACH SINGLE THING THAT comes into being in the universe affords a ready ground for praising Providence, if one possesses these two qualities–a power to see clearly the circumstances of each, and the spirit of gratitude therewith. Without these, one man will fail to see the usefulness of nature's products and another though he see it will not give thanks for them. If God had created colours and, in general, all visible things, but had not created a faculty to behold them, of what use would they be? None at all. If on the other hand He had created this faculty, but had not created objects of such a nature as to fall under the faculty of vision, even so of what use would it be? None at all. If again He had created both these, and had not created light, even so there would be no use in them. Who is it then that has adapted this to that, and that to this? Who is it that has fitted the sword to the scabbard and the scabbard to the sword? Is there no one? Surely the very structure of such finished products leads us commonly to infer that they must be the work of some craftsman, and are not constructed at random. Are we to say then that each of these products points to the craftsman, but that things visible and vision and light do not? Do not male and female and the desire of union and the power to use the organs adapted for it–do not these point to the craftsman? But if these things are so, then the fact that the intellect is so framed that we are not merely the passive subjects of sensations, but select and subtract from them and add to them, and by this means construct particular objects, nay more, that we pass from them to others which are not in mere juxtaposition–I say are not these facts sufficient to rouse men's attention and to deter them from leaving out the craftsman? If it be not so, let them explain to us what it is which makes each of these things, or how it is possible that objects so marvellously designed should have come into being by chance and at random?

Again, are these faculties found in us alone? Many in us alone–faculties which the rational creature had special need of–but many you will find that we share with irrational creatures. Do they also then understand events and things? No–for using is one thing, and understanding is another. God had need of them as creatures dealing with impressions, and of us as dealing with them and understanding them as well. That is why it is enough for them to eat and drink and rest and breed, and every function is theirs which each irrational creature fulfils; while we, to whom He gave also the power of understanding, cannot be satisfied with these functions, but, unless we act with method and order and consistently with our respective natures and constitutions, we shall no longer attain to our end. For those whose constitutions are different have also different functions and different ends. Therefore that which by constitution is capable only of using things, is satisfied to use them anyhow; but that which by constitution is capable of understanding things as well as using them, will never attain its end, unless to use it adds method also. What is my conclusion? God makes one animal for eating, and another for service in farming, another to produce cheese, and others for different uses of a like nature, for which there is no need of understanding impressions and being able to distinguish them; but He brought man into the world to take cognizance of Himself and His works, and not only to take cognizance but also to interpret them. Therefore it is beneath man's dignity to begin and to end where the irrational creatures do: he must rather begin where they do and end where nature has ended in forming us; and nature ends in contemplation and understanding and a way of life in harmony with nature. See to it then that ye do not die without taking cognizance of these things.

You travel to Olympia, that you may see the work of Phidias, and each of you thinks it a misfortune to die without visiting these sights, and will you have no desire to behold and to comprehend those things for which there is no need of travel, in the presence of which you stand here and now, each one of you? Will you not realize then who you are and to what end you are born and what that is which you have received the power to see?

'Yes, but there are unpleasant and hard things in life.'

Are there none such at Olympia? Are you not scorched with heat? Are you not cramped for room? Is not washing difficult? Are you not wet through when it is wet? Do you not get your fill of noise and clamour and other annoyances? Yet I fancy that when you set against all these hardships the magnificence of the spectacle you bear them and put up with them. And have you not received faculties, which will enable you to bear all that happens to you? Have you not received greatness of spirit? Have you not received courage? Have you not received endurance? If I am of a great spirit what concern have I in what may happen? What shall shake me or confound me or seem painful to me? Instead of using my faculty for the purpose for which I have received it, am I to mourn and lament at the events of fortune?

'Yes, but my rheum flows.'

Slave! What have you hands for then? Is it not to wipe your rheum away?

'Is it reasonable then that there should be rheum in the world?'

Well, how much better it is to wipe your rheum away than to complain! What do you think would have become of Heracles if there had not been a lion, as in the story, and a hydra and a stag and a boar and unjust and brutal men, whom he drove forth and cleansed the world of them? What would he have done, if there had been nothing of this sort? Is it not plain that he would have wrapped himself up and slept? Nay to begin with he would never have been a Heracles at all, had he slumbered all this life in such ease and luxury; and if by any chance he had been, of what good would he have been? What use would he have made of his arms and his might and his endurance and noble heart as well, had not he been stimulated and trained by such perils and opportunities?

'Was it his duty then to contrive these occasions for himself and to seek means to bring a lion, a boar, or a hydra into his country?'

That were madness and folly; but as they had come into being and were found in the world these monsters were of service to display Heracles' powers and to train them.

It is for you then, when you realize this, to look to the faculties you possess, and considering them to say, 'Zeus, send me what trial Thou wilt; for I have endowments and resources, given me by Thee, to bring myself honour through what befalls.' Nay, instead, you sit trembling for fear of what may happen, or lamenting, mourning, and groaning for what does happen, and then you reproach the gods. What else but impiety indeed can attend upon so ignoble a spirit as yours? And yet God not only gave us these faculties, which will enable us to bear all the issue of events without being humiliated or broken down by it, but, as became a good king and a true father, He gave us this gift free from all let or hindrance or compulsion–nay,

He put it wholly in our hands, not even leaving Himself any power to let or hinder us. Yet possessing thesepowers in freedom for your own you refuse to use them and will not realize what gifts you have received and from whose hand, but you sit mourning and grieving, some of you blinded to the giver Himself and refusing to recognize your benefactor, and some from meanness of spirit turning to reproaches and complaints against God. Yet I will show you that you have resources and endowment to fit you for a noble and courageous spirit: show me, if you can, what endowments you have for complaining and reproach.

CHAPTER SEVEN

On the Use of Variable Premisses and Hypothetical Arguments and the Like

MOST MEN IGNORE THE fact that the treatment of variable premisses and hypothetical arguments and again of syllogisms that conclude by way of question, and, in a word, of all such arguments is concerned with conduct. For really, whatever subject we are dealing with, our aim is to find how the good man may fitly deal with it and fitly behave towards it. It follows then that either they must say that the virtuous man will not condescend to question and answer, or that if he does he will take no care to avoid behaving lightly and at random in questioning and answering; or else, if they accept neither alternative, they must admit that we have to investigate those subjects round which question and answer chiefly turn. For what do we promise in a discussion? To establish what is true, to remove what is false, to withhold assent in what is uncertain. Is it enough then merely to learn that this is so?

'It is enough.'

Is it enough then for him who wishes not to go wrong in the use of coin merely to be told why you accept genuine drachmas and reject spurious ones?

'It is not enough.'

What then must you acquire besides? Surely you must have a faculty to test and distinguish genuine drachmas from spurious. Is it not true . then in regard to argument also that merely to hear what is said is not enough; a man must acquire the faculty to test and distinguish the true from the false and the uncertain?

'It must be so.'

This being so, what is required in argument?

'Accept what follows from the premisses you have duly granted.'

Here again, is it enough merely to know this? No, you must learn how a conclusion follows from the premisses, and how sometimes one proposition follows from one other, and sometimes from many together. May we say then that this faculty too must be acquired by him who is to behave with good sense in discussion, and who is himself to prove each point in his demonstration and to follow the demonstrations of others, and to avoid being led astray by sophistical arguments, posing as demonstrations? Thus it comes about that we are led to think it really necessary to discuss and to practise the arguments and moods which are conclusive.

But note this: there are cases where we have granted the premisses properly, and such and such a conclusion follows which, though it follows, is none the less false. What then is it fitting for me to do? Must I accept the false conclusion? How can I do that? Must I say I was wrong in granting the premisses?

'No, you may not do this either.'

That it does not follow from the premisses granted?

'No, you may not do this.'

What then is one to do in these circumstances? May we not say that just as in order to be in debt it is not enough merely to borrow, but one must remain a borrower and not have paid off the loan, so in order to be bound to admit an inference it is not enough to have granted the premisses, but one must abide by having granted them?

In a word, if they remain to the end as we granted them, we are absolutely bound to remain by our concessions and accept what follows the premisses; if, on the other hand, they do not remain as they were granted, we are also absolutely bound to abandon the concession and no longer to accept what is inconsistent with the premisses; for since we have abandoned our agreement as to the premisses, this inference which is drawn no longer concerns us or touches us. We must then examine into premisses of this sort and into such changes and alterations in them, by which they are changed in the actual process of question or answer or syllogism or the like, and so afford occasion to the foolish to be troubled because they do not see the sequence of the argument. Why must we do so? That in this sphere we may do what is fitting by avoiding what is random or confused in argument.

And we ought to do the same with hypotheses and hypothetical arguments. For it is necessary sometimes to assume a hypothesis as a step to the next argument. Must we then concede every given hypothesis or not? And if not every one, which? And, having conceded it, must we abide by it once for all and maintain it, or are we sometimes to abandon it, and are we to accept what follows from it and reject what conflicts with it?

'Yes.'

But a man says, 'If you accept a hypothesis of what is possible, I will reduce you in argument to what is impossible.'

Will the prudent man refuse to meet him in argument, and avoid examination and discussion with him? Nay, it is just the prudent man who is capable of reasoning logically and who is expert at questioning and answering, yes and who is proof against deception and sophistry. Will he then consent to argue, but take no pains to avoid being careless and casual in argument? If so, will he not cease to be the man we consider him to be? But without some such training and preparation as I suggest can he guard the sequence of his argument? Let them show that he can, and then all these speculations are idle; they were absurd and inconsistent with the conception we have formed of the good man.

Why do we persist in being lazy and indolent and sluggish, why do we seek excuses to enable us to avoid toiling early and late to perfect ourselves in logical theory?

'Do you call it parricide if I go wrong in logic?'

Slave, here is no father for you to kill. You ask what you have done, you have committed the one error which was possible in this field. Your answer is the very one I made myself to Rufus when he rebuked me because I could not find the one missing step in a syllogism. 'Well,' said I, 'I suppose I have not burnt the Capitol down'; and he answered, 'Slave, the missing step here is the Capitol.'

You are not going to tell me, are you, that setting fire to the Capitol and killing one's father are the only forms of wrongdoing? To deal with one's impressions without thought or method, to fail to follow argument or demonstration or sophism, in a word, to be unable to see what concerns himself and what does not in question and answer–is there no wrongdoing, I ask, in any of these?

CHAPTER EIGHT

That Faculties are Fraught with Danger for the Uneducated

JUST AS IT IS possible to interchange terms which are equivalent to one another, so and in just as many ways it is allowable to vary in argument the types of disputative argument and enthymeme. Take for instance this kind of argument: 'If you borrowed and did not repay, you owe me the money. You did not borrow without repaying; therefore you do not owe me the money.' And the philosopher above all others is the proper person to handle such arguments with skill. For if enthymeme is imperfect syllogism, plainly he who is trained in perfect syllogism would be equally capable in dealing with imperfect.

Why then, you ask, do we not train ourselves and one another in this style of argument? Because even now, though we do not devote ourselves to training in these matters and though we are not drawn away, so far as I have any influence, from cultivating character, nevertheless we make no advance towards goodness. What should we have to expect then, if we should add this business to our other employments? And there is more–not only should we have less leisure for more necessary things, but we should give uncommon occasion for conceit and vanity. For the faculty of disputative and plausible reasoning is a powerful one, especially if it should be developed by training and gain further dignity from mastery of language. For indeed generally every faculty is dangerous when it comes into the hands of those who are without education and without real force, for it tends to exalt and puff them up. For how would it be possible to persuade the young man who excels in these arguments that he ought not to become dependent upon them, but to make them depend upon him? Instead of this he tramples under foot all we say to him and walks among us in a high state of elation, so puffed up that he cannot bear that any one should remind him how far he has fallen short and into what errors he has lapsed.

'What do you mean? Was not Plato a philosopher?'

I reply, Was not Hippocrates a physician? But you see how eloquent Hippocrates was. Was Hippocrates so eloquent by virtue of being a physician? Why then do you mix qualities, which are casually united in the same persons? Suppose Plato was handsome and strong; ought I also to set to and strive to become handsome or strong, as though this were necessary for philosophy, just because one philosopher was handsome as well? Will you not have the discernment to see what makes men philosophers and what qualities are accidental in them? Suppose now I were a philosopher, ought you to become lame?

You ask me, do I then count these faculties as of no effect?

Heaven forbid! no more than I ignore the faculty of vision. Nevertheless if you ask me what is the true good of man, I can only say to you that it lies in a certain disposition of the will.

CHAPTER NINE

How One may Draw Conclusions from the Fact that we are God's Kinsmen

IF THESE STATEMENTS OF the philosophers are true, that God and men are akin, there is but one course open to men, to do as Socrates did: never to reply to one who asks his country, 'I am an Athenian', or 'I am a Corinthian', but 'I am a citizen of the universe.' For why do you say that you are an Athenian, instead of merely a native of the little spot on which your bit of a body was cast forth at birth? Plainly you call yourself Athenian or Corinthian after that more sovereign region which includes not only the very spot where you were born, and all your household, but also generally that region from which the race of your forbears has come down to you. When a man therefore has learnt to understand the government of the universe and has realized that there is nothing so great or sovereign or all-inclusive as this frame of things wherein men and God are united, and that from it come the seeds from which are sprung not only my own father or grandfather, but all things that are begotten and that grow upon earth, and rational creatures in particular –for these alone are by nature fitted to share in the society of God, being connected with Him by the bond of reason–why should he not call himself a citizen of the universe and a son of God? Why should he fear anything that can happen to him among men? When kinship with Caesar or any other of those who are powerful in Rome is sufficient to make men live in security, above all scorn and free from every fear, shall not the fact that we have God as maker and father and kinsman relieve us from pains and fears?

'And where am I to find food to eat, if I have nothing?' says one.

Well, what do slaves do when they leave their masters, or what do they rely on? Do they rely on fields, or servants, or silver plate? No, on nothing but themselves; nevertheless sustenance does not fail them. And shall our philosopher in his wanderings have to rest his confidence in others, instead of taking care of himself? Is he to be baser and more cowardly than the unreasoning beasts? For each one of them is content with itself, and lacks not its proper sustenance nor the way of life that is naturally suited to it.

I think that the old man who sits here to teach you ought to devote his skill not to save you from being low-minded, and from reasoning about yourselves in a low and ignoble spirit, but rather to prevent young men from arising of the type who, discovering their kinship with the gods, and seeing that we have these fetters attached to us in the shape of the body and its possessions and all that we find necessary for the course and management of our life by reason of the body, may desire to fling all these away as vexatious and useless burdens and so depart to the gods their kindred.

And so your teacher and instructor, if he were a true teacher, should engage in this conflict of argument:

You come saying, 'Epictetus, we can bear no longer to be bound with the fetters of this wretched body, giving it meat and drink and rest and purgation, and by reason of the body having to adapt ourselves to this or that set of circumstances. Are not these things indifferent and as nothing to us, and death no evil thing? Are we not kinsmen of the gods, from whom we have come hither? Suffer us to depart to the place whence we have come, suffer us to be released from these bonds that are fastened to us and weigh us down. Here are robbers and thieves and law-courts and so-called kings, who by reason of our poor body and its possessions are accounted to have authority over us. Suffer us to show them that they have authority over nothing.'

Hereupon I answer: 'Men as you are, wait upon God. When He gives the signal and releases you from this service, then you shall depart to Him; but for the present be content to dwell in this country wherein He appointed you to dwell. Short indeed is the time of your dwelling here, and easy for them whose spirit is thus disposed. What manner of tyrant or what thief or what law-courts have any fears for those who have thus set at nought the body and its possessions? Stay where you are, and depart not without reason.' Such should be the answer of the teacher to his gifted pupils. How different is what we see! There is no life in your master, and no life in you. When you have had your fill to-day, you sit groaning about the morrow, and how you are to find food. Slave, if you get food, you will have it; if not, you will depart: the door is open. Why do you whine? What room is there for tears any more? What occasion for flattery any more? Why should one envy another? Why should he gaze with wonder on them that are rich or powerful, especially if they be strong and quick to anger? For what will they do with us? We will pay no heed to what they have power to do, what we really care for they cannot touch. Who, I ask you, will be master over one who is of this spirit?

How did Socrates approach these matters? Surely as one should who is convinced of his kinship with the gods. 'If you tell me,' he says, '"We; acquit you on condition that you discourse no longer as you have done hitherto, and that you do not annoy young or old among us"', I shall answer, 'It is absurd for you to suppose that, while I am bound to maintain and guard any post to which your general appointed me, and should rather die ten thousand times than abandon it, yet if God has appointed us to a certain place and way of life we ought to abandon that.' [Plato, *Apology*, 29c, 28e] Here you see a man who is a kinsman of the gods in very truth. But as for us—we think of ourselves as if we were all belly and flesh and animal desire; such are our fears, such our passions; those that can help us to these ends we flatter, and at the same time fear.

Some one has asked me to write for him to Rome, one who, as the world thought, had had misfortunes; he had once been famous and rich, and had now lost everything and was living here. So I wrote for him in a humble tone. And he read my letter and gave it me back and said, 'I wanted your help, not your pity.' So, too, Rufus, to try me, used to say, 'Your master will do this or that to you'; and when I answered him, 'This is the lot of man', 'Why then', said he, 'do I appeal to your master when I can get everything from you?' for, indeed, it is true that what a man has of himself it is idle and futile for him to receive from another. Am I then, who can get from myself the gift of a noble and lofty spirit, to get from you a field or money or office? Heaven forbid! I will not be so blind to my true possessions. But when a man is mean and cowardly, for him one must needs write letters as for one that is dead. 'Make us a present of the corpse of so and so and his miserable quart of blood.' For indeed such a one is a mere corpse and a quart of blood and nothing more. If he were anything more, he would have realized that one man cannot make another miserable.

CHAPTER TEN

To those who nave Spent their Energies on Advancement in Rome

IF WE HAD BEEN as earnest and serious about our work as old men in Rome are about their concerns, we too might perhaps have achieved something. I know what was said to me by a man older than myself who is now in charge of the corn-supply in Rome, when he passed through here on his way back from exile; he ran down his former life and made great professions for the future, saying that when once he was back he would have no other interest except to live out the rest of his life in peace and tranquillity, 'For how little I have still left me', said he.

And I said to him, 'You will not do it; so soon as you sniff the air of Rome you will forget all your professions'; and I told him that if he got a chance of entering the Palace, he would thrust his way in and give God thanks.

'Epictetus,' he answered, 'if you find me putting one foot in the Palace, believe what you like of me.'

Well, what did he do? Before he came to Rome, a dispatch from the Emperor met him, and as soon as he got it he forgot all he had said and has gone on adding to his heap ever since. I should like to stand by him now and remind him of the words he used as he passed through, and say to him, 'How much more clever a prophet am I than you!'

What conclusion do I draw? Do I say that the creature man is not to be active? Heaven forbid! But what is it that fetters our faculty of action? Take myself first: when day comes, I remind myself a little as to what lesson I ought to read to my pupils. Then in a moment I find myself saying, 'But what do I really care what sort of lesson I give to this man or that? The first thing is for me to sleep.' And yet how can their business be compared in importance with ours? If you attend to what they are doing you will see the difference. They do nothing all day long except vote, dispute, deliberate about a handful of corn or an acre of land, and petty profits of this sort. Is there any resemblance between receiving and reading a petition such as this: 'I beg you to let me export a little corn', and a petition such as, 'I beg you to inquire from Chrysippus how the universe is governed and what position the rational creature holds in it; inquire too who you are and what is good for you, and what is evil'? What have these petitions in common? Do both demand the same attention? Is it equally shameful to neglect one and to neglect the other?

What is my conclusion? Are we elders alone indolent and sleepy? Nay, the fault is much rather with you young men. For indeed, we old folk, when we see young men playing, are only too eager and ready to join their play. Much more, if I saw them thoroughly awakened and eager to share my studies, should I be eager myself to take my studies seriously too.

CHAPTER ELEVEN

On Family Affection

WHEN AN OFFICIAL CAME to Epictetus and inquired for special directions he asked whether he had a wife and children; and when the man said, 'Yes', he asked again, How do you get on?

'Miserably', he said.

What do you mean? said he; Men do not marry and have children to the end that they may be miserable, but rather that they may be happy.

'Ah', said he, 'but I am so miserable about my poor children, that lately when my daughter was ill and was thought to be in danger I could not bear to be near her, but fled away from her, until some one brought me news that she was well.'

Well, do you think you were right to do it?

'It was natural', he said.

Nay, said the master, only convince me that it was natural, and I will convince you that everything that is natural is right.

'All fathers', he said, 'or most of us, at least, feel like that.'

I do not deny, said Epictetus, that parents feel so, but the real question is whether it is right. No doubt as far as that goes, we must say that even tumours come into being for the good of the body, and in a word that error is natural, for nearly all, or most of us at least, are prone to error. Prove to me then how it is natural.

'I cannot'; he said, 'rather do you prove to me how it is wrong or unnatural.'

He answered, Suppose we were discussing black and white, what test should we call in to distinguish between them?

'The sight', he said.

What if we were discussing things hot or cold, hard and soft, what test should we use?

'Touch.'

Well then, as we are discussing what is natural and right and the opposite, what test would you have us take?

'I do not know', said he.

Look here, it is no great loss perhaps not to know the proper test for colours and smells, nay, and flavours too, but do you think it is a small loss to man not to know what is good and what is evil, what is natural and what is unnatural?

'No, the greatest possible loss.'

Tell me now, is everything right which seems noble and fitting to certain people? To-day, for instance, are the opinions of Jews and Syrians, Egyptians and Romans, as to food all of them right?

'How can they be?'

No, I suppose if the Egyptians' views are right the other nations' must of necessity be wrong; if the Jews' opinions are good, other people's must be bad.

'Of course.'

And where there is ignorance, there is also want of insight and education as to necessary things.

'Yes.'

When once you have realized this, then, said Epictetus, you will make this your one interest in the future, and to this alone devote your mind—to discover the means of judging what is natural and to use your criterion to distinguish each particular case as it arises.

For the present I can help you just so far as this in regard to what you wish: do you think family affection is natural and good? 'Of course.'

Again, is it true that affection is natural and good, and reason not good?

'Certainly not.'

Is there a conflict then between reason and affection?

'I think not.'

If there were a conflict, then, as one of the two is natural, the other must needs be unnatural?

'Certainly', he said.

It follows then that whenever we find reason and affection united in an action, we confidently affirm that it is right and good.

'Granted', he said.

Mark what follows. I do not think you will deny that it is not reasonable to leave one's child when it is ill and to go away. The only question left for us is to consider whether it is affectionate.

'Let us consider it then.'

Was it right, I ask, for you, being affectionately disposed to your child, to run away and leave her? Is her mother not fond of the child?

'She is indeed.'

Should the mother then have left her too, or should she not?

'She should not.'

What of the nurse? Is she fond of the child?

'She is', he said.

Ought she then to have left her?

'By no means.'

Again, is not the child's attendant fond of her?

'He is.'

Ought he then to have gone away and left her? Was it right that as a consequence the child should be thus left desolate and helpless because of the great affection of you its parents and of those about it, or should die in the hands of those who had no love or care for it?

'Heaven forbid!'

Once more, it is not fair or reasonable, is it, that a man should not allow others equally affectionate with himself to do what, because he is affectionate, he thinks proper for himself. It is absurd. Tell me, would you have liked, if you were ill, your relations and every one else, even your wife and children, to show their affection for you in such a way as to leave you alone and desolate?

'Certainly not.'

Would you pray to be so loved by your own people, as to be always left alone by them when you were ill, because of their exceeding affection, or would you, if it were a question of being left alone, rather pray, supposing that were possible, to have the affection of your enemies? And if that is so, we are forced to the conclusion that your conduct was not that of affection.

What reason had you then? Was there nothing which moved and impelled you to abandon the child? How is that possible? It must have been the same sort of motive, which once made a man in Rome cover his eyes when the horse he had backed was running, and then again when the horse unexpectedly won made him faint so that he needed sponges to recover him. What is the motive? This perhaps is not the moment to define it; but it is enough that we should be convinced of this –if what philosophers say is sound–that we must not look for it somewhere outside us, but that it is always one and the same motive which causes us to do or not to do a thing, to speak or not to speak, to be elated or depressed, to fly or to pursue–the very motive which has moved you and me at this moment, you to come and sit and listen to me, and me to say what I do. What is the motive? Surely it is nothing but this–that we are so minded?

'Nothing else.'

And if things had looked different to us, we should still have done what we were minded to do and nothing else. So when Achilles mourned, his reason was, not the death of Patroclus–for another man, when his comrade dies, is not thus affected–but that he was so minded. So in your case, you ran away just because you were so minded; and again, if you stay it will be because you are so minded. And now you return to Rome, because you have a mind to do so; and if your mind changes, you will not depart thither. And in a word it is not death nor exile nor pain nor any such thing which is the cause of our action or inaction, but thoughts and judgements of the mind. Are you convinced of this or not?

'I am', he said.

Then on each occasion the effects of an action correspond to the causes. So henceforward whenever we do a thing wrong, we shall blame nothing else but the judgement which led us to do it, and we shall try to remove and extirpate this even more than we do tumours and abscesses from the body. And so also we shall assert that our right actions are determined in the same way; and we shall no longer blame neighbour or wife or children as though they caused evils to befall us, being convinced that, unless we make up our mind that things are such, we' do not act as though they were, but that whether we judge them to be so or not depends upon ourselves and not on anything outside us.

'True', he said.

From this day forward then we shall not investigate or examine the nature or condition of anything else–whether it be land or slaves or horses or dogs–but only our own judgements.

'I hope so', said he.

You see then that you must become a student–that creature whom all mock at–if you really wish to investigate your judgements. That this is not the work of an hour or a day you fully understand without my telling you.

CHAPTER TWELVE

On Contentment

CONCERNING THE GODS THERE are some who say that the Divine does not exist, others that it exists but is inactive and indifferent and takes no thought for anything, others again that God does exist and take thought but only for great things and things in the heavens, but for nothing on earth; and a fourth class say that God takes thought also for earthly and human things, but only in a general way, and has no care for individuals: and there is a fifth class, to whom belong Odysseus and Socrates, who say

> *where'er I move*
> *Thou seest me.*
>   [Homer, Iliad, X. 279]

Before all things then it is necessary to examine each of these views, to see whether it is true or untrue. For if there are no gods, how can following the gods be the end of man? If again there are gods, but they care for nothing, in that case too what good will it be to follow them? But once more, if they exist and do care, yet if there is no communication between them and men, nay what is more, if there is none between them and me, to follow them cannot be a true end. The good man then, having examined into all these questions, has submitted his mind to Him that orders the universe, as good citizens submit to the law of the city. The man who is under education ought to approach education with this purpose in his mind: 'How can I follow the gods in everything, and how can I be content with the divine governance and how can I become free?' For he is free, for whom all things happen according to his will and whom no one can hinder.

'What then? Is freedom the same as madness?'

Heaven forbid! frenzy and freedom have nothing in common.

'But', you say, 'I want everything to happen as I think good, whatever that may be.'

Then you are in a state of madness, you are out of your mind. Do you not know that freedom is a noble thing, and worthy of regard? But merely to want one's chance thoughts to be realized, is not a noble thing; it comes perilously near being the most shameful of all things. How do we act in matters of grammar? Do I want to write Dion's name as I will? No, I am taught to will the right way of writing. How is it in music? Just the same. So it is universally, in every region of art or science. Otherwise it would not be worth while to know anything, if everything conformed itself to each man's will.

Are we to say then that in this sphere alone, the greatest and most momentous of all, the sphere of freedom, it is permitted me to indulge chance desires? By no means: education is just this–learning to frame one's will in accord with events. How do events happen? They happen as the Disposer of events has ordained them. He ordained summer and winter, fruitful and barren seasons, virtue and vice and all such opposites for the sake of the harmony of the universe, and gave to each one of us a body and bodily parts and property and men to associate with.

Remembering then that things are thus ordained we ought to approach education, not that we may change the conditions of life, that is not given to us, nor is it good for us–but that, our circumstances being as they are and as nature makes them, we may conform our mind to events.

I ask you, is it possible to avoid men? How can we? Can we change their nature by our society? Who gives us that power? What is left for us then, or what means do we discover to deal with them? We must so act as to leave them to do as seems good to them, while we remain in accord with nature.

But you are impatient and discontented; if you are alone you call it a wilderness, and if you are with men you describe them as plotters and robbers, and you find fault even with your own parents and children and brothers and neighbours.

Why, when you are alone you ought to call it peace and freedom and consider yourself the equal of the gods; when you are in a large company you should not call it a crowd or a mob or a nuisance, but a high-day and a festival, and so accept all things in a spirit of content.

What punishment is there, you ask, for those who do not accept things in this spirit? Their punishment is to be as they are. Is one discontented with being alone? Let him be deserted. Is one discontented with his parents? Let him be a bad son, and mourn his lot. Is one discontented with his children? Let him be a bad father.

'Cast him into prison.'

What do you mean by prison? he is in prison already; for a man's prison is the place that he is in against his will, just as, conversely, Socrates was not in prison, for he chose to be there.

'Am I then to have a maimed leg?'

Slave, do you mean to arraign the universe for one wretched leg? Will you not make a gift of it to the sum of things? Will you not resign it? Will you not joyfully yield it up to Him who gave it? Will you be vexed and discontented with the ordinances of Zeus, laid down and ordained by Him witl- the Fates who were present at your birth and span your thread of life? Do you not know, what a little part you are, compared with the universe? I say this of your body, for in reason you are not inferior to the gods nor less than they; for the greatness of reason is judged not by length or height but by its judgements.

Will you not then set your good in that region where you are equal to the gods?

'Alas, but look what a father and mother I have got!'

Why? was it given you on entering life to choose and say, 'Let such an one marry such an one at this hour, that I may be born?' No such choice was given you: your parents had to be in existence first, and your birth had to follow. Of what parents? Of such as they were.

Well then, as your parents are what they are, is no resource left you? Surely if you did not know to what end you possess the faculty of vision, you would be unhappy and miserable if you closed your eyes, when colours were brought near you; but are you not more wretched and unhappy still for not knowing that you have a high and noble spirit to face each occasion as it arises? The objects which correspond to the faculty that you have are brought near you: yet you turn away your faculty just at the very moment when you ought to keep it open-eyed and alert. Rather give thanks to the gods that they set you above those things which they put out of your power, and made you responsible only for what is within your control. For your parents they left you without responsibility; and the same is true of brothers, body, property, death, life. For what then did they make you responsible? For that which alone is in your power, the proper handling of your impressions. Why then do you insist on dragging in these things for which you are not responsible? That is to make trouble for yourself.

CHAPTER THIRTEEN

How One may Act in All Things so as to Please the Gods

WHEN SOME ONE ASKED Epictetus how one may eat so as to please the gods, he said, If you can eat justly, and with good feeling and, it may be, with self-control and modesty, may you not also eat so as to please the gods? And when you call for hot water and the slave does not answer, or answers and brings it luke-warm, or is not to be found in the house, is it not pleasing to the gods that you should not be angry nor break into a passion?

'How then is one to bear with such persons?'

Slave, will you not bear with your own brother, who has Zeus for his forefather, and is born as a son of the same seed as you and of the same heavenly descent? You were appointed to a place of superiority like this, and are you straightway going to constitute yourself a despot? Will you not remember what you are and whom you are ruling? that they are kinsmen, born your brothers, children of Zeus?

'But I have bought them, and they have not bought me.'

Do you see where your eyes are looking? You are looking at the earth, at what is lowest and basest, at these miserable laws of the dead, and you regard not the laws of the gods.

CHAPTER FOURTEEN

That God Beholds All Men

WHEN ONE ASKED HIM how a man may be convinced that every one of his acts is seen by God, Do you not think, he said, that all things are united together?

'I do', he said.

Again, do you think that things on earth feel the influence of things in heaven?

'I do', he said.

Whence comes it that in such perfect order as at God's command, when He bids the plants to flower, they flower, when He bids them grow, they grow, when He bids them to bear fruit, they bear, when to ripen, they ripen; when again He bids them drop their fruit, they drop it, and when to let fall their leaves, they let them fall, and when He bids them gather themselves up and be still and take their rest, they are still and take their rest? Whence is it that as the moon waxes and wanes and as the sun draws near and departs afar we behold so great a change and transformation of things on the earth? If the plants then and our own bodies are so closely bound up with the universe, and so share its affections, is it not much more so with our minds? And if our minds are so bound up with God and in such close touch with Him as being part and portion of His very being, does not God perceive their every movement as closely akin to Him?

Consider this: you, a man, have power to reflect on the divine governance and on each divine operation as well as upon things human, you have the faculty of being moved in your senses and your intelligence by countless objects, sometimes assenting, sometimes rejecting, sometimes doubting; you guard in your own mind these many impressions derived from so many and various objects, and moved by them you conceive thoughts corresponding to those objects which have first impressed you, and so from countless objects you derive and maintain one after another the products of art and memory.

All this you do, and is God not able to behold all things and be present with all and to have some communication with all? Why, the sun is able to illuminate so large a part of the universe, and to leave unilluminated only so much as the shadow which the earth makes can cover: and cannot He who has created the sun itself, and who makes it to revolve–a small part of Himself as compared with the whole–has not He, I say, the power to perceive all things?

'But', says one, 'I cannot comprehend all these things at once.'

Of course no one tells you that in faculty you are equal to Zeus. Nevertheless He has set by each man his genius o guard him, and committed each man to his genius to watch over, ay and a genius which sleeps not and is not to be beguiled. To what other guardian, better or more attentive, could He have committed each one of us? Therefore, when you close your doors and make darkness within, remember never to say that you are alone: you are not alone, God is within, and your genius. What need have they of light to see what you are doing? To this God you ought to swear allegiance from the first as the soldiers swear to Caesar. They are paid servants, yet they swear that they will put the safety of Caesar above all things: and shall you not swear too, who have been counted worthy of so many and so great blessings, or having sworn shall you not keep your oath? And what shall your oath be? Never to disobey, never to accuse, never to find fault with any of God's gifts, never to let your will rebel, when you have to do or to bear what necessity demands. Can the soldier's oath be compared with ours? The soldiers swear to respect no man above Caesar, but we to respect ourselves first of all.

CHAPTER FIFTEEN

What Philosophy Professes

WHEN A MAN CONSULTED Epictetus how to persuade his brother to be angry with him no longer, he replied, 'Philosophy does not promise to secure to man anything outside him. If it did it would be admitting something beyond its subject-matter. For as wood is the material dealt with by the carpenter, bronze by the statuary, so the subject-matter of each man's art of living is his own life. What are we to say then of your brother's life? That again is the concern of his art of living: to yours it is a thing external, like land, health, good repute. Philosophy makes no promises about such things.'

'In all circumstances' (says philosophy), 'I will keep the Governing Principle in accord with nature.'

Whose Governing Principle?

'His, in whom I am.'

How then am I to prevent my brother from being angry with me? Bring him to me and I will tell him, but I have nothing to say to you about his anger.

When the man who consulted him said, 'What I am looking for is this–how I may be in accord with nature, even though he be not reconciled with me', he replied, No great thing comes suddenly into being, any more than a cluster of grapes or a fig. If you say to me now, 'I want a fig', I shall answer that it needs time. Let it flower first, then put forth its fruit and then ripen. I say then, if the fig tree's fruit is not brought to perfection suddenly in a single hour, would you gather fruit of men's minds so soon and so easily? I tell you, you must not expect it.

CHAPTER SIXTEEN

On Providence

MARVEL NOT THAT THE other creatures have their bodily needs supplied–not only meat and drink, but a bed to lie on–and that they want no shoes nor rugs nor clothes, while we want all these things. For it would not have been a good thing that these creatures, born not for themselves but for service, should have been created liable to wants. Consider what it would be for us to have to take thought not only for ourselves but for sheep and asses, how they were to dress and what shoes they were to put on, and how they should find meat and drink. But just as soldiers when they appear before their general are ready shod, and clothed and armed, and it would be a strange thing indeed if the tribune had to go round and shoe or clothe his regiment, so also nature has made the creatures that are born for service ready and prepared and able to dispense with any attention. So one small child can drive sheep with a rod.

Yet we forbear to give thanks that we have not to pay the same attention to them as to ourselves, and proceed to complain against God on our own account. I declare, by Zeus and all the gods, one single fact of nature would suffice to make him that is reverent and grateful realize the providence of God: no great matter, I mean; take the mere fact that milk is produced from grass and cheese from milk and wool from skin. Who is it that has created or contrived these things?

'No one', he says.

Oh, the depth of man's stupidity and shamelessness!

Come, let us leave the chief works of nature, and behold what she works by the way. Is anything more useless than the hairs upon the chin? Did she not use even these in the most suitable way she could? Did she not by these means distinguish male and female? Does not the nature of each one of us cry aloud from afar, 'I am a man: on these terms approach me and address me; seek nothing else. Behold the signs.' Again, in women nature took the hair from their face, even as she mingled in their voice a softer note. What! You say the creature ought to have been left undistinguished and each of us to have proclaimed, 'I am a man'? Nay, but how noble and comely and dignified is this sign, how much more fair than the cock's crest, how much more magnificent than the lion's mane! Therefore we ought to preserve the signs God has given; we ought not to abandon them, nor, so far as in us lies, to confound the sexes which have been distinguished.

Are these the only works of Providence in us? Nay, what words are enough to praise them or bring them home to us? If we had sense we ought to do nothing else, in public and in private, than praise and bless God and pay Him due thanks. Ought we not, as we dig and plough and eat, to sing the hymn to God? 'Great is God that He gave us these instruments wherewith we shall till the earth. Great is God that He has given us hands, and power to swallow, and a belly, and the power to grow without knowing it, and to draw our breath in sleep.' At every moment we ought to sing these praises and above all the greatest and divinest praise, that God gave us the faculty to comprehend these gifts and to use the way of reason.

More than that: since most of you are walking in blindness, should there not be some one to discharge this duty and sing praises to God for all? What else can a lame old man as I am do but chant the praise of God? If, indeed, I were a nightingale I should sing as a nightingale, if a swan, as a swan: but as I am a rational creature I must praise God. This is my task, and I do it: and I will not abandon this duty, so long as it is given me; and I invite you all to join in this same song.

CHAPTER SEVENTEEN

That the Processes of Logic are Necessary

Since it is reason which makes all other things articulate and complete, and reason itself must be analysed and made articulate, what is it that shall effect this? Plainly, reason itself or something else. That something else either is reason or it will be something superior to reason, which is impossible. If it is reason, who again will analyse that reason? For if it analyses itself, so can the reason with which we started. If we are going to call in something else, the process will be endless and unceasing.

'Yes,' says one, 'but the more pressing need is not logic but the discipline of men's thoughts and feelings', and the like.

If you want to hear about moral improvement, well and good. But if you say to me, 'I do not know whether you argue truly or falsely', and if I use an ambiguous word and you say to me 'distinguish', I shall grow impatient and say to you, 'this is the more pressing need.' It is for this reason, I suppose, that men put the processes of logic in the forefront, just as we put the testing of the measure before the measuring of the corn. And if we do not determine first what is the bushel and what is the scale, how shall we be able to measure or weigh anything? So in the sphere of thought if we have not fully grasped and trained to perfection the instrument by which we judge other things and understand other things, shall we ever be able to arrive at accurate knowledge? Of course, it is impossible.

'Yes,' they say, 'but the bushel is a mere thing of wood and bears no fruit.'

True, but it can measure corn.

'The processes of logic, too, are unfruitful.'

This we will consider presently: but even if one should concede this, it is enough that logic has the power to analyse and distinguish other things and in fact, as one might say, has the power to weigh and measure. Who asserts this? Is it only Chrysippus and Zeno and Cleanthes? Does not Antisthenes agree? Why, who is it that has written, 'The beginning of education is the analysis of terms'? Does not Socrates too say the same? Does not Xenophon write of him that he began with the analysis of terms, to discover what each means?

Is this then what you call great and admirable–to understand or interpret Chrysippus? Nay, no one says that. What is admirable then? To understand the will of Nature. Very well: do you understand it of yourself? If so, what more do you need? For if it is true that all error is involuntary and you have learnt the truth, you must needs do rightly hereafter.

'But,' you may say, 'I do not understand the will of Nature.'

Who then expounds it? They say 'Chrysippus.' I come and inquire what this interpreter of Nature says. I begin not to understand what he means and I seek some one to interpret. The interpreter says, 'Let us examine the sense of this phrase, as if it were Latin.'

Why, pray, should the interpreter put on airs? Even Chrysippus has no right to do so, if he is only expounding the will of Nature, and does not follow it himself: how much less his interpreter. For we have no need of Chrysippus for his own sake, but only to enable us to follow Nature: just as we have no need, for himself, of the priest who offers sacrifice, but because we think that through him we shall understand the signs which the gods give of the future, nor do we need the sacrifice for itself, but because through it the sign is given, nor do we marvel at the crow or the raven but at God who gives His signs by them.

So I come to this interpreter and priest and say, 'Examine the victim's flesh to see what sign is given me.' He takes and opens the flesh and interprets, 'Man, you have a will unhindered and unconstrained by nature. This is written here in the flesh of the sacrifice. I will show you the truth of it first in the sphere of assent. Can any one prevent you from agreeing to what is true? No one. Can any one compel you to accept the false? No one. Do you see that in this sphere your faculty is free from let and hindrance and constraint and compulsion? Is any different in the sphere of will and impulse? What, I ask, can overcome impulse except another impulse? And what can overcome the will to get or will to avoid except another will to get or to avoid?'

'If he threatens me with death,' one says, 'he compels me.'

No, it is not what he threatens you with which compels you, but your decision that it is better to do what you are bidden than to die. Once more then it is your own judgement which compels you–that is, will puts pressure on will. For if God had so created that portion of His own being which He has taken from Himself and given to us, that it could suffer hindrance or compulsion from another, He would cease to be God and to care for us as He must needs do. 'This', says the priest, 'is what I find in the sacrifice: this is God's sign to you: if you will, you are free: if you will, you will blame no one, you will accuse no one: everything shall be in accordance with your own mind and the mind of God.'

This is the prophecy which draws me to consult this seer and philosopher, and his interpretation makes me admire not him but the truths which he interprets.

CHAPTER EIGHTEEN

That we should not be Angry at Men's Errors

IF WHAT PHILOSOPHERS SAY is true, that in all men action starts from one source, feeling, as in assent it is the feeling that a thing is so, and in denial the feeling that it is not so, yes, by Zeus, and in withholding judgement, the feeling that it is uncertain: so also impulse towards a thing is originated by the feeling that it is fitting, and will to get a thing by the feeling that it is expedient for one, and it is impossible to judge one thing expedient and will to get another, and to judge one thing fitting and be impelled to another. If all this be true, why are we angry with the multitude?

'They are thieves', he says, 'and robbers.'

What do you mean by thieves and robbers?

'They are gone astray and know not what is good and what is evil.'

Ought we then to be angry with them or to pity them? Only show them their error and you will see how they desist from their faults. But if their eyes are not opened, they regard nothing as superior to their own judgement.

'What!' you say. 'Ought not this robber and this adulterer to be put to death?'

Nay, say not so, but rather, 'Should I not destroy this man who is in error and delusion about the greatest matters and is blinded not merely in the vision which distinguishes white and black, but in the judgement which distinguishes good and evil?' If you put it this way, you will recognize how inhuman your words are; that it is like saying, 'Should I not kill this blind man, or this deaf one?' For if the greatest harm that can befall one is the loss of what is greatest, and a right will is the greatest thing in every one, is it not enough for him to lose this, without incurring your anger besides? Man, if you must needs harbour unnatural feelings at the misfortune of another, pity him rather than hate him; give up this spirit of offence and hatred: do not use these phrases which the backbiting multitude use, 'These accursed and pestilent fools'.

Very well. How are you suddenly converted to wisdom? What an angry temper you show!

Why then are we angry? Because we admire the material things of which they rob us. For only cease to admire your clothes, and you are not angry with him who steals them: cease to admire your wife's beauty, and you cease to be angry with the adulterer. Know that the thief and adulterer have no place among things that are your own, but only among things that are another's and beyond your power. If you let them alone and count them as nothing you have no one to be angry with any more. But as long as you admire these things you must be angry with yourself rather than with them. For, look you, you have fine clothes, your neighbour has none: you have a window, you wish to air them. He does not know what is the true good of man, but fancies, as you do too, that it is to have fine clothes. Is he not to come then and carry them off? Why, if you show a cake to greedy men, and gobble it down all to yourself, do you expect them not to snatch at it? Do not provoke them, do not have a window, do not air your clothes.

For my part, yesterday I had an iron lamp beside my household gods, and hearing a noise I rushed to the window. I found the lamp had been carried off. I reasoned with myself, that the man who took it yielded to some plausible feeling. What do I conclude? To-morrow, I say, you will find one of earthenware. The truth is, a man loses only what he has. 'I have lost my cloak.' Yes, for you had one. 'I have got a headache.' Have you a horn-ache too? Why then are you vexed? Your losses and your pains are concerned only with what you possess.

'But the tyrant will chain me.'

Yes, your leg.

'But he will cut off.'

What? Your neck. But what will he fail to bind or cut off? Your will. That is why the men of old enjoined 'Know thyself'. What follows? You ought to practise in small things and go on from them to greater.

'I have a headache.'

Then do not say, 'Ah me!'

'I have earache.'

Do not say, 'Ah me!' And I do not mean that you may not groan, but do not groan in spirit. And if the boy brings you your leg-bands slowly, do not cry out loud and pull a long face and say, 'Every one hates me.' Who is not likely to hate such an one?

Put confidence in these thoughts for the future and walk erect and free, not relying on bulk of body like an athlete. For you do not need to be invincible by brute force like an ass.

Who then is the man who is invincible? He whom nothing beyond his will can dismay. So I go on observing him in each set of circumstances as if he were an athlete. He has overcome the first round. What will he do in the second? What if it be a hot sun, and the struggle is in Olympia?

So it is in life. If you offer a man a trifle of silver, he will scorn it. What will happen if you offer him a young. maid? What if you do it in the dark? What happens if you ply him with reputation, or abuse, or praise, or death? All these he can conquer. What will he do if he is wrestling in the hot sun, I mean, if he has drunk too much? What if he is in a frenzy, or in sleep? The man who can overcome in all these circumstances is what I mean by the invincible athlete.

CHAPTER NINETEEN

How One should behave towards Tyrants

IF A MAN POSSESSES some advantage, or thinks he does though he does not, he is bound, if he be uneducated, to be puffed up because of it. The tyrant, for instance, says, 'I am mightiest of all men.'

Well, and what can you give me? Can you enable me to get what I will to get? How can you? Can you avoid what you will to avoid, independent of circumstances? Is your impulse free from error? How can you claim any such power?

Tell me, on shipboard, do you put confidence in yourself or in the man who knows? And in a chariot? Surely in him who knows. How is it in other arts? Exactly the same. What does your power come to then?

'All men pay me attention.'

Yes, and I pay attention to my platter and work it and polish it and I fix up a peg for my oil-flask. Does that mean that these are superior to me? No, but they do me some service, and for this reason I pay them attention. Again: do I not pay attention to my ass? Do I not wash his feet? Do I not curry him? Do you not know that every man pays regard to himself, and to you only as to his ass? For who pays regard to you as a man? Show me. Who wishes to become like you? Who regards you as one like Socrates to admire and follow?

'But I can behead you.'

Well said. I forgot, of course, one ought to pay you worship as if you were fever or cholera, and raise an altar to you, like the altar to Fever in Rome.

What is it then which disturbs and confounds the multitude? Is it the tyrant and his guards? Nay, God forbid! It is impossible for that which is free by nature to be disturbed or hindered by anything but itself. It is a man's own judgements which disturb him. For when the tyrant says to a man, 'I will chain your leg,' he that values his leg says, 'Nay, have mercy,' but he that values his will says, 'If it seems more profitable to you, chain it.'

'Do you pay no heed?'

No, I pay no heed.

'I will show you that I am master.'

How can you? Zeus gave me my freedom. Or do you think that he was likely to let his own son be enslaved? You are master of my dead body, take it.

'Do you mean that when you approach me, you pay no respect to me?' No, I only pay respect to myself: if you wish me to say that I pay respect to you too, I tell you that I do so, but only as I pay respect to my water-pot.

This is not mere self-love: for it is natural to man, as to other creatures, to do everything for his own sake; for even the sun does everything for its own sake, and in a word so does Zeus himself. But when he would be called 'The Rain-giver' and 'Fruit-giver' and 'Father of men and gods', you see that he cannot win these names or do these works unless he does some good to the world at large: and in general he has so created the nature of the rational animal, that he can attain nothing good for himself, unless he contributes some service to the community. So it turns out that to do everything for his own sake is not unsocial. For what do you expect? Do you expect a man to hold aloof from himself and his own interest? No: we cannot ignore the one principle of action which governs all things–to be at unity with themselves.

What follows? When men's minds harbour wrong opinions on things beyond the will, counting them good and evil, they are bound to pay regard to tyrants. Would that it were only tyrants, and not chamberlains too! How can a man possibly grow wise of a sudden, when Caesar appoints him to the charge of the privy? How is it we straightway say, 'Felicio has spoken wisely to me'? I would fain have him deposed from the dung-heap, that he may seem foolish to you again. Epaphroditus had a shoe-maker, whom he sold because he was useless: then by some chance he was bought by one of Caesar's officials, and became Caesar's shoemaker. If you could have seen how Epaphroditus honoured him. 'How is my good Felicio, I pray you?' Then if some one asked us, 'What is your master doing?' the answer was, 'He is consulting Felicio about something.' What, had he not sold him for useless? Who has suddenly made a wise man of him? This is what comes of honouring anything outside one's will.

He has been honoured with a tribuneship. All who meet him congratulate him; one kisses his eyes, another his neck, his slaves kiss his hands. He comes into his house and finds lamps being lighted. He goes up to the Capitol and offers sacrifice. Who, I ask you, ever offered sacrifice in gratitude for right direction of the will or for impulse in accordance with nature? For we give thanks to the gods for what we think our good!

To-day one spoke to me about the priesthood of Augustus. I told him, 'Fellow, leave the thing alone; you will spend a great deal on nothing.'

'Well, but those who draw up contracts will record my name.'

Can you be there when men read it and say to them, 'That is my name,' and even supposing you can be there now, what will you do if you die?

'My name will remain.'

Write it on a stone and it will remain. But who will remember you outside Nicopolis?

'But I shall wear a golden crown.'

If you desire a crown at all, take a crown of roses and wear that: you will look smarter in that.

CHAPTER TWENTY

How Reason has the Faculty of Taking Cognizance of Itself

EVERY ART AND FACULTY has certain principal things of which it is to take cognizance. When therefore the faculty itself is of like kind with the objects of which it takes cognizance, it must of necessity have power to take cognizance of itself: when it is of unlike kind, it cannot take cognizance of itself. For instance, the shoemaker's art is concerned with hides, but itself is absolutely different from the material of hides: for this reason it does not take cognizance of itself. Grammar again is concerned with written speech: is it then written speech itself? Certainly not: therefore it cannot take cognizance of itself.

For what purpose then have we received reason from nature? That we may deal with impressions aright.

What then is reason itself?

A system framed from impressions of a certain kind. Thus it naturally has the power to take cognizance of itself.

Again, sagacity has been given us. To take cognizance of what? Things good and bad and indifferent.

What is it then itself?

Good.

And what is folly?

Bad. Do you see then that of necessity sagacity has the power of taking cognizance of itself and its opposite? Therefore the primary and highest task of the philosopher is to test impressions and distinguish them and to make use of none which is untested. Consider how we have invented an art to test the currency, in which we are admitted to have some interest. Look how many means the assayer uses to test the coin –sight, touch, smell, finally hearing: he breaks the penny and attends to the sound, and is not content with hearing its note once, but by much attention gets an ear for music.

Thus, where we think it makes a serious difference to us whether we are right or wrong, we take great pains to distinguish the possible sources of error, and yet when we have to do with our Governing Principle itself, poor thing, we gape and sleep and are ready to accept any impression that comes: for we do not notice our loss.

When you wish, therefore, to realize how little concerned you are about good and evil, and how eager about things indifferent, consider how you regard physical blindness on the one hand, and mental delusion on the other, and you will recognize that you are far from having a proper feeling in regard to things good and evil.

'Yes, but it needs much preparation and much toil and study.'

What of that? Do you expect that a brief study will enable you to acquire the greatest art? Yet the principal doctrine of philosophers itself is brief enough. If you will learn it, read Zeno's words and you will see. For it is no long matter to say man's end is to follow the gods, and the essence of good is the power of dealing rightly with impressions.

'Tell us then what is "God," and what is "impression," and what is nature in the individual, and what in the universe.'

That is a long story.

Again, if Epicurus should come and say, that the good must be in the flesh, that too means a long discussion; it means we must be taught what is the commanding faculty in us, what constitutes our substantial and true nature. If it is not probable that the good of the snail is in the shell, is it probable that man's good is in his body? Take yourself, Epicurus. What is the more masterful faculty you possess? What is it in you which deliberates, which examines everything, which examines the flesh itself and decides that it is the principal thing? Why do you light a lamp and toil for us, and write such big volumes? Is it that we may not be ignorant of the truth? Who are we? What concern have we with you? So the argument becomes a long one.

CHAPTER TWENTY ONE

To those who Wish to be Admired

WHEN A MAN HAS his proper station in life, he does not hanker after what is beyond him.

What is it, man, that you wish to have?

'I am content if I am in accord with Nature in what I will to get and will to avoid, if I follow Nature in impulse to act and to refrain from action, in purpose, and design and assent.'

Why then do you walk about as if you had swallowed a poker?

'I would fain that they who meet me should admire me, and cry aloud, "What a great philosopher!"'

Who are these by whom you wish to be admired? Are not these the men whom you generally describe as mad? What do you want then? Do you want to be admired by madmen?

CHAPTER TWENTY TWO

On Primary Conceptions

PRIMARY CONCEPTIONS ARE COMMON to all men, and one does not conflict with another. Who among us, for instance, does not assume that the good is expedient and desirable and that we ought in all circumstances to follow and pursue it? Which of us does not assume that the just is noble and becoming?

At what moment then does conflict arise? It arises in the application of primary conceptions to particular facts; when for instance one says, 'He has done well: he is brave,' and another, 'Nay, he is out of his mind.' Hence arises the conflict of men with one another. Such is the conflict between Jews and Syrians and Egyptians and Romans–not the question whether holiness must be put before all things and must in all circumstances be pursued, but whether it is holy or unholy to eat of swine's flesh. Such you will find is the conflict between Agamemnon and Achilles. Call them to come forward.

What do you say, Agamemnon? Do you say that what is right and noble ought not to be done?

'Of course it ought.'

And what do you say, Achilles? Do you not approve of doing what is noble?

'Nay, I approve of it above all things.'

Now apply these primary notions: and here the conflict begins. One says, 'I ought not to give back Chryseis to her father.' The other says, 'Nay, you ought.' Certainly one or other of them wrongly applies the primary notion of right. Again one says, 'Well, if I must give back Chryseis, I must take the prize from one of you': the other says, 'What, take away my beloved?' 'Yes, yours,' he says. 'Am I alone then to be the loser?' 'But am I alone to have nothing?' So a conflict arises.

In what then does education consist? In learning to apply the natural primary conceptions to particular occasions in accordance with nature, and further to distinguish between things in our power and things not in our power. In our power are will and all operations of the will, and beyond our power are the body, the parts of the body, possessions, parents, brothers, children, country, in a word–those whose society we share. Where then are we to place 'the good'? To what class of things shall we apply it?

'To what is in our power.'

Does it follow then that health and a whole body, and life are not good, nor children, parents, and country? No one will bear with you if you say that. Let us then transfer the name 'good' to this class of things. Is it possible for a man to be happy if he is injured and fails to win good things?

'It is impossible.'

Can he also find the proper way to live with his fellows? Nay, how is it possible? For instance, I incline by nature to my true interest. If it is my interest to have a field, it is also my interest to take it away from my neighbour: if it is my interest to have a robe, it is my interest also to steal it from the bath. This is the source of wars, factions, tyrannies, plots.

Again, how shall I be able to observe what is fitting towards Zeus, for if I am injured or unfortunate, he heeds me not? So one hears, 'What have I to do with him, if he cannot help me?' and again, 'What have I to do with him, if he wills that I should be as I am now?' It follows that I begin to hate him. Why then do we build temples and make images to Zeus as if he were an evil genius, as if he were Fever? How can we give him any more the name Saviour, Rain-giver, and Fruit-giver? Surely if we place the true nature of the good in outward things, all these consequences follow.

What are we to do then? This is the search to be made by the true student of philosophy, who is in travail with truth. These are his thoughts: 'I do not see what is good and what evil. Am I not mad? I am.' But if I put 'the good' in the region of things that my will controls, every one will laugh at me. Some grey-haired old man will arrive, with many gold rings on his fingers: then he will shake his head and say, 'Listen to me, my child: you must study philosophy, but you must keep a cool head too. All that talk is folly. You learn the syllogism from philosophers, but you know better than the philosophers what you ought to do.'

Fellow, why do you rebuke me then, if I know it? What am I to say to this slave? If I am silent, he bursts with anger. One ought to say, 'Pardon me as you would pardon lovers. I am not my own master. I am mad.'

CHAPTER TWENTY THREE

Against Epicurus

EPICURUS UNDERSTANDS AS WELL as we do that we are by nature social beings, but having once placed our good not in the spirit but in the husk which contains it he cannot say anything different. On the other hand he firmly grasps the principle that one must not admire nor accept anything which is severed from the nature of the good: and he is quite right.

How can we be social beings, if (as you say) we have no natural affection for our offspring? Why do you advise the wise man not to bring up children? Why are you afraid that they may bring him into troubles?

Does the mouse he rears indoors cause him trouble? What does he care then, if a tiny mouse begins crying in his house? But he knows that if once a child is born, it will not be in our power not to love it nor care for it.

Epicurus says that the man who is wise does not enter into politics, for he knows what sort of things the politician has to do. Of course if you are going to live among men as if they were flies, what is to prevent you? But Epicurus, as though he did not know what natural affection is, says 'Let us not bring up children.'

If a sheep does not abandon its offspring, nor a wolf, does a man abandon his? What would you have us do? Would you have us foolish as sheep? Even they do not abandon their young. Would you have us savage as wolves? Even they do not abandon theirs. Nay, who takes your advice when he sees his child fallen on the ground and crying? Why, I think that if your father and mother had foreseen that you were going to talk thus, even then they would not have cast you away from them.

CHAPTER TWENTY FOUR

How One should Contend against Difficulties

DIFFICULTIES ARE WHAT SHOW men's character. Therefore when a difficult crisis meets you, remember that you are as the raw youth with whom God the trainer is wrestling.

'To what end?' the hearer asks.

That you may win at Olympia: and that cannot be done without sweating for it. To my mind no man's difficulties ever gave him a finer trial than yours, if only you will use them for exercise, as the athlete wrestles with the young man. Even now we are sending you to Rome to spy out the land: and no one sends a coward as a spy, for that means that if he but hears a noise or sees a shadow anywhere, he will come running in confusion and saying that the enemy are close at hand. So now if you come and tell us 'The doings in Rome are fearful, death is terrible, exile is terrible, evil-speaking is terrible, poverty is terrible: fly sirs, the enemy is at hand', we shall say to you, 'Begone, prophesy to yourself, the only mistake we made was in sending a man like you to spy out the land'. Diogenes, who was sent scouting before you, has brought us back a different report: he says, 'Death is not evil, for it is not dishonour'; he says, 'Glory is a vain noise made by madmen'. And what a message this scout brought us about pain and pleasure and poverty! 'To wear no raiment', he says, 'is better than any robe with purple hem'; 'to sleep on the ground without a bed', he says, 'is the softest couch.' Moreover he proves each point by showing his own confidence, his tranquillity of mind, his freedom, and withal his body well knit, and in good condition. 'No enemy is near,' he says, 'all is full of peace.'

What do you mean, Diogenes?

'See,' he says, 'have I suffered shot or wound or rout?'

That is the right kind of scouting: but you come back to us and talk at random. Drop your cowardice and go back again, and take a more accurate observation.

What am I to do then?

What do you do, when you disembark from a ship? Do you take the helm and the oars with you? What do you take then? You take what is yours, oil-flask and wallet. So now if you remember what is yours, you will never claim what is another's.

The emperor says to you, 'Lay aside your purple hem.'

See, I wear the narrow one.

'Lay aside this also.'

See, I wear the toga only.

'Lay aside the toga.'

See, I take that off too.

'Ay, but you still rouse my envy.'

Then take my poor body, every bit of it. The man to whom I can throw away my body has no fears for me.

'But he will not leave me as his heir.'

What? Did I forget that none of these things was mine? In what sense do we call them 'mine'? Only as we call 'mine' the pallet in an inn. If then the inn-keeper dies and leaves you the pallets, well and good; if he leaves them to another, that man will have them, and you will look for another. If you do not find one you will sleep on the ground, only do so with a good cheer, snoring the while, and remembering that it is among rich men and kings and emperors that tragedies find room, and that no poor man fills a part in a tragedy except as one of the chorus. But kings begin with a prelude of good things:

Crown high the halls

[Author unknown]

and then about the third or fourth act comes–

O Cithaeron, why didst thou receive me?

[Sophocles, *Oedipus the King*, 1391]

Poor slave, where are your crowns, where your diadem? Your guards avail you naught. Therefore when you come near to one of those great men remember this, that you are meeting a tragic character, no actor, but Oedipus in person.

'Nay, but such a one is blessed, for he has a great company to walk with him.'

I too join the ranks of the multitude and have a large company to walk with.

To sum up: remember that the door is open. Do not be a greater coward than the children, but do as they do. Children, when things do not please them, say, 'I will not play any more'; so, when things seem to you to reach that point, just say, 'I will not play any more,' and so depart, instead of staying to make moan.

CHAPTER TWENTY FIVE

On the Same Theme

IF THIS IS TRUE, and if we are not silly and insincere when we say that for men good and evil lies in the region of the will, and that everything else has no concern for us, why are we disturbed or fearful any more? No one has authority over the things in which we are interested: and we pay no regard to the things over which others have authority. What more have we to trouble about?

'Nay, but give me commands' (says the student).

What command should I give you? Has not Zeus laid commands upon you? Has He not given you what is yours, free from hindrance and constraint, and what is not yours subject to hindrance and constraint? What command then have you brought with you into the world, and what manner of ordinance? Guard what is your own by all means, grasp not at the things of others. Your good faith is your own.... Who can take these qualities from you? Who shall hinder you from using them but yourself? And how will you do so? When you take no interest in what is your own, you lose it and it ceases to be yours.

When you have instructions and commands from Zeus such as these, what commands would you have from me? Am I greater or more trustworthy than He? Do you need any other commands if you keep these of His? Has He not laid these commands upon you? Look at the primary conceptions. Look at the demonstrations of philosophers. Look at the lessons you have often heard, and the words you have spoken yourself—all you have read, all you have studied.

How long, then, is it right to keep these commands and not break up the game?

As long as it is conducted properly.

Here is a king chosen by lot at the Saturnalia: for they decide to play the game of 'Kings'. He gives his orders: '*You* drink, *you* mix the wine, *yo u* sing, *you* go, *you* come'. I obey, that I may not break up the game.

'Now believe that you are in evil case.'

I do not believe it, and who will compel me to believe it?

Again, we agree to play 'Agamemnon and Achilles'. He who is given the part of Agamemnon says to me, 'Go to Achilles and drag away Briseis'. I go. 'Come.' I come.

In fact we must behave in life as we do with hypothetical arguments. 'Let us assume it is night.'

Granted.

'What follows? Is it day?'

No, for I have already assented to the assumption that it is night.

'Let us assume that you believe that it is night.'

Granted.

'Now believe that it really is night.'

This does not follow from the hypothesis.

So too it is in life. 'Let us assume that you are unfortunate.'

Granted.

'Are you then unfortunate?'

Yes.

'What then, are you in misery?'

Yes.

'Now, believe that you are in evil case.'

This does not follow from the hypothesis: and Another forbids me.

How far, then, must we submit to such commands? So far as is expedient; that is, so far as I am true to what is becoming and consistent. There are, however, some severe and sour-tempered persons who say, 'I cannot dine with this fellow, and put up with his daily narrative of how he fought in Mysia. "I told you, brother, how I mounted the hill: now I begin again at the siege."' Another says, 'I would rather dine and hear him babble on to his heart's content.' It is for you to compare these estimates: only do nothing in the spirit of one burdened and afflicted, who believes himself in evil case: for no one compels you to this. Suppose some one made the room smoke. If the smoke is moderate I will stay: if excessive, I go out: for one must remember and hold fast to this, that the door is open.

The order comes, 'Do not dwell in Nicopolis.'

I will not.

'Nor in Athens.'

I give up Athens.

'Nor in Rome.'

I give up Rome.

'Dwell in Gyara.'

I dwell in Gyara: but this seems to me a very smoky room indeed, and I depart where no one shall hinder me from dwelling: for that dwelling is open to every man. And beyond the last inner tunic, which is this poor body of mine, no one has any authority over me at all. That is why Demetrius said to Nero, 'You threaten me with death, but nature threatens you.' If I pay regard to my poor body, I have given myself over as a slave: and if I value my wretched property I am a slave, for thereby I show at once what power can master me. Just as when the snake draws in its head I say, 'Strike the part of him which he guards,' so you may be sure that your master will trample on that part of you which you wish to guard. When you remember this, whom will you flatter or fear any more?

'Nay, but I want to sit where the senators sit.'

Do you see that you are making a strait place for yourself and squeezing yourself?

'How else then shall I have a good view in the amphitheatre?'

Man, do not go to the show and you will not be crushed. Why do you trouble yourself? Or wait a little, and when the show is done, sit down in the senators' seats and sun yourself. For remember this (and it is true universally) that it is we who straiten and crush ourselves–that is to say, it is our judgements which straiten and crush us. For instance, what does it mean to be slandered? Stand by a stone and slander it: what effect will you produce? If a man then listens like a stone, what advantage has the slanderer? But if the slanderer has the weakness of him that he slanders to work upon, then he does achieve something.

'Tear his toga off him.'

Why bring *him* in? Take his toga. Tear that.

'I have done you an outrage.'

May it turn out to your good.

These were the principles that. Socrates practised: that is why his face always wore the same expression. But we are fain to study and practise everything except how to be free men and untrammelled.

'The philosophers talk paradoxes.'

But are there no paradoxes in the other arts? Nay, what is more paradoxical than to lance a man's eye that he may see? If one told this to a person unskilled in the physician's art, would he not laugh at him who said it? Is it surprising then that in philosophy also many truths seem paradoxical to those who are unskilled?

CHAPTER TWENTY SIX

What is the Law of Life

WHEN SOME ONE WAS reciting hypothetical arguments, Epictetus said: This also is a law which governs hypothesis, that we must accept what conforms with the hypothesis. But much more important is the law of living, which is this–to act in conformity with nature. For if we wish in every subject and in all circumstances to observe what is natural, it is plain that in everything we must aim at not letting slip what is in harmony with nature nor accepting what is in conflict with it. First, then, philosophers train us in the region of speculation, which is easier, and only then lead us on to what is harder: for in the sphere of speculation there is no influence which hinders us from following what we are taught, but in life there are many influences which drag us the contrary way. We may laugh, then, at him who says that he wants to try living first; for it is not easy to begin with what is harder.

And this is the defence that we must plead with parents who are angered at their children studying philosophy: 'Suppose I am in error, my father, and ignorant of what is fitting and proper for me. If, then, this cannot be taught or learnt, why do you reproach me? If it can be taught, teach me, and, if you cannot, let me learn from those who say that they know. For what think you? That I fall into evil and fail to do well because I wish to? God forbid. What, then, is the cause of my going wrong? Ignorance. Would you not then have me put away my ignorance? Who was ever taught the art of music or of steering by anger? Do you think, then, that your anger will enable me to learn the art of living?' This argument can only be used by one who has entertained the purpose of right living. But if a man studies logic and goes to the philosophers just because he wants to show at a dinner party that he knows hypothetical arguments, is he not merely trying to win the admiration of some senator who sits next him? For in such society the great forces of the world prevail, and what we call wealth here seems child's-play there.

This is what makes it difficult to get the mastery over one's impressions, where distracting forces are strong. I know a man who clung to the knees of Epaphroditus in tears and said he was in distress, for he had nothing left but a million and a half. What did Epaphroditus do? Did he laugh at him, as we should? No, he was astonished, and said, 'Unhappy man, how ever did you manage to keep silence and endure it?'

Once when he put to confusion the student who was reading hypothetical arguments, and the master who had set him to read laughed at his pupil, he said, You are laughing at yourself; you did not give the young man any preliminary training, nor discover whether he can follow the arguments, but just treat him as a reader. Why is it, he said, that when a mind is unable to follow and judge a complex argument we trust to it the task of praise and blame and of deciding on good and bad actions? If he speaks ill of any one, does the man attend to him, and is any one elated by a praise which comes from one who cannot find the logical connexion in such small matters?

This, then, is where the philosophic life begins; in the discovery of the true state of one's own mind: for when once you realize that it is in a feeble state, you will not choose to employ it any more for great matters. But, as it is, some men, finding themselves unable to swallow a mouthful, buy themselves a treatise, and set about eating it whole, and, in consequence they vomit or have indigestion. Hence come colics and fluxes and fevers. They ought first to have considered whether they have the faculty.

It is easy enough in speculation to examine and refute the ignorant, but in practical life men do not submit themselves to be tested, and we hate the man who examines and exposes us. Yet Socrates used to say that a life which was not put to the test was not worth living. [Plato, *Apology*, 38a]

CHAPTER TWENTY SEVEN

On the Ways in which Impressions Come to us: And the Aids we must Provide for Ourselves to Deal with them

IMPRESSIONS COME TO US in four ways: either things are and seem so to us; or they are not and seem not to be; or they are and seem not; or they are not and yet seem to be. Now it is the business of the true philosopher to deal rightly with all these; he ought to afford help at whatever point the pressure comes. If it is the fallacies of Pyrrho and of the Academy which crush us, let us render help against them. If it is the plausibilities of circumstances, which make things seem good which are not, let us seek help against this danger: if it is habit which crushes us, we must try to discover help against that.

What, then, can we discover to help us against habit?

Contrary habit.

You hear ignorant folk saying, 'Unhappy man that he was, he died': 'His father perished, and his mother': 'He was cut off, yes, and untimely and in a foreign land.' Now listen to the arguments on the other side; draw yourself away from these voices, set against habit the opposite habit. Set against fallacious arguments the processes of reason, training yourself to be familiar with these processes: against the plausibilities of things we must have our primary conceptions clear, like weapons bright and ready for use.

When death appears an evil we must have ready to hand the argument that it is fitting to avoid evils, and death is a necessary thing. What am I to do? Where am I to escape it? Grant that I am not Sarpedon son of Zeus, to utter those noble words, 'I would fain go and achieve glory or afford another the occasion to achieve it: if I cannot win success myself, I will not grudge another the chance of doing a noble deed'. Grant that this is beyond us, can we not compass the other?

I ask you, Where am I to escape death? Point me to the place, point me to the people, among whom I am to go, on whom it does not light, point me to a charm against it. If I have none, what would you have me do? I cannot escape death: am I not to escape the fear of it? Am I to die in tears and trembling? For trouble of mind springs from this, from wishing for a thing which does not come to pass. Wheresoever I can alter external things to suit my own will, I alter them: where I cannot, I am fain to tear any man's eyes out who stands in my way. For man's nature is such that he cannot bear to be deprived of what is good, nor can he bear to be involved in evil. And so the end of the matter is that when I cannot alter things, nor blind him that hinders me, I sit still and moan and revile whom I can–Zeus and the other gods; for if they heed me not, what have I to do with them?

'Yes, but that will be impious of you.'

Well, how shall I be worse off than I am now? In a word, we must remember this, that unless piety and true interest coincide, piety cannot be preserved in a man. Do not these principles seem to you to be urgent?

Let the Pyrrhonist and the disciple of the Academy come and maintain the contrary! For my part I have no leisure for these discussions, nor can I act as advocate to the common-sense view.

If I had some petty action concerned with a plot of land, I should have called in another to be my advocate, how much more in a matter of this concern.

With what argument, then, am I content? With what is appropriate to the subject in hand. How sensation takes place, whether through the whole body or through particular parts, I cannot render a reasoned account, though I find difficulty in both views. But that you and I are not the same persons, I know absolutely and for certain. How is that? When I want to swallow a morsel I never lift it to your mouth, but to mine. When I want to take a piece of bread, I never take rubbish instead, but go to the bread as to a mark. And even you who make nothing of the senses, act just as I do. Which of you when he wants to go to the bath goes to the mill instead?

What follows? Must we not to the best of our power hold fast to this –that is, maintain the view of common sense, and guard ourselves against all that upsets it? Yes, who disputes that? But these are matters for one who has the power and the leisure: the man who trembles, and is disturbed, and whose heart is shaken within him, ought to devote his time to something else.

CHAPTER TWENTY EIGHT

That we must not be Angry with Men: And Concerning what Things are Small and What are Great among Men

WHAT IS THE REASON that we assent to a thing? Because it seems to us that it is so. It is impossible that we shall assent to that which seems not to be. Why? Because this is the nature of the mind–to agree to what is true, and disagree with what is false, and withhold judgement on what is doubtful.

What is the proof of this?

'Feel now, if you can, that it is night.'

It is impossible.

Put away the feeling that it is day.'

It is impossible.

'Assume or put away the feeling that the stars are even in number.' It is not possible.

When a man assents, then, to what is false, know that he had no wish to assent to the false: 'for no soul is robbed of the truth with its own consent,' as Plato says, but the false seemed to him true.

Now, in the sphere of action what have we to correspond to true and false in the sphere of perception? What is fitting and unfitting, profitable and unprofitable, appropriate and inappropriate, and the like.

Cannot a man, then, think a thing is to his profit, and not choose it?

He cannot.

What of her who says

I know full well what ills I mean to do
But passion overpowers what counsel bids me.
[Euripides, *Medea*, 1078]

Here the very gratification of passion and the vengeance she takes on her husband she believes to be more to her profit than saving her children.

'Yes, but she is deceived.'

Prove to her plainly that she is deceived and she will not do it, but as long as you do not show her, what else can she follow but that which appears to her? Nothing. Why then are you indignant with her, because, unhappy woman, she is deluded on the greatest matters and is transformed from a human being into a serpent? Why do you not rather pity her–if so it may be? As we pity the blind and the lame, so should we pity those who are blinded and lamed in their most sovereign faculties.

We must remember this clearly, that man measures his every action by his impressions; of course they may be good or bad: if good, he is free from reproach; if bad, he pays the penalty in his own person, for it is impossible for one to be deluded and another to suffer for it. The man who remembers this, I say, will be angry with no one, indignant with no one, revile none, blame none, hate none, offend none.

'So you say that deeds so great and awful take their origin from this, the impressions of the mind?'

From this and nothing else. The Iliad is nothing but men's impressions and how they dealt with them. It was impressions that made Paris take away the wife of Menelaus, impressions that drew Helen to follow him. If, then, his impressions had led Menelaus to feel that it was a gain to be robbed of such a wife, what would have happened? We should have lost the Iliad, and not only that but the Odyssey too.

'What? Do these great matters depend on one that is so small?'

What are these you call 'such great matters'? Wars and factions, deaths of many men and destructions of cities. What is there great in this, pray?

'Is there nothing great?'

Why, what is there great in the death of many oxen and many sheep, and the burning and destruction of many nests of swallows and storks?

'Are these like those other horrors?'

Most like: bodies of men perished, so did bodies of oxen and sheep. Huts of men were burnt: so were storks' nests. What is great or awful here? Or if it be so, show me how a man's home differs from a stork's nest, as a dwelling.

'Is a stork, then, like a man?'

What do you say? In respect of his body, very like; save only that men's homes are built of beams and rafters and bricks, and storks' nests of sticks and clay.

'Does a man then differ in nothing from a stork?'

God forbid: but he does not differ in these matters.

'In what then does he differ?'

Search and you will find that he differs in something else. Look whether it be not that he differs in understanding what he does, in his faculty for society, in his good faith, his self-respect, his security of aim, his prudence.

Where then is man's good and man's evil, in the true sense, to be found?

In that faculty which makes men different from all else. If a man preserves this and keeps it safely fortified; if his sense of honour, his good faith, and his prudence are not destroyed, then he too is preserved; but if any of these perish or be taken by storm, then he too perishes with them. And it is on this that great events depend. Was Alexander's great failure when the Hellenes came against the Trojans and sacked Troy and when his brothers perished? By no means: for no one fails by the act of another; yet then there was destruction of storks' nests. Nay, his failure was when he lost the man of honour, the man of good faith, the man who respected manners and the laws of hospitality. When did Achilles fail? Was it when Patroclus died? God forbid: it was when he was angry, when he cried for a trumpery maiden, when he forgot that he was there not to win lady-loves, but to make war. These are man's failures–this is his siege, this is his razed city, when his right judgements are broken to the ground, and when they are destroyed.

'But when women are carried off, and children are made captive, and men themselves are slaughtered–are not these things evil?'

Where do you get this idea from? If it is true, teach it me too.

'No, I cannot: but how can you say that they are not evil?'

Let us turn to our standards, let us look to our primary notions. For I cannot be sufficiently astonished at what men do. When we want to judge weights, we do not judge at random: when we judge things straight and crooked, it is not at random: in a word, when it is important to us to know the truth on any subject, no one of us will ever do anything at random. Yet when we are dealing with the primary and sole cause of right or wrong action, of prosperity or adversity, of good or bad fortune, there alone we are random and headlong: we nowhere have anything like a scale, nowhere anything like a standard: some impression strikes me, and straightway I act on it.

Am I any better than Agamemnon or Achilles, that they should do and suffer such evils because they follow their impressions, and I should be content with mine?

Surely tragedy has no other source but this. What is the 'Atreus' of Euripides? Impressions. What is the 'Oedipus' of Sophocles? Impressions. 'Phoenix'? Impressions. 'Hippolytus'? Impressions. How do you think then we should describe the man who takes no pains to discipline his impressions? What name do we give to those who follow everything that comes into their mind?

'Madmen.'

Well, is not this exactly what we do?

CHAPTER TWENTY NINE

On Constancy

THE ESSENCE OF GOOD and of evil lies in an attitude of the will. What are external things then?

They are materials for the will, in dealing with which it will find its own good or evil.

How will it find its good?

If it does not value over much the things that it deals with. For its judgements on matters presented to it, if they be right, make the will good, and if crooked and perverse make it bad. This law God has ordained and says, 'If you want anything good, get it from yourself.'

You say, 'Not so, but from another.'

I say, No, from yourself. So when the tyrant threatens and does not invite me, I say, 'What does he threaten?' If he says, 'I will bind you', I say, 'He threatens my hands and my feet.' If he says, 'I will behead you', I say, 'He threatens my neck'. If he says, 'I will put you in prison', I say, 'He threatens all my poor flesh', and if he threatens banishment, the same.

'Does he then not threaten you at all?'

Not at all, if I feel that these things are nothing to me: but if I fear any of them, he does threaten me. Who is there left for me to fear, and over what has he control? Over what is in my power? No one controls that. Over what is not in my power? I have no concern in that.

'Do you philosophers then teach us to despise kings?'

Heaven forbid! Which of us teaches men to resist them in the matters over which they have authority? Take my bit of a body, take my property, take my good name, take my companions. If I try to persuade any of them to resist, I give him leave to accuse me indeed.

'Yes, but I want to command your judgements.'

Who has given you this authority? How can you conquer another's judgement?

'I will conquer him', he says, 'by bringing fear to bear on him.'

You are not aware that it was the judgement that conquered itself, it was not conquered by another. The will may conquer itself, but nothing else can conquer it. That is the reason too why the noblest and most just law of God is this: 'Let the better always be victorious over the worse.'

'Ten', you say, 'are better than one.'

Better for what? To bind, to slay, to carry off where they will, to take away property. Ten conquer one therefore only in so far as they are better.

'In what then are they worse?'

They are worse if the one has right judgements, and the ten have not. I ask you, can they conquer him in this? How can they? If we weigh them in the balance, must not the heavier pull down the scale?

'This is your outcome then, that Socrates should suffer the fate he did at the hands of the Athenians?'

Slave, why do you say, 'Socrates'? State the fact as it really is, That Socrates' vile body should be arrested and haled to prison by those who are stronger, and that some one should give hemlock to Socrates' vile body and it should die of chill–does this seem to you marvellous, does this seem unjust, is it for this you accuse God? Did Socrates then get nothing in exchange? In what did his true good consist? Which are we to attend to? To you or to him? Nay, what does Socrates say? 'Anytus or Meletus can slay me, but they cannot harm me' [Plato, *Apology*, 30c]: and again, 'If God so will, so be it.' [Plato, *Crito*, 43d] Prove, I say, that one who has worse judgements gains the mastery over him who is his superior in judgements. You will not prove it: far from it. For the law of nature and of God is this, 'Let the better always come out victor over the worse.' Victorious in what? In that wherein it is better. One body is stronger than another, the majority are stronger than one, the thief stronger than he who is not a thief. That is why I too lost my lamp, because in the matter of vigilance the thief was a stronger man than I. But he bought his lamp for this price: for a lamp he became a thief, for a lamp he broke his faith, for a lamp he became a brute. This seemed to his judgement to be profitable.

Very well: but now some one has laid hold on my cloak, and drags me into the market, then others raise a clamour against me, 'Philosopher, what good have your judgements done you? for, see, you are haled to prison, see, you are about to be beheaded.'

And what sort of Introduction to philosophy could I have studied, that would save me from being haled off, if a stronger man seizes my cloak, or, if ten men drag me about and cast me into prison, will save me from being cast there? Have I then learnt nothing else? I have learnt to see that everything that happens, if it is beyond the control of my will, is nothing to me. Have you not gained benefit then in this respect? Why do you seek benefit elsewhere than where you learnt that it is to be found?

I sit on then in prison and say, 'This person who clamours at me has no ear for the true meaning of things, he does not understand what is said, in a word he has taken no pains to know what philosophers do or say. Let him be.'

But the answer comes, 'Come out of your prison.'

If you have no more need of me in prison, I come out: if you need me again, I will come in. For how long? For as long as reason requires that I should abide by my vile body; but when reason demands it no longer, take it from me and good health to you! Only let me not cast it off without reason or from a faint heart, or for a casual pretext. For again God wills it not: for He has need of a world like this, and of such creatures as ourselves to move upon the earth. But if He give the signal of retreat, as He gave it to Socrates, one must obey His signal as that of the general in command.

'What then? must I say these things to the multitude?'

Why should you? Is it not sufficient to believe them yourself? For when children come up to us and clap their hands and say, 'A good Saturnalia to you to-day!' do we say 'These things are not good'? Not at all, we clap with them ourselves. So, when you cannot change a man's opinion, recognize that he is a child, clap with him, and if you do not wish to do this, you have only to hold your peace.

These things we must remember, and when called to face a crisis that is to test us we must realize that the moment is come to show whether we have learnt our lesson. For a young man going straight from his studies to face a crisis may be compared to one who has practised the analysis of syllogisms. If some one offers him one that is easy to analyse, he says, 'Nay, propound me one which is cunningly involved, that I may get proper exercise.' And so wrestlers are discontented if put to wrestle with young men of light weight: 'He cannot lift me', one says. Here is a young man of parts, yet when the crisis calls he must needs weep and say, 'I would fain go on learning.'

Learning what? If you did not learn your lesson to display it in action, what did you learn it for?

I imagine one of those who are sitting here crying out in the travail of his heart, 'Why does not a crisis come to me such as has come to him? Am I to wear my life out idly in a corner, when I might win a crown at Olympia? When will some one bring me news of a contest like that?' Such ought to be the attitude of you all. Why, among Caesar's gladiators there are some who are vexed that no one brings them out or matches them in fight, and they pray to God and go to the managers and implore them to let them fight; and shall no one of you display a like spirit? That is exactly why I should like to take ship for Rome to see how my wrestler puts his lesson into practice.

'I do not want', says he, 'an exercise of this sort.'

What? is it in your power to take the task you choose? No, a body is given you of such a kind, parents of such a kind, brothers of such a kind, a country of such a kind, a position in it of such a kind: and yet you come to me and say, 'Change the task set me.' What! have you not resources, to deal with what is given you? Instead of saying, 'It is yours to set the task, and mine to study it well', you say, 'Do not put before me such a syllogism, but such an one: do not impose on me such a conclusion, but such an one.' A time will soon come when tragic actors will imagine that they are merely mask and shoes and robe, and nothing else. Man, you have these things given you as your subject and task. Speak your pan, that we may know whether you are a tragic actor or a buffoon: for except their speech they have all else in common. Does the tragic actor disappear, if you take away his shoes and mask and bring him on the stage in the bare guise of a ghost, or is he there still? If he has a voice he is there still.

So it is in life: 'Take a post of command'; I take it, and taking it show how a philosopher behaves.

'Lay aside the senator's dress, and put on rags and appear in that character.' Very well: is it not given me still to display a noble voice? In what part then do you appear now?

As a witness called by God: 'Come and bear witness for me, for I count you worthy to come forward as my witness. Is anything good or evil which lies outside the range of the will? Do I harm any one? Do I put each man's advantage elsewhere than in himself?'

What is the witness you now bear to God?

'I am in danger, O Lord, and in misfortune; no man heeds me, no man gives me anything, all blame me and speak evil of me.'

Is this the witness you are going to bear, and so dishonour the calling that he has given you, in that he honoured you thus and counted you worthy to be brought forward to bear such weighty witness?

But suppose that he who has authority pronounces, 'I judge you to be godless and unholy', how does this affect you?

'I am judged to be godless and unholy.'

Nothing more?

'Nothing.'

If he had been giving judgement on a hypothetical proposition and had declared, 'I judge the proposition "if it be day, there is light" to be false,' how would it have affected the proposition? Who is judged here? Who is condemned? The proposition or the man who is deluded about it? Who in the world then is this who has authority to pronounce upon you? Does he know what godliness or ungodliness is? Has he made a study of it? Has he learnt it? Where and with what master? If a musician pays no heed to him when he pronounces that the lowest note is the highest, nor a geometrician when he decides that the lines from the centre of a circle to the circumference are not equal, shall he who is educated in true philosophy pay any heed to an uneducated man when he gives judgement on what is holy and unholy, just and unjust? What a great wrong for philosophers to be guilty of! Is this what you have learnt by coming to school?

Leave other people, persons of no endurance, to argue on these matters to little purpose. Let them sit in a corner and take their paltry fees, or murmur that no one offers them anything, and come forward yourself and practise what you have learnt. For it is not arguments that are wanting nowadays: no, the books of the Stoics are full of them. What then is the one thing wanting? We want the man who will apply his arguments, and bear witness to them by action. This is the character I would have you take up, that we may no longer make use of old examples in the school, but may be able to show an example from our own day.

Whose business then is it to take cognizance of these questions? It is for him that has studied at school; for man is a creature with a faculty of taking cognizance, but it is shameful for him to exercise it in the spirit of runaway slaves. No: one must sit undistracted and listen in turn to tragic actor or harp-player, and not do as the runaways do. At the very moment one of them is attending and praising the actor, he gives a glance all round, and then if some one utters the word 'master' he is fluttered and confounded in a moment. It is shameful that philosophers should take cognizance of the works of nature in this spirit. For what does 'master' mean? No man is master of another man; his masters are only death and life, pleasure and pain. For, apart from them, you may bring me face to face with Caesar and you shall see what constancy I show. But when he comes in thunder and lightning with these in his train, and I show fear of them, I am only recognizing my master as the runaway does. But so long as I have respite from them I am just like the runaway watching in the theatre; I wash, drink, sing, but do everything in fear and misery. But if I once free myself from my masters, that is from those feelings which make masters formidable, my trouble is past, and I have a master no more.

'Should I then proclaim this to all men?'

No! One should study the weakness of the uninstructed and say to them, 'This man advises me what he thinks good for himself, and I excuse him.' For Socrates too excused the gaoler who wept when he was going to drink the poison, and said, 'How nobly he has wept for us!' Does he say to the gaoler, 'That is why we dismissed the women'? No, he says that to his intimate friends, who were fit to hear it, but the gaoler he treats considerately like a child. [Plato, *Phaedo*, 116d]

CHAPTER THIRTY

What a Man should have Ready to Hand in the Crises of Life

WHEN YOU APPEAR BEFORE one of the mighty of the earth, remember that Another looks from above on what is happening and that you must please Him rather than this man. He that is above inquires of you: 'What did you say in the school about exile and prison and bonds and death and dishonour?'

I said they were 'indifferent'.

'What do you call them now, then? Have they changed?'

No.

'Have you changed then?'

No.

'Tell me then what things are indifferent.'

Things which lie outside the will's control.

'Tell me what follows.'

Things indifferent concern me not at all.

'Tell me also what you thought were "good things".'

A right will and a faculty of dealing rightly with impressions. 'And what did you think was the end?'

To follow Thee.

'Do you still say that?'

Yes. I say the same now as before.

Go on then into the palace in confidence and remember these things, and you shall see how a young man who has studied what he ought compares with men who have had no study. By the gods I imagine that you will feel thus: 'Why do we make these many and great preparations for nothing? Is this what authority meant? Are the vestibule, the chamberlains, the guards no more than this? Was it for this that I listened to those long discourses? These terrors were naught, and I made ready for them all the time as though they were great matters.'

Book Two

CHAPTER ONE

On Things in our Power and Things not in our Power

PERHAPS THE CONTENTION OF philosophers that it is possible in everything we do to combine confidence with caution may appear a paradox, but nevertheless we must do our best to consider whether it is true. In a sense, no doubt, caution seems to be contrary to confidence, and contraries are by no means compatible. But I think that what seems to many a paradox in this subject depends on a confusion, and it is this. If we really called upon a man to use caution and confidence in regard to the same things, they might fairly find fault with us as uniting qualities which cannot be united. But as a matter of fact there is nothing strange in the statement: for if it is true, as has often been said and often proved, that the true nature of good and also of evil depends on how we deal with impressions, and if things outside the will's control cannot be described as good or bad, we cannot surely call it a paradoxical demand of the philosophers if they say, 'Be confident in all that lies beyond the will's control, be cautious in all that is dependent on the will.' For if evil depends on evil choice, it is only in regard to matters of will that it is right to use caution; and if things outside the will's control, which do not depend on us, concern us in no way, we should use confidence in regard to these. And in that way we shall be at once cautious and confident and indeed confident because of our caution. For because we are cautious as to things which are really evil we shall get confidence to face things which are not so.

However, we behave like deer: when hinds fear the feathers and fly from them, where do they turn, and in what do they take refuge as a safe retreat? They turn to the nets, and so they perish because they confuse objects of fear with objects of confidence.

So it is with us. Where do we show fear? In regard to things outside our will's control. Again, when do we behave with confidence as though there were nothing to fear? In matters within the will's control. So if only we are successful in things beyond our will's control we think it is of no consequence to us to be deceived or to act rashly, or to do a shameless deed, or to conceive a shameful desire. But where death or exile or pain or infamy confronts us, there we show the spirit of retreat and of wild alarm. Wherefore, as is likely with men who are mistaken in the greatest matters, we convert our natural confidence into something bold, desperate, reckless, shameless, whereas we change our natural caution and modesty into a cowardly and abject quality, full of fears and perturbations. For if a man transfers his caution to the region of the will and the operations of the will, with the will to be cautious he will find that the will to avoid lies in his control: while if he turns his caution to what is beyond the control of our will, inasmuch as his will to avoid will be directed to what depends upon others he will of necessity be subject to fear, inconstancy, and perturbation. For it is not death or pain which is a fearful thing, but the fear of pain or death. Therefore men praise him who said

Not death, but shameful death, is to be feared.

[Author unknown]

We ought then to turn our confidence towards death, and our caution towards the fear of death: what we really do is just the contrary; we fly from death, yet we pay no heed to forming judgements about death, but are reckless and indifferent. Socrates called such fears 'bogies', and rightly too. [Plato, *Phaedo*, 77e] For just as masks seem fearful and terrible to children from want of experience, so we are affected by events for much the same reason as children are affected by 'bogies'. For what makes a child? Want of knowledge. What makes a child? Want of instruction. For so far as a child knows those things he is no worse off than we are. What is death? A bogy. Turn it round and see what it is: you see it does not bite. The stuff of the body was bound to be parted from the airy element, either now or hereafter, as it existed apart from it before. Why then are you vexed if they are parted now? For if not parted now, they will be hereafter. Why so? That the revolution of the universe may be accomplished, for it has need of things present, things future, and things past and done with. What is pain? A bogy. Turn it round and see what it is. The poor flesh is subject to rough movement, then again to smooth. If it is not to your profit, the door stands open: if it is to your profit, bear it. For in every event the door must stand open and then we have no trouble.

What then is the fruit of these judgements? A fruit which must needs be most noble and most becoming to those who are truly being educated –a mind tranquil and fearless and free. For on these matters you must not trust the multitude, who say, 'Only the free may be educated', but rather the philosophers who say, 'Only the educated are free.'

'What do you mean by that?'

I mean this. What else is freedom but power to pass our life as we will?

'True.'

Tell me, fellow men, do you wish to live doing wrong?

'We do not.'

Is no one free who does wrong?

'No one.'

Do you wish to live in fear, in pain, in distress of mind?

'By no means.'

Well, no man who suffers fear or pain or distress of mind is free, but whoever is quit of fears and pains and distresses is by the self-same road quit of slavery. How then shall we go on believing you, dearest lawgivers?

Do we allow none but the free to get education?

Nay! philosophers say that we do not allow any to be free except those whose education is complete: that is, God does not allow it.

'Well then, when a man turns his slave round before the praetor, does he do nothing?'

He does something.

'What?'

He turns his slave round before the praetor.

'Nothing else?'

Yes, he is bound to pay the twentieth for him.

'What follows? Has not the man to whom this is done gained freedom?'

No more than he has gained peace of mind. For do you who can confer this freedom own no master? Have you not a master in money, a girl lover or a boy lover, the tyrant, or a friend of the tyrant? If not, why do you tremble when you go away to face a crisis of this sort? Therefore I say many times over: What you must practise and have at command is to know what you ought to approach with confidence, and what with caution; all that is beyond the control of the will with confidence, and what is dependent on the will with caution.

'But' (says my pupil), 'have I not recited to you? Do you not know what I am doing?'

What are you engaged on? Paltry phrases. Away with your paltry phrases: show me how you stand in regard to the will to get and the will to avoid: if you do not fail to get what you will, or fall into what you will to avoid. As for those paltry periods, if you have sense you will take them away somewhere or other and make away with them.

'What do you mean? Did not Socrates write?'

Yes, who wrote so much as he? But under what conditions? He could not always have some one at hand examining his judgements or to be examined by him in turn, and therefore be examined and questioned himself and was always putting to trial some primary conception or other in a practical way. This is what a philosopher writes: but paltry phrases and periods he leaves to others, to the stupid or the blessed, those whose peace of mind gives them leisure for study or those who can draw no logical conclusions because of their folly.

To-day, when the crisis calls you, will you go off and display your recitation and harp on, 'How cleverly I compose dialogues'? Nay, fellow man, make this your object, 'Look how I fail not to get what I will. Look how I escape what I will to avoid. Let death come and you shall know; bring me pains, prison, dishonour, condemnation.' This is the true field of display for a young man come from school. Leave those other trifles to other men; let no one ever hear you say a word on them, do not tolerate any compliments upon them; assume the air of being no one and of knowing nothing. Show that you know this only, how not to fail and how not to fall. Let others practise law-suits, logical puzzles and syllogisms: let your study be how to suffer death, bondage, the rack, exile: let all this be done with confidence and trust in Him who has called you to face them, and judged you worthy of this place you hold, wherein at your appointed post you shall show what is the power of reason, the Governing Principle, when arrayed against forces which are outside the will. And, if you do this, that paradox will no longer seem impossible or paradoxical–that we must show caution and confidence at the same time, confidence in regard to things beyond the will, caution in things which depend on the will.

CHAPTER TWO

On Peace of Mind

CONSIDER, YOU WHO ARE going into court, what you want to maintain and where you want to end: for if you want to maintain your freedom of will in its natural condition, you have all security and facility to do so, and your trouble is over. If you wish to maintain authority over what is in your power and to keep it naturally free, and if you are content with this, what more need you attend to? For who is master of this, who can take it away from you? If you wish to be a man of honour and trust, who will forbid you? If you wish not to be hindered or compelled, what man will compel you to will to get what is against your judgement, and to will to avoid things that you do not think proper to avoid?

What can he do then? He will cause you troubles which seem to you formidable: but how can he make you will to avoid what is done to you? As long then as you retain in your control the will to get and the will to avoid, you need attend to nothing else. This is your introduction, this your narrative, this your proof, this your victory, this your peroration, this your ground of boasting.

That is why Socrates, in reply to one who reminded him to make ready for the court, said: 'Do you not think my whole life is a preparation for this?'

What kind of preparation?

'I have maintained', said he, 'what is my own.'

What do you mean?

'I never did an unjust act in my private or in my public life.' [Xenophon, *Apologia Socratis*, 2, 3]

But if you wish to keep what is outside you as well–your paltry body, and goods, and reputation–I advise you to begin this moment to make all possible preparation, and further to study the character of your judge and your opponent. If you must clasp his knees, clasp them; if you must weep, then weep; if you must lament, then lament. For when once you allow outward things to dominate what is your own, you had better become a slave and have done with it. Don't be drawn this way and that, wishing to be a slave one moment and free another, but be this or that simply and with all your mind, free or slave, philosopher or unenlightened, a fighting cock of spirit, or one of no spirit; either bear stroke after stroke patiently till you die, or give way at once. Let it not be your lot to suffer many blows and then give way in the end. If such conduct is shameful, get your own mind clear at once: 'Where is the nature of good and evil to be found? Where truth is. Where truth and nature are, there is caution; where truth and nature are, there is confidence.'

For what think you? If Socrates had wished to keep his outward possessions, would he have come forward and said, 'Anytus and Meletus have power to kill me, but not to harm me'? Was he so foolish as not to see that this road leads not to that end, but elsewhere? Why is it then, that he renders no account to his judges, and adds a word of provocation? Just as my friend Heraclitus, when he had an action in Rhodes concerning a plot of land and had pointed out to the judges that his arguments were just, when he came to his peroration said, 'I will not supplicate you, nor do I regard the judgement you will give; it is you who are on your trial rather than I', and so he made an end of the business. You need not speak like that, only do not supplicate. Do not add the words, 'I do not supplicate', unless, as happened to Socrates, the right time has come deliberately to provoke your judges. If, indeed, you are preparing a peroration of this sort, why do you appear in court? Why do you answer the summons? If you wish to be crucified, wait and the cross will come: but if reason requires that you should answer the summons and do your best to persuade the judge, you must act in accordance with this, but always keeping true to yourself.

On this principle it is ridiculous to say, 'Give me advice.' What advice am I to give you? Say rather, 'Enable my mind to adapt itself to the issue, whatever it may be', for the other phrase is as though a man unskilled in writing should say, 'Tell me what to write, when a name is set me to write.' For if I say 'Dion', and then yonder fellow comes forward and sets him the name not of Dion but of Theon, what is to happen? What is he to write? If you have practised writing, you can prepare yourself for anything that is dictated to you. But if you have not practised, what is the good of my making a suggestion? For if circumstances suggest something different, what will you say or what will you do? Remember then this general principle, and you will need no special suggestion. But if you fix your gaze on outward things, you must needs be tossed up and down, at the will of your master. And who is your master? He who has authority over any of those things on which you set your heart or which you will to avoid.

CHAPTER THREE
To those who Commend Persons to Philosophers

THAT IS A GOOD answer of Diogenes to one who asked him for letters of introduction: 'You are a man, and that his eyes will tell him; but whether you are good or bad he will discover, if he has skill to distinguish the good from the bad; and if he has not that skill, he will never discover it, though I should write him ten thousand letters.' A drachma might just as well ask to be introduced to some one in order to be tested. If the man is a judge of silver, you will introduce yourself. We ought, therefore, to have some faculty to guide us in life, as the assayer has in dealing with silver, that I may be able to say as he does, 'Give me any drachma you please, and I will distinguish.' Now I can deal with a syllogism and say, 'Bring any one you like, and I will distinguish between him who can analyse syllogisms and him who cannot.' Why? Because I know how to analyse them: I have the faculty a man must have who is to recognize those who can handle syllogisms aright. But when I have to deal with life, how do I behave? Sometimes I call a thing good, sometimes evil. And the reason is just this, that whereas I have knowledge of syllogisms, I have no knowledge or experience of life.

CHAPTER FOUR

To the Man Caught in Adultery

WHEN EPICTETUS WAS SAYING that man is born for mutual trust, and he who overthrows this overthrows the quality peculiar to man, there came in one of those who are reputed scholars, a man who had once been caught committing adultery in the city. If, said Epictetus, we put away this trust, for which we are born, and plot against our neighbour's wife, what are we doing? Are we not pulling down and destroying? Whom? The man of trust, of honour, of piety. Is this all? Are we not overthrowing neighbourly feeling, friendship, the city itself? What position are we taking up?

How am I to treat you, my fellow man? As a neighbour? As a friend? Of what kind? As a citizen? What trust am I to put in you? No doubt, if you were a piece of pottery, so cracked that you could not be used for anything, you would be cast out on the dunghill, and no one would stoop to take you thence: what shall we do with you then, if being a man you can fill no place becoming to a man? Granted that you cannot hold the position of a friend, can you hold that of a slave? And who will trust you? Will you not then consent to be cast upon a dunghill yourself as a useless vessel, as a thing for the dunghill?

Will you complain, 'No man pays any attention to me, a man and a scholar'?

Of course, for you are bad and useless. Wasps might as well be indignant because no one heeds them, but all avoid them and any one who can strikes and crushes them. Your sting is such that you cause pain and trouble to any one you strike with it. What would you have us do to you? There is no place to put you.

What then? Is it not true that 'women are common property by nature'? I agree, for the sucking-pig is the common property of those who are bidden to the feast. Very well, when it has been cut into portions, come, if you see fit, and snatch the portion of the guest who sits next you, steal it secretly or slip your hand over it and taste it, or if you cannot snatch any of the flesh rub your fingers on the fat and lick them. A fine companion you are for a feast or a dinner, worthy of Socrates indeed!

Again, is not the theatre common to all citizens? When they are seated there, come, if you see fit, and turn one of them out. In the same way you may say that women are common property by nature. But when the law-giver, like the giver of the feast, has apportioned them, will you not look for your own portion instead of stealing what is another's and guzzling that?

'Yes, but I am a scholar and understand Archedemus.'

Well then, understand Archedemus, be an adulterer and a man of broken trust, a wolf or an ape instead of a man; for what is there to hinder you?

CHAPTER FIVE

How a Careful Life is Compatible with a Noble Spirit

MATERIAL THINGS ARE INDIFFERENT, but how we handle them is not indifferent.

How then is one to maintain the constant and tranquil mind, and. therewith the careful spirit which is not random or hasty?

You can do it if you imitate those who play dice. Counters and dice are indifferent: how do I know what is going to turn up? My business is to use what does turn up with diligence and skill. In like manner this is the principal business of life: distinguish between things, weigh them one against the other, and say, 'External things are not in my power, my will is my own. Where am I to seek what is good and what is evil? Within me, among my own possessions.' You must never use the word good or evil or benefit or injury or any such word, in connexion with other men's possessions.

'Do you mean then that outward things are to be used without care?'

By no means. For this again is evil for the will and unnatural to it. They must be used with care, for their use is not a matter of indifference, but at the same time with constancy and tranquillity, for in themselves they are indifferent. For where the true value of things is concerned, no one can hinder or compel me. I am subject to hindrance and compulsion only in matters which lie out of my power to win, which are neither good nor evil, but they may be dealt with well or ill, and this rests with me.

It is difficult to unite and combine these qualities–the diligence of a man who devotes himself to material things, and the constancy of one who disregards them–yet not impossible. Otherwise it would be impossible to be happy. We act very much as if we were on a voyage. What can I do? I can choose out the helmsman, the sailors, the day, the moment. Then a storm arises. What do I care? I have fulfilled my task: another has now to act, the helmsman. Suppose even the ship goes down. What have I to do then? I do only what lies in my power, drowning, if drown I must, without fear, not crying out or accusing heaven, for I know that what is born must needs also perish. For I am not immortal, but a man, a part of the universe as an hour is part of the day. Like the hour I must be here and like an hour pass away. What matters it then to me how I pass, by drowning or by fever, for by some such means I must needs pass away?

You will see that those who play ball with skill behave so. No one of them discusses whether the ball is good or bad, but only how to strike it and how to receive it. Therefore balanced play consists in this–skill, speed, good judgement consist in this–that while I cannot catch the ball, even if I spread my gown for it, the expert catches it if I throw it. But if we catch or strike the ball with flurry or fear, what is the good of the game? How will any one stick to the game and see how it works out? One will say, 'Strike', and another, 'Do not strike', and another, 'You have had one stroke.' This surely is fighting instead of playing.

In that sense Socrates knew how to play the game.

'What do you mean?'

He knew how to play in the court. 'Tell me, Anytus,' said he, 'in what way you say that I disbelieve in God. What do you think that divinities are? Are they not either children of the gods, or the mixed offspring of men and gods?' And when Anytus agreed, he said, 'Who then do you think can believe in the existence of mules and not in asses?' [Plato, *Apology*, 27c] He was like one playing at ball. What then was the ball that he played with? Life, imprisonment, exile, taking poison, being deprived of his wife, leaving his children orphans. These were the things he played with, but none the less he played and tossed the ball with balance. So we ought to play the game, so to speak, with all possible care and skill, but treat the ball itself as indifferent. A man must certainly cultivate skill in regard to some outward things: he need not accept a thing for its own sake, but he should show his skill in regard to it, whatever it be. In the same way the weaver does not make fleeces, but devotes himself to dealing with them in whatever form he receives them. Sustenance and property are given you by Another, who can take them away from you too, yes and your bit of a body as well.

It is for you, then, to take what is given you and make the most of it. Then if you come off without harm, others who meet you will rejoice with you in your safety, but the man who has a good eye for conduct, if he sees that you behaved here with honour, will praise you and rejoice with you: but if he sees a man has saved his life by acting dishonourably, he will do the opposite. For where a man can rejoice with reason, his neighbour can rejoice with him also.

How is it then that some external things are described as natural and some as unnatural? It is because we regard ourselves as detached from the rest of the universe. For the foot (for instance), I shall say it is natural to be clean, but if you take it as a foot and not as a detached thing, it will be fitting for it to walk in the mud and tread upon thorns and sometimes to be cut off for the sake of the whole body: or else it will cease to be a foot. We must hold exactly the same sort of view about ourselves.

What are you? A man. If you regard man as a detached being, it is natural for him to live to old age, to be rich, to be healthy. But if you regard him as a man and a part of a larger whole, that whole makes it fitting that at one moment you should fall ill, at another go a voyage and risk your life, and at another be at your wit's end, and, it may be, die before your time. Why then are you indignant? Do you not know that, just as the foot spoke of if viewed apart will cease to be a foot, so you will cease to be a man? For what is a man? A part of a city, first a part of the City in which gods and men are incorporate, and secondly of that city which has the next claim to be called so, which is a small copy of the City universal.

'What,' you say, 'am I now to be put on my trial?'

Is another then to have a fever, another to go a voyage, another die, another be condemned? I say it is impossible in a body like ours, in this enveloping space, in this common life, that events of this sort should not happen, one to this man and another to that. It is your business then to take what fate brings and deal with what happens, as is fitting. Suppose then the judge says, 'I will judge you to be a wrongdoer'; you reply, 'May it go well with you! I did my part, and it is for you to see if you have done yours: for the judge's part too, do not forget, has its own danger!'

CHAPTER SIX

On what is Meant by 'Indifferent' Things

TAKE A GIVEN HYPOTHETICAL proposition. In itself it is indifferent, but your judgement upon it is not indifferent, but is either knowledge, or mere opinion, or delusion. In the same way though life is indifferent, the way you deal with it is not indifferent. Therefore, when you are told 'These things also are indifferent', do not be careless, and when you are urged to be careful, do not show a mean spirit and be overawed by material things.

It is a good thing to know what you can do and what you are prepared for, that in matters where you are not prepared, you may keep quiet and not be vexed if others have the advantage of you there. For when it is a question of syllogisms, you in your turn will expect to have the advantage, and if they are vexed with this you will console them with the words, 'I learnt them, but you did not. So when acquired dexterity is needed it is for you in your turn not to seek what only practice can give: leave that to those who have acquired the knack, and be content yourself to show constancy.

'Go and salute such an one.'

I have saluted him.

'How?'

In no mean spirit.

'But his house was shut upon you.'

Yes, for I have not learnt to enter by the window: when I find the door shut, I must either retire or go in by the window.

'But again one says, "Talk to him."'

I do talk to him.

'How?'

In no mean spirit.

Suppose you did not get what you wanted? Surely that was his business and not yours. Why then do you claim what is another's? If you always remember what is yours and what is not yours, you will never be put to confusion. Therefore Chrysippus well says, 'As long as the consequences are unknown to me, I always hold fast to what is better adapted to secure what is natural, for God Himself created me with the faculty of choosing what is natural.' Nay, if I really knew that it was ordained for me now to be ill, I should wish to be ill; for the foot too, if it had a mind, would wish to get muddy.

For instance, why do ears of corn grow? Is it not that they may ripen in the sun? And if they are ripened is it not that they may be reaped, for they are not things apart? If they had feelings then, ought they to pray never to be reaped at any time? But this is a curse upon corn–to pray that it should never be reaped. In like manner know that you are cursing men when you pray for them not to die: it is like a prayer not to be ripened, not to be reaped. But we men, being creatures whose fate it is to be reaped, are also made aware of this very fact, that we are destined for reaping, and so we are angry; for we do not know who we are, nor have we studied human things as those who are skilled in horses study the concerns of horses.

But Chrysantas, when he was about to strike the enemy, and heard the bugle sounding the retreat, desisted: so convinced was he that it was more to his advantage to do the general's bidding than his own. But not a man of us, even when necessity calls, is willing to obey her easily, but we bear what comes upon us with tears and groans, and we call it 'circumstances'.

What do you mean by 'circumstances', fellow men? If you mean by 'circumstances' what surrounds you, everything is circumstance: if you use the term in the sense of hardships, how is it a hardship that what was born should be destroyed? The instrument of destruction is a sword or a wheel or the sea or a potsherd or a tyrant. What matters it to you, by what road you are to go down to Hades? All roads are alike. But, if you will hear the truth, the road the tyrant sends you is shorter. No tyrant ever took six months to execute a man, but a fever often takes a year to kill one. All these complaints are mere noise and vanity of idle phrases.

'In Caesar's presence my life is in danger.'

But am not I in equal danger, dwelling in Nicopolis, where earthquakes are so many? And you too, when you sail across the Adriatic, are you not in danger of your life?

'Yes, but in thought too I am in danger.'

Your thought? How can that be? Who can compel you to think against your will? The thought of others? How can it be any danger to you for others to have false ideas?

'Yes, but I am in danger of being banished.'

What is being banished? Is it being elsewhere than in Rome? 'Yes, suppose I am sent to Gyara?'

If it makes for your good, you will go: if not, you have a place to go to instead of Gyara, a place whither he who is sending you to Gyara will also go whether he will or no. Why then do you go to Rome as though it meant so much? It is not much compared with your preparation for it: so that a youth of fine feeling may say, 'It was not worth this price—to have heard so many lectures and written so many exercises, and sat at the feet of an old man of no great merit.'

There is only one thing for you to remember, that is, the distinction between what is yours and what is not yours. Never lay claim to anything that is not your own. Tribunal and prison are distinct places, one high, the other low; but your will, if you choose to keep it the same in both, may be kept the same. So we shall emulate Socrates, but only when we can write songs of triumph in prison. As for our condition up till now, I doubt whether we should have borne with one who should say to us in prison, 'Would you like me to recite to you songs of triumph?'

'Why do you trouble me? Do you not know the ills which beset me? for this is my state.'

What is it?

'I am at the point of death.'

Yes, but are other men going to be immortal?

CHAPTER SEVEN

How to Consult Diviners

MANY OF US OFTEN neglect acts which are fitting because we consult the diviners out of season. What can the diviner see more than death or danger or disease or generally things of that sort? If then I have to risk my life for a friend, if even it is fitting for me to die for him, how can it be in season for me to consult a diviner? Have I not within me the diviner who has told me the true nature of good and evil, who has expounded the signs of both? What need have I then of the flesh of victims or the flight of birds? Can I bear with him when he says, 'This is expedient for you'? Does he know what is expedient, does he know what is good, has he learnt signs to distinguish between good things and bad, like the signs in the flesh of victims? If he knows the signs of good and evil, he knows also the signs of things noble and shameful, just and unjust. It is yours, man, to tell me what is portended–life or death, poverty or wealth; but whether this is expedient or inexpedient I am not going to inquire of you.

Why do you not lay down the law in matters of grammar? Are you going to do it here then, where all mankind are at sea and in conflict with one another? Therefore that was a good answer that the lady made who wished to send the shipload of supplies to Gratilla in exile, when one said, 'Domitian will take them away': 'I would rather', she said, 'that Domitian should take them away than that I should not send them.'

What then leads us to consult diviners so constantly? Cowardice, fear of events. That is why we flatter the diviners.

'Master, shall I inherit from my father?'

'Let us see: let us offer sacrifice.'

'Yes, master, as fortune wills.'

When he says, 'You shall inherit', we give thanks to him as though we had received the inheritance from him. That is why they go on deluding us.

What must we do then? We must come without the will to get or the will to avoid, just as the wayfarer asks the man he meets which of two ways leads anywhere, not wanting the right hand to be the road rather than the left, for he does not wish to go one particular road, but the road which leads to his goal. We ought to approach God as we approach a guide, dealing with Him as we deal with our eyes, not beseeching them to show us one sort of things rather than another, but accepting the impressions of things as they are shown us. But instead of that we tremble and get hold of the augur and appeal to him as if he were a god and say, 'Master, have pity, suffer me to come off safe.'

Slave, do you not wish for what is better for you? Is anything better than what seems good to God? Why do you do all that in you lies to corrupt the judge, and pervert your counsellor?

CHAPTER EIGHT

What is the True Nature of the Good

GOD IS BENEFICENT, but the good also is beneficent. It is natural therefore that the true nature of the good should be in the same region as the true nature of God. What then is the nature of God? Is it flesh? God forbid. Land? God forbid. Fame? God forbid. It is intelligence, knowledge, right reason. In these then and nowhere else seek the true nature of the good. Do you look for it in a plant? No. Or in an irrational creature? No. If then you seek it in what is rational why do you seek it elsewhere than in what distinguishes it from irrational things? Plants have not the faculty of dealing with impressions; therefore you do not predicate 'good' of them.

The good then demands power to deal with impressions. Is that all it demands? If that be all, you must say that other animals also are capable of good and of happiness and unhappiness. But you do not say so and you are right, for whatever power they may have to deal with impressions, they have not the power to understand how they do so, and with good reason, for they are subservient to others, and are not of primary importance.

Take the ass, for instance, is it born to be of primary importance? No; it is born because we had need of a back able to bear burdens. Nay, more, we had need that it should walk; therefore it has further received the power of dealing with impressions, for else it could not have walked. Beyond that its powers cease. But if the ass itself had received the power to understand how it deals with impressions, then it is plain that reason would have required that it should not have been subject to us or have supplied these needs, but should have been our equal and like ourselves. Will you not then seek the true nature of the good in that, the want of which makes you refuse to predicate good of other things?

'What do you mean? Are not they too God's works?'

They are, but not His principal works, nor parts of the Divine. But you are a principal work, a fragment of God Himself, you have in yourself a part of Him. Why then are you ignorant of your high birth? Why do you not know whence you have come? Will you not remember, when you eat, who you are that eat, and whom you are feeding, and the same in your relations with women? When you take part in society, or training, or conversation, do you not know that it is God you are nourishing and training? You bear God about with you, poor wretch, and know it not. Do you think I speak of some external god of silver or gold? No, you bear Him about within you and are unaware that you are defiling Him with unclean thoughts and foul actions. If an image of God were present, you would not dare to do any of the things you do; yet when God Himself is present within you and sees and hears all things, you are not ashamed of thinking and acting thus: O slow to understand your nature, and estranged from God!

Again, when we send a young man from school to the world of action, why is it that we fear that he may do something amiss–in eating, in relations with women, that he may be humbled by wearing rags, or puffed up by fine clothes?

He does not know the God that is in him, he knows not in whose company he is going. Can we allow him to say, 'I would fain have you with me'? Have you not God there? and, having Him, do you look for any one else? Will He tell you anything different from this? Why, if you were a statue wrought by Phidias–his Zeus or his Athena–you would have remembered what you are and the Craftsman who made you, and if you had any intelligence, you would have tried to do nothing unworthy of him who made you or of yourself, and to bear yourself becomingly in men's eyes. But as it is, do you, whom Zeus has made, for that reason take no thought what manner of man you will show yourself? Yet what comparison is there between the one artificer and the other or the one work and the other? What work of art, for instance, has in itself the faculties of which it gives indication in its structure? Is it not stone or bronze or gold or ivory? Even the Athena of Phidias having once for all stretched out her hand and received the Victory upon it stands thus for all time, but the works of God are endowed with movement and breath, and have the faculty of dealing with impressions and of testing them.

When this Craftsman has made you, do you dishonour his work? Nay, more, He not only made you, but committed you as a trust to yourself and none other. Will you not remember this, but even dishonour the trust committed to you?

If God had committed some orphan to your care, would you have neglected him so? Yet He has entrusted your own self to you and He says, 'I had none other more trustworthy than you: keep this man for me such as he is born to be, modest, faithful, high-minded, undismayed, free from passion and tumult.' After that, do you refuse to keep him so?

But they will say, 'Where has this man got his high looks and his lofty countenance?'

Nay, I have not got them yet as I ought: for as yet I have not confidence in what I have learnt and assented to, I still fear my own weakness. Only let me gain confidence and then you shall see a proper aspect and a proper bearing, then I will show you the statue as it is when it is finished and polished. What think you? That this means proud looks? Heaven forbid! Does Zeus of Olympia wear proud looks? No, but his gaze is steadfast, as his should be who is to say:

For my word cannot be taken back, nor can it deceive.
[Homer, *Iliad*, I. 256]

Such will I show myself to you–faithful, self-respecting, noble, free from tumult.

'Do you mean, free from death and old age and disease?'

No, but as one who dies as a god, and who bears illness like a god. These are my possessions, these my faculties; all others are beyond me. I will show you the sinews of a philosopher.

'What do you mean by sinews?'

Will to achieve that fails not, will to avoid that falls not into evil, impulse to act appropriately, strenuous purpose, assent that is not precipitate. This is what you shall see.

CHAPTER NINE

That we Adopt the Profession of the Philosopher when we cannot Fulfil that of a Man

IT IS NO ORDINARY task merely to fulfil man's promise. For what is Man? A rational animal, subject to death. At once we ask, from what does the rational element distinguish us? From wild beasts. And from what else? From sheep and the like. Look to it then that you do nothing like a wild beast, else you destroy the Man in you and fail to fulfil his promise. See that you do not act like a sheep, or else again the Man in you perishes.

You ask how we act like sheep?

When we consult the belly, or our passions, when our actions are random or dirty or inconsiderate, are we not falling away to the state of sheep? What do we destroy? The faculty of reason. When our actions are combative, mischievous, angry, and rude, do we not fall away and become wild beasts? In a word, some of us are great beasts, and others are small but base-natured beasts, which give occasion to say, 'Nay, rather let me be food for a lion.' All these are actions by which the calling of man is destroyed.

What makes a complex proposition be what it is? It must fulfil its promise: it keeps its character only if the parts it is composed of are true. What makes a disjunctive proposition? It must fulfil its purport. Is not the same true of flutes, lyre, horse, and dog? Is it surprising then that man too keeps or loses his nature on the same principle? Each man is strengthened and preserved by the exercise of the functions that correspond to his nature, the carpenter by carpentering, the grammarian by studies in grammar. If a man gets the habit of writing ungrammatically, his art is bound to be destroyed and perish. In the same way the modest man is made by modest acts and ruined by immodest acts, the man of honour keeps his character by honest acts and loses it by dishonest. So again men of the opposite character are strengthened by the opposite actions: the shameless man by shamelessness, the dishonest by dishonesty, the slanderous by slander, the ill-tempered by ill-temper, the miser by grasping at more than he gives. That is why philosophers enjoin upon us 'not to be content with learning only, but to add practice as well and then training'. For we have acquired wrong habits in course of years and have adopted for our use conceptions opposite to the true, and therefore if we do not adopt true conceptions for our use we shall be nothing else but interpreters of judgements which are not our own.

Of course any one of us can discourse for the moment on what is good and what is bad: as thus, 'Of things that are, some are good, some bad, some indifferent; good are virtues and things that have part in virtues; evil are the opposite; indifferent are wealth, health, reputation.' And then if some loud noise disturbs us while we are speaking or one of the bystanders laughs at us, we are put out of countenance. Philosopher, where are those principles you were talking of? Whence did you fetch them forth to utter? From the lips and no further.

These principles are not your own: why do you make a mess of them? Why do you gamble with things of highest moment? It is one thing (to use an illustration) to put bread and wine away into a store-cupboard, and another thing to eat. What you eat is digested and distributed, and is turned into sinews, flesh, bones, blood, complexion, breath. What you store away you have at hand and can show to others at will, but it does you no good except for the mere name of having it. What is the good of expounding these doctrines any more than those of another school? Sit down now and discourse on the doctrines of Epicurus, and you will soon discourse more effectively than Epicurus himself. Why then do you call yourself a Stoic, why do you deceive the world, why being a Hellene do you act the Jew? Do you not see in what sense a man is called a Jew, in what sense a Syrian, in what an Egyptian? When we see a man trimming between two faiths we are wont to say, 'He is no Jew, but is acting a part', but when he adopts the attitude of mind of him who is baptized and has made his choice, then he is not only called a Jew but is a Jew indeed. So we also are but counterfeit 'baptists', Jews in name only, but really something else, with no feeling for reason, far from acting on the principles we talk of, though we pride ourselves on them as though we knew them. So, being unable to fulfil the calling of Man we adopt that of the Philosopher, a heavy burden indeed! It is as though one who could not lift ten pounds were fain to lift the stone of Ajax!

CHAPTER TEN

How the Acts Appropriate to Man are to be Discovered from the Names he Bears

CONSIDER WHO YOU ARE. First, a Man; that is, one who has nothing more sovereign than will, but all else subject to this, and will itself free from slavery or subjection. Consider then from what you are parted by reason. You are parted from wild beasts, you are parted from sheep. On these terms you are a citizen of the universe and a part of it, not one of those marked for service, but of those fitted for command; for you have the faculty to understand the divine governance of the universe and to reason on its sequence. What then is the calling of a Citizen? To have no personal interest, never to think about anything as though he were detached, but to be like the hand or the foot, which, if they had the power of reason and understood the order of nature, would direct every impulse and every process of the will by reference to the whole. That is why it is well said by philosophers that 'if the good man knew coming events beforehand he would help on nature, even if it meant working with disease, and death and maiming', for he would realize that by the ordering of the universe this task is allotted him, and that the whole is more commanding than the part and the city than the citizen. 'But seeing that we do not know beforehand, it is appropriate that we should hold fast to the things that are by nature more fit to be chosen; for indeed we are born for this.'

Next remember that you are a Son. What part do we expect a son to play? His part is to count all that is his as his father's, to obey him in all things, never to speak ill of him to any, nor to say or do anything to harm him, to give way to him and yield him place in all things, working with him so far as his powers allow.

Next know that you are also a Brother. For this part too you are bound to show a spirit of concession and obedience; and to speak kindly, and not to claim against another anything that is outside the will, but gladly to sacrifice those things, that you may gain in the region where your will has control. For look what a thing it is to gain good nature at the price of a lettuce, if it so chance, or the surrender of a chair: what a gain is that!

Next, if you are a member of a city council, remember that you are a councillor; if young, that you are young; if old, that you are old; if a father, that you are a father. For each of these names, if properly considered, suggests the acts appropriate to it. But if you go and disparage your brother, I tell you that you are forgetting who you are and what is your name. I say, if you were a smith and used your hammer wrong, you would have forgotten the smith; but if you forget the brother's part and turn into an enemy instead of a brother, are you going to imagine that you have undergone no change? If instead of man, a gentle and sociable creature, you have become a dangerous, aggressive, and biting brute, have you lost nothing? Do you think you must lose cash in order to suffer damage? Does no other sort of loss damage man? If you lost skill in grammar or music you would count the loss as damage; if you are going to lose honour and dignity and gentleness, do you count it as nothing? Surely those other losses are due to some external cause outside our will, but these are due to ourselves. Those qualities it is no honour to have and no dishonour to lose, but these you cannot lack or lose without dishonour, reproach, and disaster.

What does he lose who is the victim of unnatural lust? He loses his manhood. And the agent of such lust, what does he lose? He loses his manhood like the other, and much besides. What does the adulterer lose? He loses the man of honour and self-control, the gentleman, the citizen, the neighbour. What does the angry man lose? Something else. The man who fears? Something else. No one is evil without destruction and loss.

If on the other hand you look for loss in paltry pence, all the men I have mentioned are without loss or damage, if it so chance, nay they actually receive gain and profit, when they get cash by any of these actions. But notice, that if you make money the standard in everything, you will not count even the man who loses his nose as having suffered injury.

'Yes, I do,' he says, 'for his body is mutilated.'

Well, but does the man who has lost, not his nose but his sense of smell, lose nothing? Is there no faculty of the mind, which brings gain to him that gets it and hurt to him that loses it?

'What can possibly be the faculty you mean?'

Have we no natural sense of honour?

'We have.'

Does he that destroys this suffer no damage, no deprivation, no loss of what belongs to him? Have we not a natural faculty of trust, a natural gift of affection, of beneficence, of mutual toleration? Are we then to count the man who suffers himself to be injured in regard to these as free from loss and damage?

'What conclusion do you draw? Am I not to harm him who harmed me?'

First consider what 'harm' means and remember what you heard from the philosophers. For if good lies in the will and evil also lies in the will, look whether what you are saying does not come to this: 'What do you mean? As he harmed himself by doing me a wrong, am I not to harm myself by doing him a wrong?' Why then do we not look at things in this light? When we suffer some loss in body or property, we count it hurt: is there no hurt, when we suffer loss in respect of our will?

Of course the man who is deceived or the man who does a wrong has no pain in his head or his eye or his hip, nor does he lose his estate; and these are the things we care for, nothing else. But we take no concern whatever whether our will is going to be kept honourable and trustworthy or shameless and faithless, except only so far as we discuss it in the lecture-room, and therefore so far as our wretched discussions go we make some progress, but beyond them not the least.

CHAPTER ELEVEN

What is the Beginning of Philosophy

THE BEGINNING OF PHILOSOPHY with those who approach it in the right way and by the door is a consciousness of one's own weakness and want of power in regard to necessary things. For we come into the world with no innate conception of a right-angled triangle, or of a quarter-tone or of a semi-tone, but we are taught what each of these means by systematic instruction; and therefore those who are ignorant of these things do not think that they know them. On the other hand every one has come into the world with an innate conception as to good and bad, noble and shameful, becoming and unbecoming, happiness and unhappiness, fitting and inappropriate, what is right to do and what is wrong. Therefore we all use these terms and try to fit our preconceived notions to particular facts. 'He did nobly', 'dutifully', 'un-dutifully'. 'He was unfortunate', 'he was fortunate'; 'he is unjust', 'he is just.' Which of us refrains from these phrases? Which of us puts off using them until he is taught them, just as men who have no knowledge of lines or sounds refrain from talking of them? The reason is that on the subject in question we come into the world with a certain amount of teaching, so to say, already given us by nature; to this basis of knowledge we have added our own fancies.

'Why!' says he; 'do I not know what is noble and what is shameful? Have I no conception of them?'

You have.

'Do I not fit my conception to particulars?'

You do.

'Do I not fit them well then?'

There lies the whole question and there fancy comes in. For, starting with these admitted principles, men advance to the matter in dispute, applying these principles inappropriately. For if they really possessed this faculty as well, what would prevent them from being perfect? You think that you apply your preconceptions properly to particular cases; but tell me, how do you arrive at this?

I have such a conviction.

But another has a different conviction, has he not, and yet believes. as you do, that he is applying his conception rightly?

He does.

Is it possible then for you both to apply your conceptions properly in matters on which you hold contrary opinion?

It is impossible.

Can you then point us to anything beyond your own opinion which will enable us to apply our conceptions better? Does the madman do anything else but what he thinks right? Is this criterion then sufficient for him too?

It is not.

Come, then, let us look for something beyond personal opinion. Where shall we find it?

Here you see the beginning of philosophy, in the discovery of the conflict of men's minds with one another, and the attempt to seek for the reason of this conflict, and the condemnation of mere opinion, as a thing not to be trusted; and a search to determine whether your opinion is true, and an attempt to discover a standard, just as we discover the balance to deal with weights and the rule to deal with things straight and crooked. This is the beginning of philosophy.

'Are all opinions right which all men hold?'

Nay, how is it possible for contraries to be both right?

'Well, then, not all opinions, but our opinions?'

Why ours, rather than those of the Syrians or the Egyptians, or the personal opinion of myself or of this man or that?

'Why indeed?'

So then, what each man thinks is not sufficient to make a thing so: for in dealing with weights and measures we are not satisfied with mere appearance, but have found a standard to determine each. Is there, then, no standard here beyond opinion? It is impossible surely that things most necessary among men should be beyond discovery and beyond proof?

There is a standard then. Then, why do we not seek it and find it, and having found it use it hereafter without fail, never so much as 'stretching out our finger' without it? For it is this standard, I suppose, the discovery of which relieves from madness those who wrongly use personal opinion as their only measure, and enables us thereafter to start from known principles, clearly defined, and so to apply our conceptions to particulars in definite and articulate form.

What subject, I might ask, lies before us for our present discussion? 'Pleasure.'

Submit it to the rule, put it in the balance. Ought the good to be something which is worthy to inspire confidence and trust? 'It ought.'

Is it proper to have confidence in anything which is insecure? 'No.'

Has pleasure, then, any certainty in it?

'No.'

Away with it then! Cast it from the scales and drive it far away from the region of good things. But if your sight is not keen, and you are not satisfied with one set of scales, try another.

Is it proper to be elated at what is good?

'It is.'

Is it proper, then, to be elated at the pleasure of the moment? Be careful how you say that it is proper. If you do, I shall not count you worthy of the scales.

Thus things are judged and weighed if we have standards ready to test them: and in fact the work of philosophy is to investigate and firmly establish such standards; and the duty of the good man is to proceed to apply the decisions arrived at.

CHAPTER TWELVE

On the Art of Discussion

OUR PHILOSOPHERS HAVE PRECISELY defined what a man must learn in order to know how to argue: but we are still quite unpractised in the proper use of what we have learnt. Give any one of us you like an un-skilled person to argue with, and he does not discover how to deal with him: he just rouses the man for a moment, and then if he answers him in the wrong key he cannot deal with him any longer: he either reviles him or laughs at him ever after, and says, 'He is an ignoramus, there is nothing to be got out of him.'

But the true guide, when he finds a man wandering, leads him to the right road, instead of leaving him with a gibe or an insult. So should you do. Only show him the truth and you will see that he follows. But so long as you do not show it him, do not laugh at him, but rather realize your own incapacity.

Now how did Socrates proceed? He compelled the man who was con-versing with him to be his witness, and needed no witness besides. There-fore he was able to say: 'I am satisfied with my opponent as a witness, and let every one else alone: and I do not take the votes of other people, but only of him who is arguing with me.' [Plato, *Gorgias*, 474a] For he drew out so clearly the consequences of a man's conceptions that every one realized the contradiction and abandoned it.

'Does the man who envies rejoice in his envy?'

'Not at all; he is pained rather than pleased.'

Thus he rouses his neighbour by contradiction.

'Well, does envy seem to you to be a feeling of pain at evil things? Yet how can there be envy of things evil?'

So he makes his opponent say that envy is pain felt at good things. 'Again, can a man envy things which do not concern him?' 'Certainly not.'

In this way he made the conception full and articulate, and so went away. He did not say, 'Define me envy', and then, when the man defined it, 'You define it ill, for the terms of the definition do not correspond to the subject defined.' Such phrases are technical and therefore tiresome to the lay mind, and hard to follow, yet you and I cannot get away from them. We are quite unable to rouse the ordinary man's attention in a way which will enable him to follow his own impressions and so arrive at admitting or rejecting this or that. And therefore those of us who are at all cautious naturally give the subject up, when we become aware of this incapacity; while the mass of men, who venture at random into this sort of enterprise, muddle others and get muddled themselves, and end by abusing their opponents and getting abused in return, and so leave the field. But the first quality of all in Socrates, and the most characteristic, was that he never lost his temper in argument, never uttered anything abusive, never anything insolent, but bore with abuse from others and quieted strife. If you would get to know what a faculty he had in this matter, read the Banquet of Xenophon and you will see how many strifes he has brought to an end. Therefore the poets too with good reason have praised this gift most highly:

And straightway with skill he brought to rest a mighty quarrel.
[Hesiod, *Theogony*, 87]

What follows? The occupation is not a very safe one nowadays, and especially in Rome. For he who pursues it will certainly not have to do it in a corner, but he must go up to a consular or a rich man, if it so chance, and ask him: 'You there, can you tell me to whose care you trust your horses?'

'Yes.'

Do you trust them to a chance corner and one unskilled in horse-keeping?

'Certainly not.'

Again, tell me to whom you trust your gold or your silver or your clothes.

'Not to a chance corner either.'

And your body–have you ever thought of trusting that to anybody to look after it?

'Certainly.'

He too, no doubt, is one skilled in the art of training or of medicine, is he not?

'Certainly he is.'

Are these then your best possessions or have you got something be-sides, better than all?

'What can you mean?'

I mean, of course, that which makes use of all these possessions and tests each one, and thinks about them.

'Do you mean the soul?'

You are right; that is exactly what I do mean.

'Yes, I certainly think that this is a better possession than all the rest.'

Can you tell me, then, in what manner you have taken care of your soul? for it is not likely that one so wise as you. and of such position in the state, should lightly and recklessly allow the best possession you have to be neglected and go to ruin.

'Certainly not.'

Well, have you taken care of it yourself? Did any one teach you how, or did you find out for yourself?

When you do this, the danger is, you will find, that first he will say: 'My good sir, what concern is it of yours? Are you my master?' Then, if you persist in annoying him he will lift his hand and give you a drubbing.

That (says Epictetus) was a pursuit I had a keen taste for once, before I was reduced to my present condition.

CHAPTER THIRTEEN

Concerning Anxiety

WHEN I SEE A man in a state of anxiety, I say, 'What can this man want? If he did not want something which is not in his power, how could he still be anxious? It is for this reason that one who sings to the lyre is not anxious when he is performing by himself, but when he enters the theatre, even if he has a very good voice and plays well: for he not only wants to perform well, but also to win a great name, and that is beyond his own control.

In fact, where he has knowledge there he has confidence. Bring in any unskilled person you like, and he pays no heed to him. On the other hand he is anxious whenever he has no knowledge and has made no study of the subject. What does this mean? He does not know what 'the people' is, nor what its praise is worth: he has learnt to strike the bottom note or the top note, but he does not know what the praise of the multitude is, nor what value it has in life; he has made no study of that. So he is bound to tremble and grow pale.

When I see a man, then, in this state of fear I cannot say that he is no performer with the lyre, but I can say something else of him, and not one thing but many. And first of all I call him a stranger and say, This man does not know where in the world he is; though he has been with us so long, he does not know the laws and customs of the City–what he may do and what he may not do–no, nor has he called in a lawyer at any time to tell him and explain to him what are the requirements of the law. Of course he does not draw up a will without knowing how he ought to draw it up, or without calling in one who knows, nor does he lightly put his seal to a guarantee or give a written security; but he calls in no lawyer when he is exercising the will to get and will to avoid, impulse and intention and purpose. What do I mean by 'having no lawyer'? I mean that he does not know that he is wishing to have what is not given him, and wishing not to have what he cannot avoid, and he does not know what is his own and what is not his own. If he did know, he would never feel hindrance or constraint or anxiety; how could he? Does any one fear about things which are not evil?

'No.'

Or again about things which are evil but are in his power to prevent? 'Certainly not.'

If, then, nothing beyond our will's control is either good or evil, and everything within our will's control depends entirely on ourselves, so that no one can take any such thing away from us or win it for us against our will, what room is left for anxiety? Yet we are anxious for our bit of a body, for our bit of property, for what Caesar will think, but are not anxious at all for what is within us. Am I anxious about not conceiving a false thought? No, for that depends on myself.

Or about indulging an impulse contrary to nature?

No, not about this either. So, when you see a man pale, just as the physician, judging from his colour, says, 'This man's spleen is out of order, or that man's liver', so do you say, 'This man is disordered in the will to get and the will to avoid, he is not in the right way, he is feverish'; for nothing else changes the complexion and causes a man to tremble and his teeth to chatter,

and droop the knee and sink upon his feet.
[Homer, *Iliad*, XIII, 281]

Therefore Zeno was not distressed when he was going to meet Antigonus, for Antigonus had no authority over any of the things that Zeno admired, and Zeno paid no attention to the possessions of Antigonus. Antigonus was anxious when he was going to meet Zeno, and with good reason, for he wanted to please him, and this lay beyond his control; but Zeno did not wish to please Antigonus, any more than any artist cares to please one who has no skill.

Do I want to please you? Why should I? Do you know the standards by which man judges man? Have you made it your study to learn what a good man is and what a bad man is, and what makes each of them so? Why, then, are you not good yourself?

'Not good? What do you mean?' he replies.

Why, no good man whines or groans or laments, no good man grows pale or trembles or says, 'How will he receive me? What hearing will he give me?'

Slave, he will do as he thinks good. What concern have you in what does not belong to you? Is it not his fault if he gives a bad reception to what you offer?

'His fault, certainly.'

But can the fault be one man's and the harm another's?

'No.'

Why, then, are you anxious about another's concerns?

'Nay, but I am anxious to know how I am to address him.' What, is it not in your power to address him as you will? 'Yes, but I am afraid I may lose my self-possession.'

Are you afraid of losing your self-possession when you are going to write the name Dion?

'Certainly not.'

What is the reason? Is it not, that you have practised writing?

Of course it is. Or again, when you are about to read, would you not be in like case?

'Exactly.'

What is the reason? The reason is that every art contains within it an element of strength and confidence. Have you not practised speaking, then? What else did you study at school? You studied syllogisms and variable arguments. What for? Was it not that .you might converse with skill, and does not 'with skill' mean in good season, with security and good sense, and, more than that, without failure or hindrance, and, to crown all, with confidence?

'Yes.'

Well, if you are a rider and have to confront a man on foot in the plain, where you have the advantage of practice and he has not, are you anxious?

'Nay, but he has power to put me to death.'

Miserable man, tell the truth and be not a braggart nor claim to be a philosopher. Know who are your masters. As long as you give them this hold over your body, you must follow every one who is stronger than you.

But Socrates, who spoke to the Tyrants, to his judges, and in prison, in the tone we know, had studied speaking to some purpose. So had Diogenes, who spoke in the same tone to Alexander, to Philip, to the pirates, to his purchaser. . . . Leave this to those who have made it their concern, to the confident: and do you go to your own concerns and never leave them again. Go and sit in your corner and weave syllogisms and propound them to others,

No ruler of a state is found in you.
[Author unknown]

CHAPTER FOURTEEN

On Naso

ONCE WHEN A ROMAN came in with his son and was listening to one of his lectures Epictetus said: 'This is the method of my teaching', and broke off short. And when the Roman begged him to continue, he replied:–Every art, when it is being taught, is tiresome to one who is unskilled and untried in it. The products of the arts indeed show at once the use they are made for, and most of them have an attraction and charm of their own; for though it is no pleasure to be present and follow the process by which a shoemaker learns his art, the shoe itself is useful and a pleasant thing to look at as well. So too the process by which a carpenter learns is very tiresome to the unskilled person who happens to be by, but his work shows the use of his art. This you will see still more in the case of music, for if you are by when a man is being taught you will think the process of all things the most unpleasant, yet the effects of music are pleasant and delightful for unmusical persons to hear.

So with philosophy; we picture to ourselves the work of the philosopher to be something of this sort: he must bring his own will into harmony with events, in such manner that nothing which happens should happen against our will, and that we should not wish for anything to happen that does not happen. The result of this is that those who have thus ordered their life do not fail to get what they will, and do not fall into what they will to avoid: each man spends his own life free from pain, from fear, and from distraction, and maintains the natural and acquired relations which unite him to his fellows–the part of son, father, brother, citizen, husband, wife, neighbour, fellow traveller, ruler, subject.

Such is the business of the philosopher as we picture it. The next thing is that we seek how we are to achieve it. Now we see that the carpenter becomes a carpenter by learning certain things, the helmsman becomes a helmsman by learning certain things. May we, then, infer that in the sphere of conduct too it is not enough merely to wish to become good, but one must learn certain things? We have, then, to look and see what these things are. The philosophers say that the first thing one must learn is this: 'that God exists and provides for the universe, and it is impossible for a man to act or even to conceive a thought or reflection without God knowing. The next thing is to learn the true nature of the gods. For whatever their nature is discovered to be, he that is to please and obey them must needs try, so far as he can, to make himself like them.' If God is faithful, he must be faithful too; if free, he must be free too; if beneficent, he too must be beneficent: if high-minded, he must be high-minded: he must, in fact, as one who makes God his ideal, follow this out in every act and word.

'At what point, then, must we begin?'

If you attempt this task, I will tell you, that you must first understand terms.

'What? Do you imply that I do not understand terms now?' You do not.

'How then do I use them?'

You use them as illiterate persons deal with written sounds, as cattle deal with impressions: for it is one thing to use them, and another to understand. If you think you understand them, let us take any term you like and put ourselves to the test, to see if we understand.

'But it is vexatious when one is getting old, and has served, if it so chance, one's three campaigns, to be put through an examination.'

I know that as well as you. You have come to me now as if you were in want of nothing: and indeed what could you be imagined as wanting? You are rich, you have children, it may be, and a wife and many servants, the Emperor knows you, you possess many friends in Rome, you perform the acts appropriate to you, you know how to return good for good and evil for evil. What do you lack? If I show you that you lack what is most necessary and important for happiness, and that hitherto you have paid attention to everything rather than to acting appropriately, and if I conclude my criticism by saying that you do not know what God or man is, or what good or evil is, though perhaps you may bear being told of your ignorance in other ways, you cannot bear with me when I say that you do not know your own self; how can you submit to examination and abide my question? You cannot bear it at all: you go away at once in disgust. And yet what evil have I done

you? Unless indeed the mirror does harm to the ugly man, by showing him what sort of man he is: unless the physician too insults the
sick man, when he says to him, 'Sir, you think there is nothing wrong
with you, but you are in a fever; take no food to-day and drink water';
and no one says, 'What shocking insolence!' But if you say to a man,
'There is fever in your will to get, your will to avoid is degraded, your
designs are inconsistent, your impulses out of harmony with nature,
your conceptions random and false', he goes away at once and says,
'He insulted me!'

Our condition may be compared to the gathering at a public festival.
Cattle and oxen are brought thither for sale, and the mass of men come to
buy or to sell; only some few come to look at the assembled people

CHAPTER FIFTEEN

On those who Cling Stubbornly to their Judgements

THERE ARE SOME WHO when they hear these precepts–that a man must be steadfast, and that the will is by nature a free thing and not subject to compulsion, whereas all else is subject to hindrance and compulsion, being in bondage and dependence–imagine that they must abide without swerving by every judgement that they have formed. No–first of all the judgement arrived at must be sound.

For I would have the body firmly braced, but it must be the firmness of health and good condition; if you show me that you have the firmness of a madman and boast of that, I shall say to you, 'Look, man, for some one to cure you.' This is not firmness, but the opposite.

Let me describe another state of mind to be found in those who hear these precepts amiss. A friend of mine, for instance, determined for no reason to starve himself. I learnt of it when he was in the third day of his fasting, and went and asked him what had happened.

'I have decided', said he.

Yes, but, for all that, say what it was that persuaded you; for if your decision was right, here we are at your side ready to help you to leave this life, but, if your decision was against reason, then change your mind.

'A man must abide by his decisions.'

What are you doing, man? Not all decisions, but right decisions. For instance, if you were convinced at the moment that it was right, abide by that opinion if you think fit, and do not change it, but say, 'one must abide by one's decisions.'

Will you not lay this foundation to begin with–that is, examine your decision and see whether it is sound or unsound, and then afterwards build on it your firmness and unshaken resolve? But if you lay a rotten and crumbling foundation you will not be able to build even a tiny building; the more courses and the stronger that you lay upon it the quicker will it collapse. You are removing from life without any reason our familiar friend, our fellow citizen in the great City and the small, and then, though you are guilty of murder and of killing one who has done no wrong, you say, 'I must abide by my decisions.' If perchance it occurred to you to kill me, would you be bound to abide by your decisions?

Well, I had much ado to persuade that friend to change his mind. But it is impossible to move some of the men of to-day, so that I think that I know now what I did not know before, the meaning of the familiar saying, 'A fool is not to be persuaded nor broken of his folly.' May it never be my lot to have for friend a wise fool: nothing is more difficult to handle.

'I have decided.'

So have the madmen, but the more firmly they persist in false judgements the more hellebore do they require. Will you not act as the sick man should, and call in the physician? As he says, 'I am sick, master; help me: consider what I ought to do, it is for me to obey you', so you should say, 'I do not know what I ought to do, but I have come to learn.' Oh no, you say: 'Talk to me about other things; this I have decided.' Other things indeed! What is greater or more to your advantage than that you should be convinced that it is not sufficient to have decided and to refuse all change of mind? This is the firmness of madness, not of health.

'If you force me to this, I would fain die.'

Why, man, what has happened?

'I have decided.'

Lucky for me that you have not decided to kill me.

'I do not take fees.'

Why?

'I have decided.'

Let me tell you that the same energy with which you now refuse to take fees may incline you one day (what is to prevent it?) to take them and to say again, 'I have decided.'

Just as in an ailing body, which suffers from a flux, the flux inclines now to this part and now to that, so it is with a weak mind: no one can tell which way it sways, but when this swaying and drift has energy to back it, then the mischief becomes past help and remedy.

CHAPTER SIXTEEN

That we do not Practise Applying our Judgements About Things Good and Evil

WHERE LIES THE GOOD?

In a man's will.

Where lies evil?

In the will.

Where is the neutral sphere?

In the region outside the will's control.

Well, now, does any one of us remember these principles outside the lecture-room? Does any man practise by himself to answer facts as he would answer questions? For instance, is it day? 'Yes.' Again, is it night? 'No.' Again, are the stars even in number? 'I cannot say.' When money is shown you have you practised giving the proper answer, that it is not a good thing? Have you trained yourself in answers like this, or only to meet fallacious arguments? Why are you surprised, then, that you surpass yourself in the sphere where you have practised, and make no progress where you are unpractised?

Why is it that the orator, though he knows that he has written a good speech, and has got by heart what he has written, and brings a pleasant voice to his task, still feels anxiety in spite of all? The reason is that merely to declaim his speech does not content him. What does he want then? To be praised by his audience. Now he has been trained to be able to declaim, but he has not been trained in regard to praise and blame. For when did he hear from any one what praise is and what blame is: what is the nature of each, what manner of praise must be pursued, and what manner of blame must be avoided? When did he go through this training in accordance with these principles?

Why, then, are you still surprised that he is superior to others in the things he has been taught, and on a level with the mass of men in the things he has not studied? He is like the singer accompanying the lyre who knows how to play, sings well, and wears a fine tunic, and yet trembles when he comes on; for though he has all this knowledge he does not know what the people is or the clamour or mockery of the people. Nay, he does not even know what this anxiety is that he is feeling, whether it depends on himself or on another, whether it can be suppressed or not. Therefore, if men praise him, he leaves the stage puffed up; if they mock him, his poor bubble of conceit is pricked and subsides.

Very much the same is our position. What do we admire? External things. What are we anxious about? External things. And yet we are at a loss to know how fears or anxiety assail us! What else can possibly happen when we count impending events as evil? We cannot be free from fear, we cannot be free from anxiety. Yet we say, 'O Lord God, how am I to be rid of anxiety?' Fool, have you no hands? Did not God make them for you? Sit still and pray forsooth, that your rheum may not flow. Nay, wipe your nose rather and do not accuse God.

What moral do I draw? Has not God given you anything in the sphere of conduct? Has He not given you endurance, has He not given you greatness of mind, has He not given you manliness? When you have these strong hands to help you, do you still seek for one to wipe your rheum away?

But we do not practise such conduct nor pay attention to it. Find me one man who cares how he is going to do a thing, who is interested not in getting something but in realizing his true nature. Who is there that when walking is interested in his own activity, or when deliberating is interested in the act of deliberation, and not in getting that for which he is planning? And then if he succeeds he is elated and says, 'What a fine plan that was of ours! Did not I tell you, my brother, that if we have thought a thing out it is bound to happen so?' But if he fails he is humbled and miserable, and cannot find anything to say about what has happened. Which of us ever called in a prophet in order to realize his true nature? Which of us ever slept in a temple of dreams for this? Name the man. Give me but one, that I may set eyes on him I have long been seeking for, the man who is truly noble and has fine feeling; be he young or old, give me one.

Why, then, do we wonder any more that, whereas we are quite at home in dealing with material things, when we come to express ourselves in action we behave basely and unseemly, are worthless, cowardly, unenduring, failures altogether? But if we kept our fear not for death or exile, but for fear itself, then we should practise to avoid what we think evil. As it is we are glib and fluent in the lecture-room, and if any paltry question arises about a point of conduct, we are capable of pursuing the subject logically; but put us to the practical test and you will find us miserable shipwrecks. Let a distracting thought occur to us and you will soon find out for what we were studying and training. The result of our want of practice is that we are always heaping up terrors and imagining things bigger than they really are. When I go a voyage, as soon as I gaze down into the deep or look round on the sea and find no land, I am beside myself, imagining that if I am wrecked I must swallow all this sea, for it never occurs to me that three quarts are enough for me. What is it alarms me? The sea? No, but my judgement about it. Again, when an earthquake happens, I imagine that the city is going to fall on me. What! Is not a tiny stone enough to knock my brains out?

What, then, are the burdens that weigh upon us and drive us out of our minds? What else but our judgements? When a man goes away and leaves the companions and the places and the society that he is used to, what else is it that weighs upon him but judgement? Children, when they cry a little because their nurse has left them, forget her as soon as they are given a bit of cake.

'Do you want us to be like children too?'

No, not at all; it is not by cake I would have you influenced, but by true judgements. What do I mean? I mean the judgements that a man must study all day long, uninfluenced by anything that does not concern him, whether it be companion or place or gymnasia, or even his own body; he must remember the law and keep this before his eyes.

What is the law of God?

To guard what is your own, not to claim what is another's; to use what is given you, not to long for anything if it be not given; if anything be taken away, to give it up at once and without a struggle, with gratitude for the time you have enjoyed it, if you would not cry for your nurse and your mammy. For what difference does it make what a man is a slave to, and what he depends on? How are you better than one who weeps for a mistress, if you break your heart for a paltry gymnasium and paltry colonnades and precious young men and that sort of occupation? Here comes a man complaining that he is not to drink the water of Dirce any more.

What! is not the Marcian water as good as that of Dirce?

'Nay, but I was used to the other.'

Yes, and you will get used to this in turn. I say, if such things are go-ing to influence you, go away and cry for it, and try to write a line like that of Euripides,

The baths of Nero and the Marcian spring
[This line parodies Euripides, *The Phoenissae*]

See how tragedy arises when fools have to face everyday events!

'When shall I see Athens again, then, and the Acropolis?'

Unhappy man, are you not content with what you see day by day? Can you set eyes on anything better or greater than the sun, the moon, the stars, the whole earth, the ocean? And if you really understand Him that governs the universe and if you carry Him about within you, do you still long for paltry stones and pretty rock? What will you do, then, when you are going to leave the very sun and moon? Shall you sit cry-ing like little children? What were you doing, then, at school? What did you hear? What did you learn? Why did you write yourself down a philosopher when you might have written the truth, saying, 'I did a few Introductions and read Chrysippus' sayings, but I never entered the door of a philosopher. What share have I in the calling of Socrates, who lived and died so nobly, or of Diogenes? Can you imagine one of them weeping or indignant, because he is not going to see this man or that or be in Athens or in Corinth, but in Susa, if it so chance, or Ecbatana? Does he who may leave the banquet when he will and play no longer, vex himself while he stays on? Does he not stay at play just as long as it pleases him? Do you suppose the man I describe would endure inter-minable exile or condemnation to death?

Will you not be weaned at last, as children are, and take more solid food, and cease to cry 'nurse' and 'mammy', cries for old women's ears? 'But I shall distress them', you say, 'by departing.'

You will distress them? No, you will not distress them; what distress-es them and you is judgement. What can you do then? Get rid of your judgement: theirs, if they do well, they will get rid of themselves, or they will sorrow for it and have themselves to thank. Man, be bold at last, even to despair, as the phrase is, that you may have peace and freedom and a lofty mind. Lift up your neck at last, as one released from slavery. Have courage to look up to God and say, 'Deal with me hereafter as Thou wilt, I am as one with Thee, I am Thine. I flinch from nothing so long as Thou thinkest it good. Lead me, where Thou wilt, put on me what raiment Thou wilt. Wouldst Thou have me hold office, or eschew it, stay or fly, be poor or rich? For all this I will defend Thee before men. I will show each thing in its true nature, as it is.'

Nay, stay rather in the cow's belly and wait for your mammy's milk to fill you. What would have become of Heracles, if he had stayed at home? He would have been Eurystheus, and no Heracles.

But tell me, how many friends and companions had he, as he went about the world? No nearer friend than God: and that is why he was believed to be son of Zeus, and was so. Obedient to Him, he went about the world, cleansing it of wrong and lawlessness.

Do you say you are no Heracles, nor able to get rid of other men's evils, not even a Theseus, to cleanse Attica of ills?

Cleanse your own heart, cast out from your mind, not Procrustes and Sciron, but pain, fear, desire, envy, ill will, avarice, cowardice, passion uncontrolled. These things you cannot cast out, unless you look to God alone, on Him alone set your thoughts, and consecrate yourself to His commands. If you wish for anything else, with groaning and sorrow you will follow what is stronger than you, ever seeking peace outside you, and never able to be at peace: for you seek it where it is not, and refuse to seek it where it is.

CHAPTER SEVENTEEN

How we must Adjust our Primary Conceptions to Particular Things

WHAT IS THE FIRST business of the philosopher? To cast away conceit: for it is impossible for a man to begin learning what he thinks he knows. When we go to the philosophers we all bandy phrases freely of things to be done and not to be done, of things good and bad, noble and base; we make them the ground of our praise and blame, accusation and disparagement, pronouncing judgement on noble and base conduct and distinguishing between them. But what do we go to the philosophers for? To learn in their school what we think we do not know. What is that? Principles. For we want to learn what the philosophers talk of, some of us because we think their words witty and smart, and others in hope to make profit of them. It is absurd, then, to think that a man will learn anything but what he wishes to learn, or in fact that he will make progress if he does not learn. But the mass of men are under the same delusion as Theopompus the rhetor, when he criticized Plato because he wanted to define every term. What are his words?

'Did none of us before you talk of "good" or "just," or did we use the terms vaguely and idly without understanding what each of them meant?'

Who told you, Theopompus, that we had not natural notions and primary conceptions of each of these? But it is impossible to adjust the primary conceptions to the appropriate facts, without making them articulate and without considering just this–what fact must be ranged under each conception.

You may say just the same thing, for instance, to physicians. Which of us did not use the words 'healthy' and 'diseased' before Hippocrates was born? Were those terms we used mere empty sounds? No, we have a conception of 'healthy', but we cannot apply it. Therefore one physician says, 'Take no food', and another 'Give food', and one says, 'Cut the vein', and another, 'Use the cupping-glass.' What is the reason? Nothing but incapacity to apply the conception of 'the healthy' to particulars in the proper way.

So it is here in life. Which of us does not talk of 'good' and 'bad', 'expedient' and 'inexpedient'? Which of us has not a primary conception of each of these? Is that conception, then, articulate and complete? Prove it. How am I to prove it? Apply it properly to particular facts. To begin with, Plato makes his definitions conform to the conception of 'the useful', you to the conception of 'the useless'. Is it possible, then, for both of you to be right? Of course not. Does not one man apply his primary conception of 'good' to wealth while another does not? Another applies it to pleasure, another to health. To sum up, if all of us who use these terms really know them adequately as well, and if we need take no pains to make our conceptions articulate, why do we quarrel and make war and criticize one another?

Indeed, I need not bring forward our contentions with one another and make mention of them. Take yourself alone; if you apply your preconceptions properly, why do you feel miserable and hampered? Let us dismiss for the moment the Second Department of study, that concerned with impulses and with what is fitting in relation to them. Let us dismiss also the Third Department, that of assents. I grant you all this. Let us confine' ourselves to the First Department, where we have almost sensible demonstration that we do not apply our preconceptions properly. Do you now will things possible, and possible for you? Why, then, do you feel hindered and miserable? Do you now refuse to shun what is necessary? Why, then, do you fall into trouble and misfortune? Why does a thing not happen when you will it, and happen when you do not will it, for this is the strongest proof of misery and misfortune? I will a thing, and it does not happen; what could be more wretched than I? I will it not and it happens; again, what is more wretched than I?

It was because she could not endure this that Medea was led to kill her children: and the act showed a great nature; for she had a right conception of what it means for one's will not to be realized. 'Then', said she, 'I shall thus take vengeance on him who did me wrong and outrage. Yet what is the good of putting him in this misery? What am I to do then? I kill my children, but I shall also be punishing myself. What do I care?' This is the aberration of a mind of great force; for she did not know where the power lies to do what we will; that we must not get it from outside, nor by disturbing or disarranging events. Do not will to have your husband, and then nothing that you will fails to happen. Do not will that he should live with you in all circumstances, do not will to stay in Corinth: in a word, will nothing but what God wills. Then who shall hinder you, who compel you? You will be as free as Zeus Himself.

When you have a leader such as this, and identify your will with His, you need never fear failure any more. But, once make a gift to poverty and wealth of your will to get and your will to avoid, and you will fail and be unfortunate. Give them to health and you will be unhappy: or to office, honour, country, friends, children–in a word, if you give them to anything beyond your will's control. But give them to Zeus and to the other gods; hand them to their keeping, let them control them, and command them, and you can never be miserable any more. But if, O man of no endurance, you are envious, pitiful, jealous, timorous, and never go a day without bewailing yourself and the gods, how can you call yourself a philosopher any more? Philosophy indeed! Just because you worked at variable syllogisms? Will you not unlearn all this, if you can, and begin at the beginning again, and realize that so far you never touched the matter, and, beginning here, build further on this foundation, so that nothing shall be when you will it not, nothing shall not be when you will it? Give me one young man who has come to school with this purpose, ready to strive at this, like one at the games, saying, 'For my part let all else go for nothing: I am content if I shall be allowed to spend my life unhindered and free from pain, and to lift my neck like a free man in face of facts, and to look up to heaven as God's friend, fearing nothing that can happen.' Let one of you show himself in this character, that I may say, 'Come to your own, young man: for it is your destiny to adorn philosophy, these possessions are yours, the books and theories are for you.' Then, when he has worked at this subject and made himself master of it, let him come again and say to me, 'I wish to be free from passion and disquiet, and to know in a religious and philosophic and devoted spirit how it is fitting for me to behave towards the gods, towards my parents, my brothers, my country, and towards foreigners.'

Enter now on the Second Department: this is yours too.

'Yes, but now I have studied the Second Department; next I should wish to be secure and unshaken, and that not only in my waking hours, but in my sleep and in my cups and when distraught.'

Man, you are a god, you have great designs!

'No,' he replies, 'I want to understand what Chrysippus says in his treatise on "The Liar".'

That's your design, is it, my poor fellow? Take it and go hang! What good will it do you? You will read all the treatise with sorrow and repeat it to others with trembling.

That is just how you behave. 'Would you like me to read to you, brother, and you to me?' 'Man, you are a wonderful writer': and, 'You have a great turn for Xenophon's style', and, 'You for Plato's', and, 'You for Antisthenes'. And after all, when you have related your dreams to one another, you return again to the same behaviour as before: the same will to get and will to avoid, the same impulses and designs and purposes, the same prayers, the same interests. Then you never look for any one to remind you of the truth, but are vexed if any one reminds you. Then you say, 'He is an unamiable man; he did not weep when I left home nor say, "What difficulties you are going to! my son, if you return safe, I will light some lamps." This is what an amiable man would say.' Great good you will get if you return safe! It is worth while lighting a lamp for such as you, for you ought no doubt to be free from disease and death!

We must, then, as I say, put off this fancy of thinking that we know anything useful, and we must approach philosophy as we approach the study of geometry and music: otherwise we shall not come near making progress, even if we go through all the Introductions and treatises of Chrysippus and Antipater and Archedemus.

CHAPTER EIGHTEEN

How we must Struggle against Impressions

EVERY HABIT AND EVERY faculty is confirmed and strengthened by the corresponding acts, the faculty of walking by walking, that of running by running. If you wish to have a faculty for reading, read; if for writing, write. When you have not read for thirty days on end, but have done something else, you will know what happens. So if you lie in bed for ten days, and then get up and try to take a fairly long walk, you will see how your legs lose their power. So generally if you wish to acquire a habit for anything, do the thing; if you do not wish to acquire the habit, abstain from doing it, and acquire the habit of doing something else instead. The same holds good in things of the mind: when you are angry; know that you have not merely done ill, but that you have strengthened the habit, and, as it were, put fuel on the fire. When you yield to carnal passion you must take account not only of this one defeat, but of the fact that you have fed your incontinence and strengthened it. For habits and faculties are bound to be affected by the corresponding actions; they are either implanted if they did not exist before, or strengthened and intensified if they were there already. This is exactly how philosophers say that morbid habits spring up in the mind. For when once you conceive a desire for money, if reason is applied to make you realize the evil, the desire is checked and the Governing Principle recovers its first power; but if you give it no medicine to heal it, it will not return to where it was, but when stimulated again by the appropriate impression it kindles to desire quicker than before. And if this happens time after time it ends by growing hardened, and the weakness confirms the avarice in a man. For he who has a fever and gets quit of it is not in the same condition as before he had it, unless he has undergone a complete cure. The same sort of thing happens with affections of the mind. They leave traces behind them like weals from a blow, and if a man does not succeed in removing them, when he is flogged again on the same place his weals turn into sores. If, then, you wish not to be choleric, do not feed the angry habit, do not add fuel to the fire. To begin with, keep quiet, and count the days when you were not angry. I used to be angry every day, then every other day, then every three days, then every four. But if you miss thirty days, then sacrifice to God: for the habit is first weakened and then wholly destroyed.

I kept free from distress to-day, and again next day, and for two or three months after; and when occasions arose to provoke it, I took pains to check it.

Know that you are doing well.

To-day when I saw a handsome woman I did not say to myself, 'Would that she were mine!' and 'Blessed is her husband!' For he who says that will say, 'Blessed is the adulterer!' Nor do I picture the next scene: the woman present and disrobing and reclining by my side. I pat myself on the head and say, 'Bravo, Epictetus, you have refuted a pretty fallacy, a much prettier one than the so-called "Master"'. And if, though the woman herself, poor thing, is willing and beckons and sends to me, and even touches me and comes close to me, I still hold aloof and conquer: the refutation of this fallacy is something greater than the argument of 'The Liar', or the 'Resting' argument. This is a thing to be really proud of, rather than of propounding the 'Master' argument.

How, then, is this to be done? Make up your mind at last to please your true self, make up your mind to appear noble to God; set your desires on becoming pure in the presence of your pure self and God. 'Then when an impression of that sort assails you', says Plato [*Laws*, 854b], 'go and offer expiatory sacrifices, go as a suppliant and sacrifice to the gods who avert evil': it is enough even if 'you withdraw to the society of the good and noble' and set yourself to compare them with yourself, whether your pattern be among the living or the dead. Go to Socrates and see him reclining with Alcibiades and making light of his beauty. Consider what a victory, what an Olympic triumph, he won over himself–and knew it–what place he thus achieved among the followers of Heracles! a victory that deserves the salutation, 'Hail, admirable victor, who hast conquered something more than these worn-out boxers and pancratiasts and the gladiators who are like them!' If you set these thoughts against your impression, you will conquer it, and not be carried away by it. But first of all do not be hurried away by the suddenness of the shock, but say, 'Wait for me a little, impression. Let me see what you are, and what is at stake: let me test you'. And, further, do not allow it to go on picturing the next scene. If you do, it straightway carries you off whither it will. Cast out this filthy impression and bring in some other impression, a lovely and noble one, in its place. I say, if you acquire the habit of training yourself thus, you will see what shoulders you get, what sinews, what vigour; but now you have only paltry words and nothing more.

The man who truly trains is he who disciplines himself to face such impressions. Stay, unhappy man! be not carried away. Great is the struggle, divine the task; the stake is a kingdom, freedom, peace, an unruffled spirit. Remember God, call Him to aid and support you, as voyagers call in storm to the Dioscuri. Can any storm be greater than that which springs from violent impressions that drive out reason? For what is storm itself but an impression? Take away the fear of death, and you may bring as much thunder and lightning as you will, and you will discover what deep peace and tranquillity is in your mind. But if you once allow yourself to be defeated and say that you will conquer hereafter, and then do the same again, be sure that you will be weak and miserable; you will never notice hereafter that you are going wrong, but will even begin to provide excuses for your conduct: and then you will confirm the truth of Hesiod's words, 'A dilatory man is ever wrestling with calamities'. [*Works and Days*, 413]

CHAPTER NINETEEN

To those who Take up the Principles of the Philosophers Only to Discuss them

THE 'MASTER' ARGUMENT APPEARS to have been propounded on some such basis as this.

There are three propositions which are at variance with one another–i.e., any two with the third–namely, these: (1) everything true as an event in the past is necessary; (2) the impossible does not follow from the possible; (3) what neither is true nor will be is yet possible. Diodorus, noticing this conflict of statements, used the probability of the first two to prove the conclusion, 'Nothing is possible which neither is nor will be true'. Some one else, however, will maintain another pair of these propositions. 'What neither is nor will be true is yet possible', and, 'The impossible does not follow from the possible', while rejecting the third, 'Everything true in the past is necessary', as appears to be the view of Cleanthes and his school, who have been supported to a large extent by Antipater. Others maintain the third pair, 'What neither is true nor will be is yet possible', and 'Everything true as an event in the past is necessary', and reject 'The impossible does not follow from the possible'. But to maintain all three propositions at once is impracticable, because every pair is in conflict with the third.

If, then, some one ask me, 'But which of these do you maintain?' I shall answer him that I do not know, but the account I have received is that Diodorus maintained one pair, and the school of Panthoides and Cleanthes, I fancy, the second, and the school of Chrysippus the third.

'What do you hold then?'

I have never given my mind to this, to put my own impression to the test and compare different views and form a judgement of my own on the subject: therefore I am no better than a grammarian.

'Who was Hector's father?'

Priam.

'Who were his brothers?'

Paris and Deiphobus.

'And who was their mother?'

Hecuba. That is the account I have received.

'From whom?'

From Homer: and Hellanicus also writes on the same subject, I believe, and others of the same class.

So it is with me and the 'Master' argument: I go no further. But if I am a vain person I cause the utmost amazement among the company at a banquet by enumerating those who have written on the subject. 'Chrysippus also has written admirably in the first book of his treatise "On the possible". Cleanthes, too, has written a special book on this, and Archedemus. And Antipater also has written, not only in his book on "The possible", but also specially in his work on "the Master" argument. Have you not read the treatise?'

'I have not read it.'

Read it.

And what good will he get from it? He will only be more silly and tiresome than he is now. For what have you got by reading it? What judgement have you formed on the subject? You will only tell us of Helen and Priam and the island of Calypso, which never was nor will be.

And indeed in the field of literature it does not matter much that you should master the received account and have formed no judgement of your own. But we are much more liable to this fault in matters of conduct than in literary matters.

'Tell me about things good and evil.'

Listen.

From Ilion to the Cicones I came,
Wind-borne.

[Homer, *Odyssey*, IX. 39]

'Of things that are, some are good, some bad, some indifferent. The virtues and all that share in them are good, vices and all that share in them are bad, and all that comes between is indifferent–wealth, health, life, death, pleasure, pain.'

How do you know?

'Hellanicus says so in his history of Egypt.' For you might just as well say that as say 'Diogenes or Chrysippus or Cleanthes said so in his Ethics'. I ask, have you put any of these doctrines to the test, and formed a judgement of your own? Show us how you are wont to bear yourself in a storm on shipboard. Do you remember this distinction of good and bad when the sail cracks and you cry aloud to heaven, and some bystander, untimely merry, says 'Tell me, by the gods, what have you been telling us lately? Is it a vice to suffer shipwreck? Does it partake of vice?' Will you not take up a belaying pin and give him a drubbing? 'What have we to do with you, fellow? We are perishing, and you come and mock us.'

Again, if you are sent for by Caesar and are accused, do you remember the distinction? As you enter with a pale face, and trembling withal suppose some one comes up and says to you, 'Why do you tremble, man? What are you concerned about? Does Caesar put virtue and vice in the hearts of those who come before him?'

'Why do you mock me, as though I had not miseries enough?'

Nay, philosopher, tell me why you tremble. Is it not of death you stand in danger, or prison or pain of body or exile or disgrace, nothing else? Is it wickedness, or anything that partakes of wickedness? And what did you tell us that all these were?

'Man, what have I to do with you? My own evils are enough for me.'

Well said, indeed: for your own evils are indeed enough–meanness, cowardice, the boasting spirit, which you showed when you sat in the lecture-room. Why did you pride yourself on what was not your own? Why did you call yourself a Stoic?

Watch your own conduct thus and you will discover to what school you belong. You will find that most of you are Epicureans and some few Peripatetics, but with all the fibre gone from you. Where have you shown that you really hold virtue to be equal to all else, or even superior? Show me a Stoic if you can! Where or how is he to be found? You can show me men who use the fine phrases of the Stoics, in any number, for the same men who do this can recite Epicurean phrases just as well and can repeat those of the Peripatetics just as perfectly; is it not so?

Who then is a Stoic?

Show me a man moulded to the pattern of the judgements that he utters, in the same way as we call a statue Phidian that is moulded according to the art of Phidias. Show me one who is sick and yet happy, in peril and yet happy, dying and yet happy, in exile and happy, in disgrace and happy. Show him me. By the gods I would fain see a Stoic. Nay you cannot show me a finished Stoic; then show me one in the moulding, one who has set his feet on the path. Do me this kindness, do not grudge an old man like me a sight I never saw till now. What! you think you are going to show me the Zeus of Phidias or his Athena, that work of ivory and gold? It is a soul I want; let one of you show me the soul of a man who wishes to be at one with God, and to blame God or man no longer, to fail in nothing, to feel no misfortune, to be free from anger, envy, and jealousy–one who (why wrap up my meaning?) desires to change his manhood for godhead, and who in this poor dead body of his has his purpose set upon communion with God. Show him to me. Nay, you cannot. Why, then, do you mock yourselves, and trifle with others? Why do you put on a character which is not your own, and walk about like thieves and robbers in these stolen phrases and properties that do not belong to you?

And so now I am your teacher, and you are at school with me: and my purpose is this, to make you my completed work, untouched by hindrance or compulsion, or constraint, free, tranquil, happy, looking to God in everything small or great; and you are here to learn and practise these things. Why, then, do you not finish the work, if indeed you also have the purpose you should have, and if I have the purpose and the proper equipment also? What is it that is wanting? When I see a craftsman and material ready to his hand, I look for the finished work. Now here, too, is the craftsman, and here is the material. What do we lack? Is not the subject teachable? It is teachable. Is it not within our power then? Nay, it is the one thing of all others which is in our power. Wealth is not in our power, nor health, nor anything else, in a word, except the proper use of impressions. This alone, by nature's gift, is unhindered and untrammelled. Why, then, do you not finish the work? Tell me the reason: for it lies either in me or in you or in the nature of the thing. The achievement itself is possible, and rests with us alone. It follows then that the reason lies in me or in you, or, more truly, in both. What is my conclusion? Let us begin, if you only will, to carry out such purpose here and now. Let us leave behind what is past. Only let us begin; have trust in me, and you shall see.

CHAPTER TWENTY

Against Followers of Epicurus and of the Academy

EVEN THOSE WHO CONTRADICT propositions that are true and evident are obliged to make use of them. And indeed one may almost give as the strongest proof that a thing is evident that even he who contradicts it finds himself obliged to make use of it. For instance, if one should deny that any universal statement is true, plainly he cannot help asserting the contrary.

'No universal statement is true.'

Slave, this is not true either: for what else is your assertion than, 'If a statement is universal, it is false?' Again, if one comes forward and says, 'Know that nothing is knowable, but that everything is unprovable,' or another says, 'Believe me, and it will be to your advantage; you ought not to believe a man at all'; or again, if another says, 'Learn from me, man, that it is impossible to learn anything; I tell you this, and will teach you, if you will.' What difference is there between such persons and–whom shall I say?–those who call themselves Academics? 'Men, give your assent to the statement that no man assents!'

'Believe us that no man believes any one!'

So too Epicurus, when he wishes to get rid of the natural fellowship of men with one another, makes use of the very principle of which he is getting rid. For what does he say? 'Men, be not deceived, be not misled or deluded. There is no natural fellowship of rational beings with one another: believe me. Those who state the contrary deceive you and mislead your reason.'

What concern, then, is it of yours? Let us be deceived. Will you come off any the worse if the rest of us are all convinced that we have a natural fellowship with one another and that we are bound by all means to guard it? Nay, your position will be much better and more secure. Man, why do you take thought for our sake, why do you keep awake for us, why do you light your lamp, why do you rise early, why do you write such big books? Is it to prevent any of us being deluded into thinking that the gods have any care for mankind, or to prevent us from supposing that the nature of the good is anything but pleasure? For if this is so, be off with you and go to sleep; do as the worm does, for this is the life of which you pronounce yourself worthy: eating, drinking, copulation, evacuation, and snoring.

What does it matter to you, what opinions others will hold on these matters, or whether they are right or wrong? What have we to do with you? You take interest in sheep because they offer themselves to be shorn and milked and finally to be slaughtered by us. Would it not be desirable if men could be charmed and bewitched by the Stoics into slumber, and offer themselves to you and those like you to be shorn and milked? These sentiments were proper enough to utter to your fellow Epicureans; ought you not to conceal them from outsiders, and take special pains to convince them before all things that we are born with a sociable nature, that self-control is a good thing, that so you may secure everything for yourself? Or do you say we must maintain this fellowship towards some and not towards others? Towards whom, then, must we observe it? Towards those who observe it in their turn, or towards those who transgress it? And who transgress it more completely than you who have laid down these doctrines?

What, then, was it that roused Epicurus from his slumbers and compelled him to write what he wrote? What else but that which is the most powerful of all human things, Nature, which draws a man to her will though he groan and resist? For (she says), because you hold these unsociable opinions, write them down and bequeath them to others and stay up late for them and by your own act accuse the very principles you maintain. What! we speak of Orestes pursued by the Furies and roused from his slumbers, but are not the Furies and Torments that beset Epicurus more exacting? They roused him from his sleep and would not allow him to rest, but compelled him to announce his miseries, as madness and wine compel the priests of Cybele. So powerful and unconquerable a thing is human nature. How can a vine be moved to act, not as a vine but as an olive, or again an olive not as an olive but as a vine? It is impossible, inconceivable. So it is impossible for man utterly to destroy the instincts of man; even those who have their bodily organs cut off cannot cut off the desires of men. In the same way Epicurus, though he cut off all the attributes of a man and a householder and a citizen and a friend, could not cut off human desires. No, he could not do it, any more than the indolent Academics could cast away or blind their senses, though they have made this the chief object of their life. Is not this sheer misfortune? A man has received from Nature measures and standards for the discovery of truth, and instead of busying himself to add to them and to work out further results, he does exactly the opposite, and tries to remove and destroy any faculty which he possesses for discovering the truth.

What say you, philosopher? What is your view of religion and piety?

'If you will, I will prove that it is good.'

Prove it then, that our fellow citizens may take heed and honour the Divine and cease at last from being indifferent as to the highest matters.

'Have you the proofs then?'

I have, and am thankful for it!

'Since you find such an interest in these things, now hear the contrary: "The gods do not exist, and if they do, they pay no regard to men and we have no communion with them, and thus religion and piety, of which the multitude talk, are a lie of pretentious persons and sophists, or it may be of lawgivers, for the fear and deterrence of wrongdoers."'

Bravo, philosopher! What a service you confer on our citizens! Our young men are already inclining to despise divine things, and you recover them for us!

'What is the matter? Does not this please you? Now learn, how justice is nothing, how self-respect is folly, how "father" and "son" are empty words.'

Bravo, philosopher! Stick to your task, persuade our young men, that we may have more to agree with you and share your views. These, no doubt, are the arguments which have brought well-governed cities to greatness, these are the arguments which made Lacedaemon, these are the convictions which Lycurgus wrought into the Spartans by his laws and training: that slavery is no more shameful than noble, and freedom no more noble than shameful! For these beliefs no doubt those who died at Thermopylae died! And for what principles but these did the Athenians give up their city?

And yet the men who state these theories marry and beget children and share in city life and appoint themselves priests and prophets. Of what? Of what has no existence! And they question the Pythian prophetess themselves, to learn lies, and they interpret oracles to others. Is not this the height of shameless imposition?

Man, what are you doing? You convict yourself of falsehood day by day: will you not abandon these crude fallacies? When you eat where do you put your hand, to your mouth or to your eye? When you bathe into what do you go? When did you ever call the jug a saucer or the ladle a spit?

If I were slave to one of these men, I would torture him, even if I had to stand a flogging from him every day. Put a drop of oil, boy, in the bath.' I would get some fish sauce and pour it over his head. 'What is that? By your fortune I had an impression, very like oil, indistinguishable from it. 'Give me gruel here.' I would fill a dish with vinegar sauce and bring it him.

'Did I not ask for gruel?'

Yes, master, this is gruel.

'Is not this vinegar sauce?'

How is it more that than gruel?

'Take it and smell, take it and taste.'

How can you know if the senses play us false? If I had three or four fellow slaves who shared my mind I should give him such a dressing that he would hang himself, or change his opinion. Such men trifle with us; they take advantage of all the gifts of nature, while in theory they do away with them.

Grateful and self-respecting men indeed! they eat bread every day, to say nothing else, and yet dare to assert that we know not whether there is a Demeter or Kore or Pluto: not to say that they enjoy day and night and the changes of the year, the stars and sea and land and the service that men render, yet not one of these things makes them take notice in the least. No, their only aim is to vomit their paltry problem, and having thus exercised their stomach to go away and have a bath. But they have not given the slightest thought to what they are going to say: what subject they are going to speak about, or to whom, and what they are going to get from these arguments: whether any young man of noble spirit may be influenced by them or has been influenced already and may lose all the germs of nobility in him: whether we may be giving an adulterer opportunity to brazen out his acts: whether one who is embezzling public funds may find some excuse to lay hold of in these theories: whether one who neglects his parents may get from them fresh courage.

What, then, do you hold good or evil, base or noble? Is it this doctrine, or that? It is useless to go on disputing with one of these men, or reasoning with him, or trying to alter his opinion. One might have very much more hope of altering the mind of a profligate than of men who are absolutely deaf and blind to their own miseries.

CHAPTER TWENTY ONE

Concerning Inconsistency of Mind

THERE ARE SOME ADMISSIONS which men readily make, others they do not. Now no one will admit that he is thoughtless or foolish: on the contrary, you will hear every one say, 'Would that I had luck as I have wits!' But men readily admit that they are cowards and say, 'I am a bit of a coward, I admit, but for the rest you will find me no fool'. A man will not readily own to incontinence, to injustice not at all, never to envy or fussiness, while most men will own to being pitiful. You ask what is the reason? The most vital reason is a confusion and want of consistency in men's views of what is good and evil, but, apart from this, different persons are affected by different motives; speaking generally, people are not ready to own to qualities which to their mind appear base. Cowardice and a sense of pity they imagine show good nature, silliness a slavish mind, and social faults they are least ready to admit. In most of the errors which they are inclined to confess to, it is because they think there is an involuntary element, as in the cowardly and the pitiful. So if any one does own to incontinence, he brings in passion, to give him the excuse of involuntary action. Injustice is in no circumstances conceived as involuntary. There is an involuntary element, they think, in jealousy, and for this reason this too is a fault which men confess.

Moving, then, as we do among men of this character, so bewildered, so ignorant of what they are saying, or of what evil is theirs, or whether they have any, or what is the reason of it, or how they are to be relieved, we ought ourselves, I think, to be constantly on our guard, asking ourselves, 'Am I too perhaps one of them? What impression have I of myself? How do I bear myself? Do I too bear myself as a man of prudence and self-control? Do I too sometimes say that I am educated to meet every emergency? Am I conscious, as the man who knows nothing should be, that I know nothing? Do I come to my teacher as to the oracles, prepared to obey, or do I too come to school like a driveller, to learn nothing but history and to understand the books which I did not understand before, and if it so chance, to expound them to others?'

Man, you have had a boxing match with your slave at home, and turned your house upside down and disturbed your neighbours, and now do you come to me with a solemn air like a wise man and sit and criticize the way I interpret language, and how I rattle out anything that comes into my head? Do you come in a spirit of envy, depressed because nothing is brought you from home, and while the discussion is going on, sit thinking of nothing yourself but how you stand with your father or your brother? 'What are men at home saying about me? They are think-ing now that I am making progress and say, "He will come back knowing everything". I did indeed wish to return one day if I could, having learnt everything, but it needs hard work, and no one sends me anything and the baths are shockingly bad in Nicopolis, and I am badly off in my lodg-ings and in the lecture-room.'

Then they say, 'No one gets any good from the lecture-room!'

Why, who comes to the lecture-room? Who comes to be cured? Who comes to have his judgements purified? Who comes that he may grow conscious of his needs? Why are you surprised, then, that you carry away from school the very qualities you bring there, for you do not come to put away your opinions or to correct them, or to get others in exchange? No, far from it! What you must look to is whether you get what you come for. You wish to chatter about principles. Well, do you not come away with lighter tongues than before? Does not school afford you material for displaying your precious principles? Do you not analyse variable syllogisms? Do you not pursue the assumptions of 'The Liar' and hypothetical propositions? Why then do you go on being vexed at getting what you come for?

'Yes, but if my child or my brother die, or if I must be racked and die myself, what good will such things do me?'

What! is this what you came for? Is this what you sit by me for? Did you ever light your lamp or sit up late for this? Or, when you have gone out for a walk, have you ever put a conception before your mind instead of a syllogism and pursued this with your companion? When have you ever done so? Then you say, 'Principles are useless.' To whom? To those who use them wrongly. For collyrium is not use-less to those who anoint themselves at the right time and in the right way, plasters are not useless, leaping-weights are not useless, but only useless to some, and again useful to others.

If you ask me now, 'Are syllogisms useful?' I shall say they are useful, and if you wish I will prove it.

'What good have they done me then?'

Man, did you ask whether they were useful in general, or useful to you? Suppose a man suffering from dysentery asked me, 'Is vinegar useful?' I shall say it is. 'Is it useful to me?' I shall say: 'No; seek first to get your flux stayed, and your ulcerations healed.' It is the same with you. You must first attend to your ulcers, and stay your flux, and arrive at peace in your mind and bring it to school undistracted, and then you will discover how wonderful the power of reason is.

CHAPTER TWENTY TWO

On Friendship

A MAN NATURALLY LOVES those things in which he is interested. Now do men take an interest in things evil? Certainly not. Do they take interest in what does not concern them? No, they do not. It follows then that they are interested in good things alone, and if interested in them, therefore love them too. Whoever then has knowledge of good things, would know how to love them; but how could one who cannot distinguish good things from evil and things indifferent from both have power to love? Therefore the wise man alone has power to love.

'Nay, how is this?' says one. 'I am not wise, yet I love my child.'

By the gods, I am surprised, to begin with, at your admission that you are not wise. What do you lack? Do you not enjoy sensation, do you not distinguish impressions, do you not supply your body with the food that is suited to it, and with shelter and a dwelling? How is it then that you admit that you are foolish? I suppose because you are often disturbed and bewildered by your impressions, and overcome by their persuasive powers, so that the very things that at one moment you consider good you presently consider bad and afterwards indifferent; and, in a word, you are subject to pain, fear, envy, confusion, change: that is why you confess yourself to be foolish. And do you not change in your affections? Do you believe at one time that wealth and pleasure and mere outward things are good, and at another time that they are evil, and do you not regard the same persons now as good, now as bad, and sometimes feel friendly towards them, sometimes unfriendly, and now praise, now blame them?

'Yes. I am subject to these feelings.'

Well then; do you think a man can be a friend to anything about which he is deceived?

'Not at all.'

Nor can he whose choice of a friend is subject to change bear good will to him?

'No, he cannot.'

Can he who first reviles a man and then admires him?

'No, he cannot.'

Again, did you never see curs fawning on one another and playing with one another, so that you say nothing could be friendlier? But to see what friendship is, throw a piece of meat among them and you will learn. So with you and your dear boy: throw a bit of land between you, and you will learn how your boy wishes to give you a speedy burial, and you pray for the boy to die. Then you cry out again, 'What a child I have reared! He is impatient to bury me.' Throw a pretty maid between you and suppose you both love her, you the old man, and he the young man. Or suppose you throw a bit of glory between you. And if you have to risk your life, you will use the words of Admetus' father:

> *You love the light; shall not your father love it?*
> [Euripides, *Alcestis*, 691]

Do you think that he did not love his own child when it was small, and was not distressed when it had the fever, and did not often say, 'Would it were I who had the fever instead!'? yet when the event came close upon him, see what words they utter! Were not Eteocles and Polynices born of the same mother and the same father? Were they not reared together, did they not live together, drink together, sleep together, often kiss one another, so that if one had seen them he would, no doubt, have laughed at the paradoxes of philosophers on friendship. Yet when the bit of meat, in the shape of a king's throne, fell between them, see what they say:

> E. *Where wilt stand upon the tower?*
> P. *Wherefore dost thou ask me this?*
> E. *I will face thee then and slay thee.*
> P. *I desire thy blood no less.*
> [Euripides, *The Phoenissae*, 621]

Yes, such are the prayers they utter!

For be not deceived, every creature, to speak generally, is attached to nothing so much as to its own interest. Whatever then seems to hinder his way to this, be it a brother or a father or a child, the object of his passion or his own lover, he hates him, guards against him, curses him. For his nature is to love nothing so much as his own interest; this is his father and brother and kinsfolk and country and god. At any rate, when the gods seem to hinder us in regard to this we revile even the gods and overthrow their statues and set fire to their temples, as Alexander ordered the shrines of Asclepius to be burnt when the object of his passion died. Therefore if interest, religion and honour, country, parents and friends are set in the same scale, then all are safe; but if interest is in one scale, and in the other friends and country and kindred and justice itself, all these are weighed down by interest and disappear. For the creature must needs incline to that side where 'I' and 'mine' are; if they are in the flesh, the ruling power must be there; if in the will, it must be there; if in external things, it must be there.

If then I identify myself with my will, then and only then shall I be a friend and son and father in the true sense. For this will be my interest–to guard my character for good faith, honour, forbearance, self-control, and service of others, to maintain my relations with others. But if I separate myself from what is noble, then Epicurus' statement is confirmed, which declares that 'there is no such thing as the noble or at best it is but the creature of opinion'.

It was this ignorance that made the Athenians and Lacedaemonians quarrel with one another, and the Thebans with both, and the Great King with Hellas, and the Macedonians with Hellas and the King, and now the Romans with the Getae; and yet earlier this was the reason of the wars with Ilion. Paris was the guest of Menelaus, and any one who had seen the courtesies they used to one another would not have believed one who denied that they were friends. But a morsel was thrown between them, in the shape of a pretty woman, and for that there was war! So now, when you see friends or brothers who seem to be of one mind, do not therefore pronounce upon their friendship, though they swear to it and say it is impossible for them to part with one another. The Governing Principle of the bad man is not to be trusted; it is uncertain, irresolute, conquered now by one impression, now by another. The question you must ask is, not what others ask, whether they were born of the same parents and brought up together and under the charge of the same slave; but this question only, where they put their interest–outside them or in the will. If they put it outside, do not call them friends, any more than you can call them faithful, or stable, or confident, or free; nay, do not call them even men, if you are wise. For it is no human judgement which makes them bite one another and revile one another and occupy deserts or market-places like wild beasts and behave like robbers in the law-courts; and which makes them guilty of profligacy and adultery and seduction and the other offences men commit against one another. There is one judgement and one only which is responsible for all this–that they set themselves and all their interests elsewhere than in their will. But if you hear that these men in very truth believe the good to lie only in the region of the will and in dealing rightly with impressions, you need trouble yourself no more as to whether a man is son or father, whether they are brothers, or have been familiar companions for years; I say, if you grasp this one fact and no more, you may pronounce with confidence that they are friends, as you may that they are faithful and just. For where else is friendship but where faith and honour are, where men give and take what is good, and nothing else?

'But he has paid me attention all this time: did he not love me?'

How do you know, slave, whether he has paid you this attention, as a man cleans his boots, or tends his beast? How do you know whether, when you have lost your use as a paltry vessel, he will not throw you away like a broken plate?

'But she is my wife and we have lived together this long time.'

How long did Eriphyle live with Amphiaraus, ay, and was mother of many children?–But a necklace came between them.

'What do you mean by a necklace?'

Man's judgement about good and evil. This was the brutish element, this was what broke up the friendship, which suffered not the wife to be true to her wedlock, nor the mother to be a mother indeed. So let every one of you, who is anxious himself to be friend to another, or to win another for his friend, uproot these judgements, hate them, drive them out of his mind. If he does that, then first he will never revile himself or be in conflict with himself, he will be free from change of mind, and self-torture; secondly he will be friendly to his neighbour, always and absolutely, if he be like himself, and if he be unlike, he will bear with him, be gentle and tender with him, considerate to him as one who is ignorant and in error about the highest matters; not hard upon any man, for he knows of a certainty Plato's saying, 'No soul is robbed of the truth save involuntarily'.

But if you fail to do this, you may do everything else that friends do – drink together and live under the same roof and sail in the same ship and be born of the same parents; well, the same may be true of snakes, but neither they nor you will be capable of friendship so long as you retain these brutish and revolting judgements.

CHAPTER TWENTY THREE

On the Faculty of Expression

EVERY ONE CAN READ a book with the more pleasure and ease the plainer the letters in which it is written. So too every one can listen more easily to discourse which is expressed in becoming and distinguished language. We must therefore not say that the faculty of expression is nothing. To say so is at once irreligious and cowardly; irreligious because it means disparaging God's gifts, just as though one should deny the usefulness of the faculty of vision or hearing or even the faculty of speech. Was it for nothing then that God gave you your eyes? Was it for nothing He mingled with them a spirit so powerful and cunningly devised, that even from a distance they can fashion the shapes of what they see? And what messenger is so swift and attentive as they? Was it for nothing that He made the intervening air so active and sensitive that vision passes through it as through a tense medium? Was it for nothing that He made light, without the presence of which all the rest would have been useless?

Man, be not ungrateful, nor again forget higher things! Give thanks to God for sight and hearing, yes, and for life itself and what is conducive to life–for grain and fruit, for wine and oil; but remember that He has given you another gift superior to all these, the faculty which shall use them, test them, and calculate the value of each. For what is it that pronounces on each of these faculties, and decides their value? Is it the faculty itself, in each case? Did you ever hear the faculty of vision saying anything about itself, or the faculty of hearing? No, these faculties are ordained as ministers and slaves to serve the faculty which deals with impressions. And if you ask what each is worth, whom do you ask? Who answers you? How then can any other faculty be superior to this, which uses the rest as its servants and itself tests each result and pronounces on it? Which of those faculties knows what it is and what it is worth, which of them knows when it ought to be used and when it ought not? What is the faculty that opens and closes the eyes and brings them near some objects and turns them away, at need, from others? Is it the faculty of vision? No, it is the faculty of will. What is it that closes and opens the ears? What is it that makes us curious and questioning, or again unmoved by discourse? Is it the faculty of hearing? It is no other faculty but that of the will.

I say, when the will sees that all the other faculties which surround it are blind and deaf and are unable to see anything else beyond the very objects for which they are ordained to minister to this faculty and serve it, and this alone has clear sight and surveys the rest and itself and estimates their value, is it likely to pronounce that any other faculty but itself is the highest? What is the function of the eye, when opened, but to see? But what is it tells us whether we ought to look at a man's wife or how? The faculty of will. What tells us whether we ought to believe or disbelieve what we are told, and if we believe whether we are to be excited or not? Is it not the faculty of will? This faculty of eloquence I spoke of, if such special faculty there be, concerned with the framing of fair phrases, does no more than construct and adorn phrases, when there is an occasion for discourse, just as hairdressers arrange and adorn the hair. But whether it is better to speak or be silent, and to speak in this way or that, and whether it is proper or improper–in a word, to decide the occasion and the use for each discourse, all these are questions for one faculty only, that of the will. Would you have it come forward and pronounce against itself?

'But', says the objector, 'what if the matter stands thus, what if that which ministers can be superior to that which it serves, the horse to the horseman, the hound to the hunter, the lyre to him that plays it, the servants to the king they serve?' The answer is: What is it that uses other things? The will. What is it that attends to everything? The will. What is it that destroys the whole man, now by starvation, now by a halter, now by a headlong fall? The will. Is there then anything stronger in men than this? Nay, how can things that are subject to hindrance be stronger than that which is unhindered? What has power to hinder the faculty of vision? Will and events beyond the will. The faculty of hearing and that of speech are subject to the same hindrance. But what can hinder the will? Nothing beyond the will, only the perversion of the will itself. Therefore vice or virtue resides in this alone. Yet being so mighty a faculty, ordained to rule all the rest, you would have it come forward and tell us that the flesh is of all things most excellent. Why, if the flesh itself asserted that it was the most excellent of things, one would not tolerate it even then. But as it is, Epicurus, what is the faculty that pronounces this judgement? Is it the faculty which has written on 'The End' or 'Physics' or 'The Standard'? The faculty which made you grow your beard as a philosopher? which wrote in the hour of death 'I am living my last day and that a blessed one'? Is this faculty flesh or will? Surely it is madness to admit that you have a faculty superior to this. Can you be in truth so blind and deaf?

What follows? Do we disparage the other faculties? God forbid. Do we say that there is no use nor advancement save in the faculty of will? God forbid! That were foolish, irreligious, ungrateful toward God. We are only giving each thing its due. For there is use in an ass, but not so much as in an ox; there is use in a dog, but not so much as in a servant; there is use in a servant, but not so much as in a fellow-citizen; there is use in them too, but not so much as in those who govern them. Yet because other faculties are higher we must not depreciate the use which inferior faculties yield. The faculty of eloquence has its value, but it is not so great as that of the will; but when I say this, let no one suppose that I bid you neglect your manner of speech, any more than I would have you neglect eyes or ears or hands or feet or clothes or shoes.

But if you ask me, 'What then is the highest of all things,' what am I to say? The faculty of speech? I cannot say that. No, the faculty of will, when it is in the right way. For it is this which controls the faculty of speech and all other faculties small and great. When this is set in the right course, a man becomes good; when it fails, man becomes bad; it is this which makes our fortune bad or good, this which makes us critical of one another or well content; in a word, to ignore this means misery, to attend to it means happiness.

Yet to do away with the faculty of eloquence and deny its existence is indeed not only ungrateful to those who have given it, but shows a coward's spirit. For he who denies it seems to me to fear that, if there is a faculty of eloquence, we may not be able to despise it. It is just the same with those who deny that there is any difference between beauty and ugliness. What! are we to believe that the sight of Thersites could move men as much as the sight of Achilles, and the sight of Helen no more than the sight of an ordinary woman? No, these are the words of foolish and uneducated persons, who do not know one thing from another, and who fear that if once one becomes aware of such differences, one may be overwhelmed and defeated.

No, the great thing is this–to leave each in possession of his own faculty, and so leaving him to see the value of the faculty, and to understand what is the highest of all things and to pursue this always, and concentrate your interest on this, counting all other things subordinate to this, yet not failing to attend to them too so far as you may. For even to the eyes you must attend, yet not as though they were the highest, but to these also for the sake of the highest; for the highest will not fulfil its proper nature unless it uses the eyes with reason, and chooses one thing rather than another.

What then do we see men doing? They are like a man returning to his own country who, finding a good inn on his road, stays on there because it pleases him. Man, you are forgetting your purpose! You were not travelling to this, but through it.

'Yes, but this is a fine inn.'

And how many other fine inns are there, and how many fine meadows? But they are merely to pass through; your purpose is yonder; to return to your country, to relieve your kinsfolk of their fears, to fulfil your own duties as a citizen, to marry, beget children, and hold office in due course. For you have not come into the world to choose your pick of fine places, but to live and move in the place where you were born and appointed to be a citizen. The same principle holds good in what we are discussing. Our road to perfection must needs lie through instruction and the spoken word; and one must purify the will and bring into right order the faculty which deals with impressions; and principles must be communicated in a particular style, with some variety and epigram. But this being so, some people are attracted by the very means they are using and stay where they are, one caught by style, another by syllogisms, a third by variable arguments, and a fourth by some other seductive inn by the way; and there they stay on and moulder away, like those whom the Sirens entertain.

Man, the purpose set before you was to make yourself capable of dealing with the impressions that you meet as nature orders, so as not to fail in what you will to get, nor to fall into what you will to avoid, never suffering misfortune or bad fortune, free, unhindered, unconstrained, conforming to the governance of God, obeying this, well pleased with this, criticizing none, blaming none, able to say these lines with your whole heart,

Lead me, O Zeus, and thou my Destiny.

[Cleanthes]

Having this purpose before you, are you going to stay where you are just because a pretty phrase or certain precepts please you, and choose to make your home there, forgetting what you have left at home, and say, 'These things are fine'? Who says they are not fine? But they are fine as things to pass through, as inns by the way. What prevents you from being unfortunate, though you speak like Demosthenes? Though you can analyse syllogisms like Chrysippus, what prevents you from being wretched, mournful, envious–in a word, bewildered and miserable? Nothing prevents you. Do you see then that these were inns of no value; and the goal set before you was different? Certain persons when I say this think I am disparaging the study of rhetoric or of principles. No, I am not depreciating that, but only the tendency to dwell unceasingly on such matters and to set your hopes on them. If any man does his hearers harm by bringing this truth home to them, count me among those who do this harm. But when I see that what is highest and most sovereign is something different, I cannot say that it is what it is not in order to gratify you.

CHAPTER TWENTY FOUR

To One whom he did not Think Worthy

SOME ONE SAID TO him, 'I often came to you, desiring to hear you and you never gave me an answer, and now, if it may be, I beg you to say something to me'.

Do you think, he replied, that there is an art of speaking, like other arts, and that he who has it will speak with skill and he who has it not, without skill?

'I think so.'

Is it true then that he who by his speech gains benefit himself and is able to benefit others would speak with skill, and he who tends to be harmed himself and harm others would be unskilled in the art of speaking?

'Yes, you would find that some are harmed, some benefited.'

But what of the hearers? Are they all benefited by what they hear, or would you find that of them too some are benefited and some harmed?

'Yes, that is true of them too', he said.

Here too then it is true that those who hear with skill are benefited, and those who hear without skill are harmed?

He agreed.

Is there then a skill in hearing as well as in speaking?

'So it appears.'

If you will, look at the question thus. Whose part do you think it is to touch an instrument musically?

'The musician's.'

And whose part do you think it is to make a statue properly?

'The sculptor's.'

Does it not seem to you to require any art to look at a statue with skill?

'Yes, this requires art too.'

If then right speaking demands a skilled person, do you see that hearing with profit also demands a skilled person? As for perfection and profit in the full sense, that, if you like, we may for the moment dismiss, as we are both far from anything of that sort; but this I think every one would admit, that he who is to listen to philosophers must have at least some practice in listening. Is it not so?

Show me then what it is you would have me speak to you about. What are you able to hear about? About things good and bad? Good what? A good horse?

'No.'

A good ox?

'No.'

What then? A good man?

'Yes.'

Do we know then what man is, what his nature is, what the notion is? Are our ears open in any degree with regard to this? Nay, do you understand what Nature is, or can you in any measure follow me when I speak? Am I to demonstrate to you? How am I to do it? Do you really understand what demonstration is, or how a thing is demonstrated, or by what means, or what processes are like demonstration without being demonstrations? Do you know what is true or what is false, what follows what, what is in conflict, or disagreement or discord with what? Can I rouse you to philosophy? How can I show you the conflict of the multitude, their disputes as to things good and evil, useful and harmful, when you do not so much as know what conflict is? Show me then what good I shall do you by conversing with you.

'Rouse my interest.'

As the sheep when he sees the grass that suits him has his desire roused to eat, but if you set a stone or loaf by him he will not be roused, so there are in us certain natural inclinations toward discourse, when the appropriate hearer appears and provokes the inclination; but if he lies there like a stone or a piece of grass, how can he rouse a man's will? Does the vine say to the farmer, 'Attend to me'? No, its very appearance shows that it will be to his profit to attend to it and so calls out his energies. Who does not answer the call of winning and saucy children to play with them and crawl with them and talk nonsense with them, but who wants to play or bray with an ass? However small he may be, he is still an ass.

'Why then do you say nothing to me?'

There is only one thing I can say to you, that he who is ignorant who he is and for what he is born and what the world is that he is in and who are his fellows, and what things are good and evil, noble and base; who cannot understand reasoning or demonstration, or what is true or what false, and is unable to distinguish them, such a man will not follow nature in his will to get or to avoid, in his impulses or designs, in assent, refusal, or withholding of assent; to sum up, he will go about the world deaf and blind, thinking himself somebody, when he is really nobody. Do you think there is anything new in this? Ever since the race of men began, have not all errors and misfortunes arisen from this ignorance?

Why did Agamemnon and Achilles quarrel with one another? Was it not because they did not know what was expedient or inexpedient? Did not one say that it was expedient to give back Chryseis to her father, and the other that it was not? Did not one say that he ought to take the other's prize, and the other that he ought not? Did not this too make them forget who they were and for what they had come?

Let be, man, what have you come for? To win women for your love or to make war?

'To make war.'

With whom? Trojans or Greeks?

'Trojans.'

Why then do you leave Hector and draw your sword on your own king? And you, best of men, have you left your duties as a king,

trusted with clans and all their mighty cares,

[Homer, *Iliad*, II. 25]

to fight a duel for a paltry damsel with the most warlike of your allies, whom you ought by all means to respect and guard? Do you show yourself inferior to the courteous high priest who pays all attention to you noble gladiators? Do you see what ignorance as to things expedient leads to?

'But I too am rich.'

Are you any richer than Agamemnon?

'But I am handsome as well.'

Are you any handsomer than Achilles?

'But I have a fine head of hair.'

Had not Achilles a finer, and golden hair too, and he did not comb and smooth it to look fine?

'But I am strong.'

Can you lift a stone as big as Hector or Ajax could?

'But I am noble too.'

Was your mother a goddess, or your father of the seed of Zeus? What good do these things do Achilles, when he sits weeping for his darling mistress?

'But I am an orator.'

And was not he? Do not you see how he handled Odysseus and

Phoenix, the most eloquent of the Hellenes, how he shut their mouths? This is all I can say to you, and even this I have no heart for. 'Why?'

Because you do not excite my interest. Is there anything in you to excite me as men who keep horses are excited at sight of a well-bred horse? Your poor body? You make an ugly figure. Your clothes? They are too luxurious. Your air, your countenance? There is nothing to see. When you wish to hear a philosopher, do not say to him, 'You say nothing to me,' but only show yourself worthy to hear and you will see how you will rouse him to discourse!

CHAPTER TWENTY FIVE

How the Art of Reasoning is Necessary

WHEN ONE OF HIS audience said, 'Convince me that logic is useful,' he said,

Would you have me demonstrate it?

'Yes.'

Well, then, must I not use a demonstrative argument?

And, when the other agreed, he said, How then shall you know if I impose upon you? And when the man had no answer, he said, You see how you yourself admit that logic is necessary, if without it you are not even able to learn this much–whether it is necessary or not.

CHAPTER TWENTY SIX

What is the Distinctive Character of Error

EVERY ERROR IMPLIES CONFLICT; for since he who errs does not wish to go wrong but to go right, plainly he is not doing what he wishes. For what does the thief wish to do? What is to his interest. If then thieving is against his interest, he is not doing what he wishes. But every rational soul by nature dislikes conflict; and so, as long as a man does not understand that he is in conflict, there is nothing to prevent him from doing conflicting acts, but, whenever he understands, strong necessity makes him abandon the conflict and avoid it, just as bitter necessity makes a man renounce a falsehood when he discovers it, though as long as he has not this impression he assents to it as true.

He then who can show to each man the conflict which causes his error, and can clearly bring home to him how he fails to do what he wishes and does what he does not wish, is powerful in argument and strong to encourage and convict. For if one shows this, a man will retire from his error of himself; but as long as you do not succeed in showing this, you need not wonder if he persists in his error, for he acts because he has an impression that he is right. That is why Socrates too, relying on this faculty, said, 'I am not wont to produce any other witness to support what I say, but am content with him to whom I am talking on each occasion; it is his vote that I take, his evidence that I call, and his sole word suffices instead of all.' For Socrates knew what moves the rational soul, and that it will incline to what moves it, whether it wishes to or not. Show the conflict to the rational Governing Principle and it will desist. If you do not show it, blame yourself rather than him who refuses to obey.

Book Three

CHAPTER ONE

On Adornment

WHEN A YOUNG STUDENT of rhetoric came into his lecture-room with his hair elaborately arranged and paying great attention to his dress in general: Tell me, said he, do you not think that some dogs and horses are beautiful and some ugly, and is it not so with every creature?

'I think so', he said.

Is not the same true of men, some are beautiful, some ugly?

'Certainly.'

Now do we give the attribute 'beautiful' to each of them in their own kind on the same grounds or on special grounds in each case? Listen and you will see what I mean. Since we see that a dog is born for one thing and a horse for another, and a nightingale, if you like to take that, for another, speaking generally one would not be giving an absurd opinion in saying that each of them was beautiful when it best fulfilled its nature; and since the nature of each is different, I think that each of them would be beautiful in a different way, would it not?

'Yes.'

So that what makes a dog beautiful makes a horse ugly, and what makes a horse beautiful makes a dog ugly, seeing that their natures are different?

'So it seems.'

Yes, for what makes a pancratiast beautiful does not, I imagine, make a good wrestler, and makes a very ridiculous runner; and one who is beautiful for the pentathlon makes a very ugly appearance as a wrestler?

'True', he said.

What then makes a man beautiful if it is not that which in its kind makes dog and horse beautiful?

'It is just that', he said.

What then makes a dog beautiful? The presence of a dog's virtue. What makes a horse beautiful? The presence of a horse's virtue. What makes a man beautiful? Is it the presence of a man's virtue? Therefore, young man, if you would be beautiful, make this the object of your effort, human virtue. And what is human virtue? Consider whom you praise, when you praise men dispassionately; do you praise the just or the unjust?

'The just.'

Do you praise the temperate or the intemperate?

'The temperate.'

The continent or the incontinent?

'The continent.'

Therefore if you make yourself such an one, be sure that you will make yourself beautiful, but as long as you neglect this you cannot help being ugly, though you should use every device to appear beautiful.

But beyond this I do not know what more to say to you; for, if I say what I think, I shall vex you and you will go out and perhaps never return, but if I say nothing, consider what my conduct will be then; you come to me to get good, and I shall be refusing to do you good; you come to me to consult a philosopher, and I shall be refusing you a philosopher's advice. Besides, it is cruelty towards you to leave you uncorrected. If some day hereafter you come to your senses you will accuse me with god reason: 'What did Epictetus find in me, that when he saw me coming in to him in such a shameful state he should do nothing for me a say never a word to me? Did he so utterly despair of me? Was I n young? Was I not fit to listen to discourse? How many other young men make many mistakes like me in their youth? I hear that one Polemo, who had been the most intemperate of young men, underwent such a wonderful change. Grant that he did not think I should be a Polemo: he could have set my hair right, have taken away my bangles, have stopped me pulling my hairs out, but seeing that I had the aspect of–whom shall I say?–he said nothing.' I do not say whose aspect this is, but you will say it for yourself when you come to look into your own heart, and you will learn what it means and what sort of men they are who adopt it.

If hereafter you bring this charge against me, what defence shall I be able to make?

Yes, but suppose I do speak, and he will not obey?

Did Laius obey Apollo? Did he not go away in his drunken stupor and dismiss the oracle from his mind? What then? Did Apollo withhold the truth from him for that reason? Indeed I do not know whether you will obey me or not, but Apollo knew most certainly that Laius would not obey, and yet he spoke. Why did he speak? Nay, why is he Apollo, why does he give oracles, why has he set himself in this position, to be a Prophet and a Fountain of truth, so that men from all the world come to him? Why is 'Know thyself' written up over his shrine, though no one understands it?

Did Socrates persuade all who came to him to attend to their characters Not one in a thousand! Nevertheless when appointed to this post, as he says, by the ordinance of God, he refused to desert it. Nay, what did he say to his judges? 'If you acquit me', he says, 'on these terms, that I cease to do what I do now, I shall not accept your offer, nor give up my ways, but I shall go to any one I meet, young or old, and put to him these questions that I put now, and I shall question you my fellow citizens far more than any others because you are nearer akin to me.' [Plato, *Apology*, 29c]

Are you so fussy and interfering, Socrates? What do you care what we do?

'What language to use! You are my fellow and kinsman, yet you neglect yourself and provide the city with a bad citizen, your kinsmen with a bad kinsman, and your neighbours with a bad neighbour!'

'Who are you, then?'

To this question it is a weighty answer to say, 'I am he who is bound to take interest in men.' For ordinary cattle dare not resist the lion; but if the bull comes up to withstand him, say to hire, if you think fit, 'Who are you?' and 'What do you care?' Man! in every class of creatures nature produces some exceptional specimen; it is so among cattle, dogs, bees, horses. Do not say then to the exception, 'What are you then?' If you do, he will get a voice somehow and say, 'I am like the purple in a garment: do not require me to be like the rest, nor blame my nature, because it made me different from the rest.'

What then? Am I fit to play this part? How can I be? And are you fit to hear the truth? Would that it were so! Nevertheless since I am condemned, it seems, to wear a white beard and a cloak, and since you come to me as to a philosopher, I will not treat you cruelly as though I despaired of you, but will say, Young man, who is it that you want to make beautiful? First get to know who you are, and then adorn yourself. You are a man, that is, a mortal creature which has the power to deal with impressions rationally. What does 'rationally' mean? Perfectly, and in accordance with nature. What then is your distinctive possession? Your animal nature? No. Your mortality? No. Your power to deal with impressions? No. Your reasoning faculty is the distinctive one: this you must adorn and make beautiful. Leave your hair to Him that formed it in accordance with His will. Tell me, what other names have you? Are you man or woman?

'Man.'

Adorn Man then, not Woman. Woman is born smooth and tender, and if she has much hair on her body it is a prodigy, and exhibited in Rome as a prodigy. But in a man it is a prodigy not to be hairy: if he is born smooth it is a prodigy, and if he make himself smooth by shaving and plucking, what are we to make of him? Where are we to show him, and what notice are we to put up? 'I will show you a man who prefers to be a woman.' What a shocking exhibition! Every one will be astonished at the notice: by Zeus, I think that even the men who pluck out their hairs do so without understanding that this is what they are doing! Man, what complaint have you to make of Nature? Is it that she made you a man? Ought she to have made all to be women? Why, if all were women, there would be no one to adorn yourself for.

If you are not satisfied with your condition as it is, do the thing completely. Remove–what shall I call it?–that which is the cause of your hairiness; make yourself a woman out and out, and not half-man, half-woman, and then we shall not be misled. Whom do you wish to please? Your darling womenkind? Then please them as a man.

'Yes, but they like smooth men.'

Go and hang yourself! If they liked unnatural creatures, would you become one? Is this your function, is this what you were born for, that profligate women should take pleasure in you? Is it with this character that we are to make you a citizen of Corinth, and, if it so chance, City-warden, or Governor of the Ephebi, or General, or Steward of the games? Well, and when you have married a wife, are you going to pluck yourself smooth? For whom and for what? And when you have begotten boys, are you going to bring them into our citizenship as plucked creatures too? Noble citizen and senator and orator! Is this the kind of young man we are to pray to have bred and reared for us?

Nay, by the gods, young man! but when once you have heard these words, go and say to yourself: 'These are not the words of Epictetus: how could they be? but some kind god speaks through him; for it would never have occurred to Epictetus to say this, as he is not wont to speak to any one. Come then, let us obey God, that we may not incur God's wrath.'

Why, if a raven croaks and gives you a sign, it is not the raven that gives the sign, but God through him: and if He gives you a sign through a human voice, will He not be making man tell you this, that you may learn the power of the divine, and see that it gives signs to some in this way, and to others in that, and of the highest and most sovereign matters gives signs through the noblest messenger? What else is the meaning of the poet, when he says

Since we warned him
By Hermes Argus-slayer, clear of sight,
To slay him not nor woo his wedded wife?
                       [Homer, *Odyssey*, I. 39]

And as Hermes was sent down to tell him this, so now the gods have sent 'Hermes the Argus-slayer, their messenger,' and tell you this–not to pervert what is good and right, and not to interfere with it, but to leave man man and woman woman, the beautiful person a beautiful person, and the ugly person an ugly person. For you are not flesh, nor hair, but a rational will: if you get this beautiful, then you will be beautiful.

So far I do not dare to tell you that you are ugly, for I think you would hear anything rather than that. But see what Socrates says to Alcibiades, most beautiful and charming of men: 'Strive then to attain beauty.' What does he say to him? Does he say, 'Arrange your hair and smooth your legs'? God forbid! but 'Set your will in order, rid it of bad judgements.'

'How treat the poor body then?'

According to its nature: that is God's concern, trust it to Him. 'What then? Is the body to be unclean?'

God forbid! but cleanse your true, natural self: let man be clean as man, woman as woman, child as child.

Nay, let us pluck out the lion's mane, lest it be unclean, and the cock's comb, for he too must be clean!

Clean? yes, but clean as a cock, and the lion as a lion, and the hound of the chase as such a hound should be.

1) In What Matters should the Man who is to Make Progress Train himself: and (2) That we Neglect What is Most Vital

THERE ARE THREE DEPARTMENTS in which a man who is to be good and noble must be trained. The first concerns the will to get and will to avoid; he must be trained not to fail to get what he wills to get nor fall into what he wills to avoid. The second is concerned with impulse to act and not to act, and, in a word, the sphere of what is fitting: that we should act in order, with due consideration, and with proper care. The object of the third is that we may not be deceived, and may not judge at random, and generally it is concerned with assent.

Of these the most important and the most pressing is the first, which is concerned with strong emotions, for such emotion does not arise except when the will to get or the will to avoid fails of its object. This it is which brings with it disturbances, tumults, misfortunes, bad fortunes, mournings, lamentations, envies; which makes men envious and jealous–passions which make us unable to listen to reason.

The second is the sphere of what is fitting: for I must not be without feeling like a statue, but must maintain my natural and acquired relations, as a religious man, as son, brother, father, citizen.

The third department is appropriate only for those who are already making progress, and is concerned with giving certainty in the very things we have spoken of, so that even in sleep or drunkenness or melancholy no untested impression may come upon us unawares.

'This', says a pupil, 'is beyond us.'

But the philosophers of to-day have disregarded the first and second departments, and devote themselves to the third–variable premisses, syllogisms concluding with a question, hypothetical syllogisms, fallacious arguments.

'Of course,' he says, 'when a man, is engaged on these subjects he must take pains to escape being deceived.' But whose business is it to do this? It is only for the man who is already good.

In logic then you fall short: but have you reached perfection in other subjects? Are you proof against deceit in regard to money? If you see a pretty girl, do you resist the impression? If your neighbour comes in for an inheritance, do you not feel a twinge? Do you lack nothing now but security of judgement? Unhappy man, even while you are learning this lesson you are in an agony of terror lest some one should think scorn of you, and you ask whether any one is talking about you! And if some one comes and tells you, 'We were discussing who was the best philosopher, and one who was there said, "There is only one philosopher, So-and-so (naming you)"', straightway your poor little four-inch soul shoots up to two cubits! Then if another who is by says, 'Nonsense! It is not worth while to listen to So-and-so: what does he know? He has the first rudiments, nothing more', you are beside yourself, and grow pale and cry out at once, 'I will show him the man I am, he shall see I am a great philosopher.' Why, the facts themselves are evidence; why do you want to show it by something else? Do you not know that Diogenes pointed out one of the sophists thus, making a vulgar gesture? Then, when the man was furious, 'That is So-and-so,' said he, 'I have shown him to you.' A man is not indeed like a stone or a log, that you can show what he is by just pointing a finger, but you show what he is as a man, when you show what are his judgements.

Let us look at your judgements too. Is it not clear that you set no value on your will, but look outside to things beyond your will?–what So-and-so will say, what men will think of you, whether they will think you a scholar, one who has read Chrysippus or Antipater, for if you have read them and Archedemus as well, you have read everything. Why are you still in agony, lest you should fail to show us what manner of man you are? Would you like me to say what manner of man you showed yourself to us? A man who comes before us mean, critical, quick-tempered, cowardly, blaming everything, accusing every one, never quiet, vainglorious–that is what you showed us! Go away now and read Archedemus; then if a mouse fall and make a noise, you die of fright! For the same sort of death awaits you, as–whom shall I say?–Crinis! He too was proud of understanding Archedemus!

Unhappy man, will you not leave these things alone, which do not concern you? They are suited only to those who can learn them without confusion, to those who are able to say, 'I feel no anger, pain, or envy; I am under no hindrance, no constraint. What is left for me to do? I have leisure and peace of mind. Let us see how we ought to deal with logical changes: let us see how one may adopt a hypothesis and not be led to an absurd conclusion.'

These are matters well enough for men like that. It is fitting for sailors who are in good trim to light a fire, and take their dinner, if luck serves, and to sing and dance: but you come to me when the ship is sinking and begin hoisting the topsails!

What is the Material with which the Good Man Deals: and What should be the Object of our Training

THE MATERIAL OF THE good man is his own Governing Principle, as the body is the material of the physician and trainer, the land of the farmer; and it is the function of the good man to deal with his impressions naturally. And just as it is the nature of every soul to assent to what is true and dissent from what is false, and withhold judgement in what is uncertain, so it is its nature to be moved with the will to get what is good and the will to avoid what is evil, and to be neutral towards what is neither good nor evil. For just as neither the banker nor the greengrocer can refuse the Emperor's currency, but, if you show it, he must part, willy-nilly, with what the coin will buy, so it is also with the soul. The very sight of good attracts one towards it, the sight of evil repels. The soul will never reject a clear impression of good, any more than we reject Caesar's currency. On this depends every motion of man and of God. Therefore the good is preferred to every tie of kinship.

I have no concern with my father, but with the good!

'Are you so hard-hearted?'

It is my nature; this is the currency which God has given me. Therefore if the good is different from the noble and just, then father and brother, country and all such things disappear.

I say, am I to neglect my good, that you may get it? am I to make way for you? Why should I?

'I am your father.'

But not my good.

'I am your brother.'

But not my good. If we make the good consist in right will, the mere maintenance of such relations becomes good: further, he who resigns some of his external possessions attains the good.

'My father is taking away my money.'

But he is not harming you.

'My brother will have the greater part of the land.'

Let him have as much as he likes: does he gain in character? Is he more modest, trustworthy, brotherly? Who can eject one from *that* possession? Not even Zeus: nor did He wish to eject me; He put my character in my keeping and gave it me as He had it himself, unhindered, unfettered, unrestrained.

Inasmuch then as different people have a different currency, a man shows his coin and gets what it will buy. A thief has come to the province as Proconsul. What coin does he use? Money. Show him money, and carry off what you will. An adulterer has come. What currency does he use? Pretty girls. 'Take your coin', says he, 'and sell me the thing I want.' Give, and buy. Another's heart is set on minions. Give him the coin and take what you will. Another is a sportsman. Give him a fine horse or dog. With sighs and groans he will sell you what you like for it: for he is constrained from within, by Another, who has ordained this currency.

It is by this principle above all that you must guide yourself in training. Go out as soon as it is dawn and whomsoever you may see and hear, question yourself and answer as to an interrogator.

What did you see? A beautiful woman or boy. Apply the rule: Is this within the will's control or beyond it? Beyond. Away with it then!

What did you see? One mourning at his child's death. Apply the rule: Is death beyond the will, or can the will control it? Death is beyond the will's control. Put it out of the way then!

Did a Consul meet you? Apply the rule: What is a consulship? Is it beyond the will's control or within it? Beyond it. Take it away: the coin will not pass; reject it, you have no concern with it.

I say, if we did this and trained ourselves on this principle every day from dawn to night, we should indeed achieve something. As it is, we are caught open-mouthed by every impression we meet, and only in the lecture-room, if then, does our mind wake up a little. Then we go into the street and if we see a mourner we say, 'He is undone'; if a Consul, 'Lucky man'; if an outlaw, 'Miserable man'; if a poor man, 'Wretched man, he has nothing to buy food with.'

These mistaken judgements we must eradicate, and concentrate our efforts on doing so. For what is weeping and lamenting? A matter of judgement. What is misfortune? Judgement. What is faction, discord, criticism, accusation, irreligion, foolishness? All these are judgements, nothing else, and judgements passed on things beyond the will, as though they were good and evil. Only let a man turn these efforts to the sphere of the will, and I guarantee that he will enjoy peace of mind, whatever his circumstances may be.

The soul is like a dish full of water, and the impressions like the rays of light which strike the water. Now when the water is disturbed the light seems to be disturbed too, but it is not really disturbed. So when a man has a fit of dizziness, the arts and virtues are not put to confusion, but only the spirit in which they exist: when this is at rest, they come to rest too.

CHAPTER FOUR

Against One who was Indecorously Excited in the Theatre

WHEN THE PROCURATOR OF Epirus offended decorum by the way he showed interest in a comedian, the people reviled him for this; thereupon when he brought word of this to Epictetus and expressed annoyance at those who reviled him: Why! he said, what harm were they doing? They too showed their interest as you did!

'What!' said he, 'is this the way they show interest?'

Yes, he said, when they saw you, their Governor, the friend and Procurator of Caesar, showing your interest in this way, would you not expect them to do the same? If it is not right to show interest in that way, leave off doing it yourself: but if it is right, why are you angry at their imitating you? For whom else but you, their superiors, have the people to imitate? Whom are they to look to when they come to the theatre but you? 'See', they say, 'how Caesar's Procurator behaves in the theatre. He cries out: then I will cry out too. He jumps from his seat. I will do so too. His claque of slaves shout from their scattered seats: I have no slaves, I will cry as loud as I can to make up for it.' You ought to know then that when you enter the theatre you enter it as a pattern and example to all other spectators how to behave. Why then did they revile you? Because every man hates what stands in his way. They wanted So-and-so to be crowned, you wanted another; they stood in your way and you in theirs. You were found to be stronger than they; they did what they could, they reviled what stood in their way. What would you have then? That you should do what you wish, and they should not even say what they wish? Nay, what wonder they should talk so? Do not farmers revile Zeus, when He stands in their way? Do not sailors revile

– 178 –

Him? Do they not revile Caesar without ceasing? What follows? Does not Zeus know? Does not Caesar have reported to him what men say? What does he do then? He knows that if he punishes all who revile him he will have no one left to rule over. What is my conclusion? When you enter the theatre you ought not to say, 'Let me have Sophron crowned', but, 'Let me keep my will in accord with Nature in this matter, for no one is dearer to me than myself: it is absurd then that I should be injured, that another may be victorious on the stage.'

Whom then do I want to win? The victor: and so the victory will always be in accordance with my wish.

'But I wish Sophron to be crowned.'

Hold as many contests as you please in your own house and proclaim him there victor in the Nemean, Pythian, Isthmian and Olympic games: but in public do not claim more than your share, nor steal what is public property. If you do, you must put up with being reviled: for when you do as the people do, you put yourself on their level.

CHAPTER FIVE

Against those who Make Illness an Excuse for Leaving the Lecture-Room

'I AM ILL HERE,' says one, 'and want to go away home.'

What, were you never ill at home? Do you not consider whether you are doing anything here to improve your will, for if you are doing no good, you might just as well never have come? Go away, and attend to your affairs at home: for if your Governing Principle cannot be brought into accord with Nature, no doubt your bit of land will prosper; you will add to your bit of money! You will tend your old father, frequent the market-place, serve as a magistrate, do anything that comes next, poor wretch, in your wretched way. But if you understand that you are getting rid of bad judgements and gaining others in their place, and that you have transferred your attention from things outside the will's control to things within it, and that now if you cry, 'Ah me!' it is not for your father or your brother but for yourself that you cry, then why should you take account of illness any more? Do you not know that disease and death are bound to overtake us whatever we are doing? They overtake the farmer at his farming, the sailor on the seas. What would you like to be doing when they overtake you? For you must needs be overtaken, whatever you are doing. If you can find anything better than this to be doing when you are overtaken, do it by all means!

For my own part I would wish death to overtake me occupied with nothing but the care of my will, trying to make it calm, unhindered, unconstrained, free. I would fain be found so employed, that I may be able to say to God, 'Did I transgress Thy commands? Did I use the faculties Thou gayest me to wrong purpose? Did I use my senses or my primary notions in vain? Did I ever accuse Thee? Did I ever find fault with Thy ordinance? I fell sick, when it was Thy will: so did others, but I rebelled not. I became poor when Thou didst will it, but I rejoiced in my poverty. I held no office, because it was Thy will: I never coveted office. Didst Thou ever see me gloomy for that reason? Did I ever come before Thee but with a cheerful face, ready for any commands or orders that Thou mightest give? Now it is Thy will for me to leave the festival. I go, giving all thanks to Thee, that Thou didst deign to let me share Thy festival and see Thy works and understand Thy government.' May these be my thoughts, these my studies, writing or reading, when death comes upon me!

'But I am ill, and shall not have my mother to hold my head.'

Go to your mother then; for you deserve to be ill, with her to hold your head.

'But I had a nice bed to lie on at home.'

Go to your nice bed then; sick or well you deserve to lie on a bed of that sort! Pray do not lose what you can do there.

But what does Socrates say? 'As one man', he says, 'delights to improve his field, and another his horse, so I delight in following day by day my own improvement.'

'In what? In paltry phrases?'

Man, hold your peace.

'In pretty precepts then?'

Enough of that.

'Nay, but philosophers busy themselves with nothing else, so far as I see.'

Is it nothing (do you think?) never to accuse any one, God or man, never to blame any, to go in and out with the same countenance? These are the things which Socrates knew, and yet he never said that he knew or taught anything; and if any one asked for phrases or precepts, he would take him away to Protagoras or Hippias. In the same way if any one had come looking for greenstuff, he would have taken him to the gardener. Which of you then makes this the purpose of his life? Why, if you did, you would gladly suffer sickness and hunger and death. If any one of you was ever in love with a pretty girl, he knows that I speak true!

CHAPTER SIX
Scattered Sayings

WHEN ONE OF HIS acquaintances asked why more progress was made in old days, although the processes of reason have been more studied by the men of to-day, he answered, On what has the effort been spent, and in what was the greater progress in the past? For you will find that progress to-day corresponds exactly to the effort spent. The fact is that to-day men have spent their effort on the analysis of syllogisms, and progress is made in that: in old days men spent their effort on maintaining their mind in accord with Nature, and they made progress in that. Therefore do not confound the processes, nor seek to spend effort on one thing and make progress in another. If you look whether any of us who sets himself to keep in accord with Nature and to live his life so, fails to make progress, you will find there is none.

'The good man can suffer no defeat.'

Of course, for he engages in no contest where he is not superior. 'Take my lands, if you will: take my servants, take my office, take my poor body, yet you will not make me fail to get what I will or fall into what I will to avoid.' This is the only contest for which he enters–that which is concerned with the sphere of the will, and therefore he cannot fail to be invincible.

When some one asked him what 'general perception' meant, he replied, You might describe the faculty which only distinguishes sounds as 'general' hearing, but the faculty which distinguishes musical sounds you would not call 'general' but 'technical'. In the same way there are certain things which all men who are not utterly perverted can see in virtue of their general faculties. It is this mental constitution to which the name 'general perception' is given.

It is not easy to give stimulus to young men who have no grit: 'you cannot lift a cream-cheese by a hook' [Musonius Rufus]; but young men of parts hold fast to reason even if you try to deter them. That is why Rufus generally tried to deter them, and made this his test of those who were gifted and those who were not; 'for', said he, 'just as the stone, if you throw it up, will fall to the earth by its own nature, so the gifted soul is all the more inclined towards its natural object, the more you try to beat it off.'

CHAPTER SEVEN

Dialogue with the Commissioner of the Free Cities, who was an Epicurean

WHEN THE COMMISSIONER, who was an Epicurean, came into his lecture-room, It is proper, said Epictetus, that we who are ignorant should inquire of you philosophers what is the Best Thing in the world, just as those who come to a strange city make inquiry of the citizens who know the place; that having learnt what it is we may pursue it for ourselves, and come to the sight of it, as foreigners visit the sights of the cities. For all, one may say, are agreed that man has to do with three things, soul and body and external things; it only remains for you to answer the question, 'What is the *best* in man?' What shall we say to men? Shall we say, 'The flesh'? and was it for this that Maximus sailed as far as Cassiope to see his son on his way? Was it to have pleasure in the flesh? When the Commissioner denied it, saying, 'God forbid!' Epictetus went on, Is it not proper to devote our efforts to what is best in us?

'It is most proper.'

What have we then better than the flesh?

'The soul', he said.

And which are better, the goods of the best element in us or the goods of the inferior?

'Those of the best.'

Are the goods of the soul in the sphere of the will or beyond it?

'Within the sphere of the will.'

Is the pleasure of the soul then within the sphere of the will?

'Yes', he said.

And what gives rise to it? Does it arise of itself? That is inconceivable; for we must assume the existence of the good as something which has value in itself, by partaking in which we shall have pleasure in the soul.

To this too he agreed.

What then will give rise to this pleasure of the soul in us? If the goods of the soul give rise to it, then the nature of the good is discovered; for it is impossible that the good and that which gives us rational delight should be different from one another, or that the consequence should be good unless that on which it depends is good. For the primary end must be good, if that which follows on it is to be rational. But you cannot say this if you have any sense, for you will be saying what is inconsistent with Epicurus, and with the other judgements of your school. You will be reduced to saying that the pleasure of the soul is pleasure in bodily things: these, as it now appears, are of primary value and are identical with the nature of the good.

Therefore Maximus acted foolishly, if he had any motive in sailing but the flesh, that is the highest principle. He acts like a fool too if, as a judge, he refrains from other men's goods when he can take them. If you think fit to do it, the only point for us to look to is that it be done secretly, securely, without any one's knowledge. For even Epicurus himself does not set down stealing as evil, but only detected stealing: and he says 'Do not steal', only because 'it is impossible to be sure of escaping detection'. But I tell you that if it be done cleverly and cautiously, we shall escape detection. Further, we have powerful friends in Rome, both men and women, and the Greeks are feeble folk: no one will have the courage to go to Rome to prosecute. Why do you refrain from your own good? It is foolish and silly. Nay, even if you tell me you refrain, I will not believe you; for just as it is impossible to assent to what appears false and to reject what is true, so it is impossible to hold aloof from what appears good. Now wealth is a good thing, and, so to speak, most productive of pleasure. Why should not one acquire it? Why should we not corrupt our neighbour's wife, if we can do it without detection; and if her husband talks nonsense, why should we not break his neck as well? This, if you wish to be a philosopher of the right sort, to be perfect and consistent with your own judgements. Otherwise you will be no better than we so-called Stoics, for we too say one thing and do another: we say noble words and do shameful deeds! You will be suffering from the opposite perversion, of uttering shameful judgements, and doing noble deeds!

Before God, I ask you, can you imagine a city of Epicureans? 'I shall not marry' (says one).

'Nor shall I,' (says another) 'for it is wrong to marry.'

Yes, and it is wrong to get children, and wrong to be a citizen!

What is to happen then? Where will your citizens come from? Who will educate them? Who will be Governor of the Ephebi? Who will manage the Gymnasia? Yes, and what will be their education? Will it be the education the Lacedaemonians or Athenians received? Take me a young man and bring him up in accordance with your judgements. The judgements are bad, subversive of the city, ruinous to family life, not even fit for women. Man, leave these principles alone. You live in an imperial city: you must hold office, judge justly, refrain from other men's property: no woman but your wife must seem fair in your eyes, no boy, no silver or gold plate. You must look for judgements that will be in keeping with such conduct, and will enable you to refrain with pleasure from things so persuasive to attract and to overcome you. If on the other hand we back up their persuasive power by this philosophy, such as it is, that we have discovered, thrusting us forward and confirming us in the same direction, what is to become of us? What is the best part of a piece of plate, the silver or the art spent on it? The hand in itself is mere flesh, it is the products of the hand that claim precedence. So too appropriate actions are of three kinds: the first class relative to k mere existence, the second relative to particular conditions, the third commanding and absolute. On this principle too we ought not to honour man's material being, his rags of flesh, but his leading characteristics. What are these? Citizenship, marriage, procreation of children, worship of God, care of parents, and in general, will to get and to avoid, impulse to act and not to act, each in its proper and natural manner.

What is our nature? To be free, noble, self-respecting. What other animal blushes? What other can have a conception of shame? We must subordinate pleasure to these principles, to minister to them as a servant, to evoke our interests and to keep us in the way of our natural activities.

'But I am rich, and have need of nothing.'

Why then do you still pretend to be a philosopher? Gold and silver plate are enough for you: what need have you of judgements? 'Nay, but I also sit as judge over the Greeks.'

What! you know how to judge? What made you know that? 'Caesar wrote me a patent.'

Let him write to you to judge questions of music: what use will it be to you? But let that pass. How did you get made a judge? Whose hand did you kiss? Was it Symphorus' or Numenius'? In whose antechamber did you sleep? To whom did you send gifts? After all, do you not see that being judge is worth no more nor less than Numenius is worth?

'Well, but I can put any one I wish in prison.'

As you may a stone!

'But I can cudgel to death any one I wish.'

As you can an ass! This is not governing men. Govern us as rational creatures by showing us what is expedient, and we will follow it: show us what is inexpedient and we will turn away from it. Make us admire and emulate you, as Socrates made men do. He was the true ruler of men, for he brought men to submit to him their will to get and to avoid, their impulse to act and not to act.

'Do this, refrain from this, or I will put you in prison.' This is not how rational beings are ruled. But, 'Do this as Zeus ordained: if not, you will suffer penalty and harm.' What kind of harm? No harm but that of failing to do your duty: you will destroy the trustworthy, self-respecting, well-behaved man in you. Look not for any greater harm than this!

CHAPTER EIGHT

How we should Train ourselves to Deal with Impressions

As WE TRAIN OURSELVES to deal with sophistical questions, so we ought to train ourselves day by day to deal with impressions: for these too propound questions to us.

'The son of So-and-so is dead.'

Answer, That is beyond the will, not an evil.

'So-and-so's father has disinherited him: what do you think?'

It is outside the will, not an evil.

'Caesar has condemned him.'

That is outside the will, not an evil.

'Something has made him grieve.'

That is an act of will, and evil.

'He has endured nobly.'

That is an act of will, and good.

If we acquire this habit, we shall make progress, for we shall never assent to anything but that of which we get a convincing impression.

The son dies. What happens?

The son dies.

Nothing more?

Nothing.

The ship is lost. What happens?

The ship is lost.

He is led to prison. What happens?

He is led to prison. Each man may add, 'He has fared ill', but if so, that is his own affair.

'Still', you say, 'Zeus does wrong to act so.'

Why? Do you mean because He made you patient, noble-minded, because He saved these things from being evil, because He puts it in your power to endure these troubles and still be happy, because He 'opens the door' to you, when your position is impossible? Leave the scene, man, and do not complain.

If you would know the attitude of the Romans to philosophers, listen to this. Italicus, a man of the highest repute as a philosopher among them, in my presence expressed his indignation at his lot, which he thought intolerable, by saying, 'I cannot bear it: you are ruining me, you will make me like him', and pointed to me!

CHAPTER NINE

To a Rhetor Going up to Rome for a Trial

WHEN A MAN, who was going to Rome for an action regarding his official position, came in to see him, he inquired the reason for his journey, and when the man went on to ask him his opinion on the matter, 'If you ask me', he said, 'what you will do in Rome, whether you will succeed or fail, I have no precept to offer: but if you ask me how you will do, I can say this, that if your judgements are right you will do well, if wrong, you will do ill. For every man's action is determined by a judgement. What is it that made you desire to be elected patron of the Cnossians?' Judgement.

What is the reason you now go to Rome? Judgement. Yes, and in stormy weather and at your own risk and charges?

'Necessity compels me.'

Who tells you this? Your judgement. If then judgements are the cause of everything and a man has bad judgements, the result resembles the cause, whatever this be. Have we all then sound judgements? Have you and your opponent? Then how are you at variance? Have you sound judgements any more than he? Why? You think so. So does he, and so do madmen. Opinion is a bad criterion. No! Show me that you have examined your judgements and paid attention to them. You are now sailing to Rome to be patron of the Cnossians and are not content to stay at home with the honours you had before, but desire some greater and more distinguished honour. When did you ever take the trouble to sail like this in order to examine your judgements and reject any that are bad? Whom have you ever consulted for this purpose? What time or what part of your life have you charged with this duty? Review the seasons of your life in your own mind, if you respect me. Did you examine your judgements when you were a boy? Did not you do what you did then as you do everything now? And when you grew to be a youth and listened to the teachers of rhetoric and wrote declamations of your own, what did you imagine that you lacked? And when in early manhood you began to enter public life and to plead in cases and to have a reputation, did you ever think any one your equal? Would you ever have let any one examine you and show that your judgements were bad? What then would you have me tell you?

'Give me some help in the matter.'

I have no precepts to offer for your purpose: and if you have come to me for this, you have come to me as you would come to a greengrocer or a shoemaker and not as to a philosopher.

'For what purpose then have philosophers precepts to offer?'

For this: that, whatever the issue may be, we should keep our Governing Principle in accord with Nature to our life's end. Do you think this a small matter?

'No, the greatest of all.'

Well then: will a little time suffice for this, and can it be acquired in a passing visit? Acquire it if you can!

Then you will go away and say, 'I met Epictetus, it was like meeting a stone, or a statue.'

Yes, for you just saw me and no more. Man can only meet man properly when he gets to understand his convictions and shows him his own in turn. Get to know my judgements, and show me yours, and then say that you have met me. Let us question one another: if one of my judgements is bad, remove it: if you have anything to say, put it forward. That is how to meet a philosopher. That's not your way, but 'We are passing through: while we wait to charter our ship, we can see Epictetus; let us see what he is saying.' Then when you leave you say, 'Epictetus was nothing: he talked bad Greek, outlandish stuff.' Of course, of what else are you competent to judge, coming in like that?

'But', he goes on, 'if I let myself be absorbed in these things, I shall be like you without land, like you without silver cups, like you without fine cattle.'

To this perhaps it is sufficient to answer, I have no need of them: but if you get a large property, you still need something else, and willy-nilly you are poorer than I.

'What do you mean that I need?'

You need what you have not got–tranquillity, a mind in accord with Nature, and free from perturbation. Whether I am Patron or not, what does it matter? It does matter to you. I am richer than you: I am not in an agony as to what Caesar will think of me: I do not flatter any one for that. This is what I have instead of your silver and gold plate. You have vessels of gold, but your reason–judgements, assent, impulse, will –is of common clay. But mine are in accord with Nature, and that being so, why should I not make a special study of reasoning? I have leisure, and my mind is not distracted. How can I occupy my mind that is thus free? I cannot find an occupation more worthy of man than that. When you have nothing to do, you are troubled in spirit, and enter a theatre, or wander aimlessly. Why should not the philosopher devote his efforts to developing his own reason? You devote yourself to crystal vases, I to the syllogism called 'the Liar': you to murrhine vessels, I to the syllogism of 'Denial'. To you all that you have appears small: to me all I have appears great. Your desire can never be fulfilled, mine is fulfilled already. Your case is like that of children putting their hand into a narrow-necked jar and pulling out raisins and almonds. If a child fills his hand full, he cannot pull it out and then he cries. Let a few go, child, and you will get it out. So I say to you, 'Let your desire go.' Do not crave much, and you will obtain.

CHAPTER TEN

How One should Bear Illnesses

WE SHOULD HAVE EACH judgement ready at the moment when it is needed: judgements on dinner at dinner-time, on the bath at bathing-time, on bed at bedtime.

> *Admit not sleep into your tender eyelids*
> *Till you have reckoned up each deed of the day–*
> *How have I erred, what done or left undone?*
> *So start, and so review your acts, and then*
> *For vile deeds chide yourself, for good be glad.*
> [Ascribed to Pythagoras]

Keep hold of these lines for practical use, not to declaim them as a cry like 'Paean Apollo'. Again in a fever we must be ready with judgements for that; if we fall into a fever we must not give up and forget everything, and say, 'If I ever study philosophy again, may the worst befall me! I must go off somewhere and attend to my poor body.' Well, but does not fever come there? What does studying philosophy mean? Does it not mean preparing to face events? Do you not understand then that what you are saying comes to this, 'If I go on preparing to bear events quietly, may the worst befall me'? That is as though a man should give up competing for the pancration because he has been struck. But there it is possible to leave off and so escape a beating: but what profit do we get if we leave off studying philosophy?

What ought one to say then as each hardship comes? 'I was practising for this, I was training for this.' God says to you, 'Give me a proof, whether you have kept the rules of wrestling–eaten the proper food, trained, and obeyed the trainer.' After that, are you going to play the coward when the moment of action comes? If now is the time for fever, take your fever in the right way; if for thirst, thirst in the right way, if for hunger, hunger aright. Is it not in your power? Who will hinder you? The physician will hinder you from drinking, but he cannot hinder you from thirsting aright: he will hinder you from eating, but he cannot hinder you from hungering in the right way. 'But am I not a student?'

Why are you a student? Slave, is it not that you may be happy and have peace of mind? Is it not that you may conform to nature and so live your life? What hinders you in a fever from keeping your Governing Principle in accord with Nature? Here is the test of the matter, this is how the philosopher is proved. For fever too is a part of life, like walking, sailing, travelling. Do you read when you are walking? No. Nor do you in a fever: but if you walk aright, you have done your part as a walker; if you bear your fever aright, you have done your part as a sick man. What does bearing fever rightly mean? It means not to blame God or man, not to be crushed by what happens, to await death in a right spirit, to do what you are bidden; when the physician comes in, not to be afraid of what he may say, and if he says, 'You are doing well', not to be overjoyed: for what good is there in that? What good had you when you were in health? It means not to be disheartened if he says, 'You are doing badly'; for what does 'doing badly' mean? It means drawing near the dissolution of the soul from the body. What is there to fear in that? If you do not draw near now, shall you not draw near later? Is the world going to be turned upside down by your death? Why then do you coax the physician? Why do you say, 'Master, if you will, I shall get well'? Why do you give him occasion to lift his brow in arrogance? As you give the shoemaker his due in regard to the foot, the builder in regard to the house, why do you not give the physician his due (and no more) in regard to the paltry body, for the body is not mine and is naturally dead? This is what the moment requires from the man in a fever: if he fulfils these requirements, he has what is his own.

It is not the business of the philosopher to guard these outward things–paltry wine or oil or body–but to guard his Governing Principle. How is he to regard outward things? Only so far that he does not concern himself with them unreasonably. What occasion is left then for fear? What occasion for anger, what occasion for fear concerning things that are not our own, nor of any value? For the two principles we must have ready at command are these: that outside the will there is nothing good or evil, and that we must not lead events but follow them. 'My brother ought not to have behaved so to me.' No, but it is his business to look to that; however he may behave, I will deal with him as I ought. This is my part, that is another's: this no one can hinder, that is subject to hindrance.

CHAPTER ELEVEN

Scattered Sayings

THERE ARE CERTAIN PUNISHMENTS ordained as it were by law for those who disobey the government of God. Whoever judges anything to be good except what depends upon the will, let him be liable to envy, desire, flattery, distraction. Whoever judges anything else to be evil (save acts of the will), let distress be his, and mourning, lamentation, misfortune. And yet, though we suffer punishments so severe, we cannot refrain.

Remember what the poet says about the stranger:

Stranger, though baser man than thou should come,
He must be honoured, for the hand of Zeus
Guards stranger folk and poor.
                    [Homer, *Odyssey*, XIV. 56]

One should be ready to apply this to a father: 'Though a baser one than thou should come, I may not dishonour a father; for all depend on Zeus, God of our fathers', and to a brother, 'for all depend on Zeus, God of kindred'. In the same way we shall find that Zeus is Protector of all other relations of life.

CHAPTER TWELVE
On Training

WE OUGHT NOT TO train ourselves in unnatural or extraordinary actions, for in that case we who claim to be philosophers shall be no better than mountebanks. For it is difficult to walk on a tight-rope, and not only difficult but dangerous as well: ought we for that reason to practise walking on a tight-rope or setting up a palm-tree, or embracing statues? By no means. Not everything that is difficult and dangerous is suitable for training, but only that which is conducive to what is set before us as the object of our effort. What is set before us as the object of our effort? To move without hindrance in the will to get and the will to avoid. And what does that mean? Not to fail in what we will nor to fall into what we avoid. To this end, therefore, let our training be directed: for since it is impossible without great and continuous effort to secure that the will to get fail not and the will to avoid be not foiled, know that, if you allow training to be directed to things lying outside and beyond the will, you will not get what you will to get nor avoid what you will to avoid.

And since habit has established a strong predominance, because we have acquired the habit of turning our will to get and our will to avoid only to what lies outside our control, we must set a contrary habit to counteract the former, and where impressions are most likely to go wrong there employ training as an antidote.

I am inclined to pleasure: in order to train myself I will incline beyond measure in the opposite direction. I am disposed to avoid trouble: I will harden and train my impressions to this end, that my will to avoid may hold aloof from everything of this kind. For how do we describe the man who trains? He is the man who practises avoiding the use of his will to get, and willing to avoid only what is in the sphere of the will and who exercises himself in what is hard to overcome. And so different men have to train for different objects. What is it to the purpose here to set up a palm-tree, or to carry about a hut of skins or a pestle and mortar? Man, train yourself, if you are arrogant, to bear with being reviled, and not to be annoyed when you are disparaged. Then you will make such progress that, even if you are struck, you will say to your-self, 'Imagine that you have embraced a statue.' Next train yourself to use wine properly, not for heavy drinking–for there are men misguided enough to train for this–but first to abstain from wine, and to leave alone pretty maids and sweet cakes. Then, if the proper time comes, you will enter the lists, if at all, to try yourself and learn whether your impressions overcome you as before. But to begin with, fly far from enemies that are stronger than you. The battle is an unequal one when it is between a pretty maid and a young man beginning philosophy. 'Pot and stone', as the saying is, 'do not agree.'

Next after the will to get and the will to avoid comes the sphere of im-pulse for action and against action: where the object is to obey reason, not to do anything at the wrong time or place, or offend the harmony of things in any other way.

Third comes the sphere of assents, concerned with things plausible and attractive. For, as Socrates bade men 'not live a life without examina-tion', so you ought not to accept an impression without examination, but say, 'Wait, let me see who you are and whence you come', just as the night-watch say, 'Show me your token.' 'Have you the token given by nature, which the impression that is to be accepted must have?'

And to conclude, the methods which are applied to the body by those who exercise it, may themselves conduce to training, if they tend in this direction, that is, if they bear upon the will to get and the will to avoid. But if their object is display, they are the marks of one who has swerved from the right line, whose aims are alien, one who is looking for spectators to say, 'What a great man!' This is why Apol-lonius was right in saying, 'If you wish to train for your soul's sake, when you are thirsty in hot weather take a mouthful of cold water and spit it out and tell no one!'

CHAPTER THIRTEEN

What a 'Forlorn' Condition Means, and a 'Forlorn' Man

THE 'FORLORN' STATE is the condition of one without help. For a man is not forlorn simply because he is alone, any more than a man in a crowd is unforlorn. At any rate when we lose a brother or a son or a friend, in whom we rest our trust, we say that we have been left forlorn, though often we are in Rome, with that great throng meeting us in the streets, and those numbers living about us, and sometimes we have a multitude of slaves. For according to its conception the term 'forlorn' means that a man is without help, exposed to those who wish to harm him. For this reason, when we are travelling, we call ourselves forlorn most of all, when we fall among robbers. For it is not the sight of a man as such that relieves us from being forlorn, but the sight of one who is faithful and self-respecting and serviceable. For if being alone is enough to make one forlorn, you must say that Zeus Himself is forlorn at the Conflagration of the Universe and bewails Himself: 'Unhappy me! I have neither Hera nor Athena nor Apollo nor, in a word, brother or son or grandson or kinsman.' And in fact this is what some say that He does, when left alone in the Conflagration: for they cannot conceive of the mode of life of a solitary Being: they start with a natural principle, the fact that men are by nature drawn by ties of fellowship and mutual affection, and enjoy converse with their kind. But nevertheless a man must prepare himself for solitude too–he must be able to suffice for himself, and able to commune with himself. Just as Zeus communes with Himself and is at peace with Himself and reflects upon the nature of His government, and occupies Himself with thoughts appropriate to Himself, so should we be able to talk to ourselves, without need of others, or craving for diversion: we should study the divine government and the relation in which we stand to other things: we should consider what was our attitude to events before, and what it is now: what the things are which still afflict us: how they may be cured, how removed: if any things need to be brought to perfection, perfect them as reason requires.

For see: Caesar seems to provide us with profound peace; there are no wars nor battles any more, no great bands of robbers or pirates: we are able to travel by land at every season, and to sail from sunrise to sunset. Can he then provide us also with peace from fever, from shipwreck, from fire or earthquake or thunderbolt? Go to, can he give us peace from love? He cannot. From mourning? He cannot. From envy? No! he cannot give us peace from any of them. But the reasoning of philosophers promises to give us peace from these troubles also. What does it say? 'Men, if you attend to me, wherever you may be, whatever you may be doing, you will feel no distress, no anger, no compulsion, no hindrance, but will live undisturbed and free from all distractions.' When a man has this peace proclaimed to him, not by Caesar (how could he proclaim it?) but proclaimed by God, through the voice of reason, is he not content when he is alone? When he considers and reflects, 'Now no evil can befall me, robber exists not for me, earthquake exists not: all is full of peace and tranquillity: every road, every city, every meeting, neighbour, companion–all are harmless.' Another, Who takes care of me, supplies food and raiment; He has given me senses and primary conceptions; and when He does not provide necessaries, He sounds the recall, He opens the door and says, "Come." Where? To nothing you need fear, but to that whence you were born, to your friends and kindred, the elements. So much of you as was fire shall pass into fire, what was earth shall pass into earth, the spirit into spirit, the water into water. There is no Hades, nor Acheron, nor Cocytus, nor Pyriphlegethon, but all is full of gods and divine beings. When one has this to think upon, and when he beholds the sun and moon and stars, and enjoys land and sea, he is not forlorn any more than he is destitute of help.

'Nay,' you say, 'but what if one come upon me alone and murder me?' Fool, he murders not you, but your paltry body.

How can we speak any more then of being forlorn and helpless? Why do we make ourselves worse than children? For what do children do when they are left alone? They pick up potsherds and dust and build something or other and then pull it down and build something else again, and so they never lack diversion. If you sail away, am I to sit and shed tears because I am left alone and forlorn? Shall I not in that case have my potsherds and my dust? But they do this in their foolishness: do we in our wisdom make ourselves miserable?

Great power is always dangerous in a beginner. We must then bear such things according to our strength, but always according to nature. A certain course may suit a strong man but not a consumptive. Be content to practise the life of an invalid, that you may one day live the life of a healthy man. Take scant food, drink water: refrain from willing to get anything for a while, that you may one day direct your will rationally. If you do so, then, when you have some good in you, you will direct your will aright.

'No,' you say, 'we want at once to live as wise men and benefit mankind.'

Benefit indeed! What are you after? Did you ever benefit yourself? 'But I want to stir them up.'

Have you stirred yourself up first? You want to benefit them; then show them in your own life what sort of men philosophy makes, and cease to talk folly. When you eat, benefit those who eat with you, when you drink, benefit those who drink, by yielding and giving way to all, by bearing with them: that is the way to benefit them and not by venting your own phlegm upon them!

CHAPTER FOURTEEN

Scattered Sayings

As BAD ACTORS CANNOT sing alone, but only in a large company, so some men cannot walk alone. Man, if you are worth anything, you must walk alone, and talk to yourself and not hide in the chorus. Learn to bear mockery, look about you, examine yourself, that you may get to know who you are.

When a man drinks water, or puts himself in training in any way, he tells everybody at every opportunity, 'I am a water-drinker.' What? Do you drink water for the sake of drinking it? Man, if it is to your profit to drink it, drink; if not, your conduct is absurd. I say, if you drink water because it does you good, say nothing to those who dislike it. What? Are these the people of all others that you wish to please?

Actions have varying degrees of value: some are based on first principles, others are determined by circumstances, or compromise, or compliance, or manner of life.

There are two qualities that men must get rid of–conceit and diffidence. Conceit is to think that one needs nothing beyond oneself: diffidence is to suppose that one cannot live the untroubled life in the midst of so many difficulties. Now conceit is removed by cross-questioning, and that was what Socrates began with: that the thing is not impossible you must discover by thought and search. This search will do you no harm: and indeed philosophy means very little else but this–to search how it is practicable to exercise the will to get and the will to avoid without hindrance.

'I am better than you, for my father is of consular rank.' Another says, 'I have been tribune, and you have not.' If we were horses you would say, 'My sire was swifter', or, 'I have plenty of barley and fodder', or, 'I have fine trappings.' If you said that, you may imagine me replying, 'Very well then, let us try our paces.' Come, is there nothing in men, like the pace of a horse, which will enable us to distinguish the better from the worse? Are there not self-respect, honour, justice? Show yourself superior in these qualities, that you may be superior as a man should be. If you say to me, 'I am great at kicking', I shall answer, 'That is the boast of an ass!'

CHAPTER FIFTEEN

That we should Approach Everything with Consideration

IN EVERYTHING YOU DO consider what comes first and what follows, and so approach it. Otherwise you will come to it with a good heart at first because you have not reflected on any of the consequences, and afterwards when difficulties come in sight you will shamefully desist.

'I wish to win at the Olympic games.'

'So do I, by the gods, for it is a fine thing.'

Yes, but consider the first steps to it and what follows: and then, if it is to your advantage, lay your hand to the work. You must be under discipline, eat to order, touch no sweets, train under compulsion, at a fixed hour, in heat and cold, drink no cold water, nor wine, except to order; you must hand yourself over completely to your trainer as you would to a physician. Then, when the contest comes, you get hacked, sometimes dislocate your hand, twist your ankle, swallow plenty of sand, get a flogging, and with all this you are sometimes defeated. First consider these things and then enter on the athlete's career, if you still wish to do so: otherwise, look you, you will be behaving like the children, who one day play at athletes, another at gladiators, then sound the trumpet, next dramatize anything they see and admire. You will be just the same–now athlete, now gladiator, then philosopher, then orator, but nothing with all your soul. Like an ape you imitate everything you see, and one thing after another takes your fancy, but nothing that is familiar pleases you, for you undertake nothing with forethought; you do not survey the whole subject and examine it beforehand, but you take it up half-heartedly and at random. In the same way some people when they see a philosopher, and hear some one speaking like Euphrates (and indeed who can speak as he can?) wish to be philosophers themselves.

Man, consider first, what it is you are undertaking: then consider your own powers, and what you can bear. If you want to be a wrestler, look to your shoulders, your thighs, your loins. For different men are born for different things. Do you suppose that you can be a philosopher if you do as you do now? Do you suppose that you can eat and drink as you do now, and indulge your anger and displeasure just as before? Nay, you must sit up late, you must work hard, conquer some of your desires, abandon your own people, be looked down on by a mere slave, be ridiculed by those who meet you, get the worst of it in everything–in office, in honour, in justice. When you have carefully considered these drawbacks, then come to us, if you think fit: if you are willing to pay this price for peace of mind, freedom, tranquillity. If not, do not come near: do not be like the children, first a philosopher, then a tax-collector, then an orator, then one of Caesar's procurators. These callings do not agree. You must be one man, good or bad: you must develop either your rational soul, or your outward endowments, you must be busy either with your inner man, or with things outside, that is, you must choose between the position of a philosopher and that of an ordinary man.

When Galba was killed some one said to Rufus, 'Now the world is governed by Providence, isn't it?' To which he answered, 'Did I base my proof that the world is governed by Providence upon a casual thing like Galba's death?'

CHAPTER SIXTEEN

That we must be Cautious in our Social Relations

THE MAN WHO MIXES with other people a good deal either for talk or for a wine-party or generally for social purposes, must needs either grow like them himself or convert them to his likeness; for if you put a quenched coal by one that is burning, either it will put the burning 'one out, or will catch fire from it. As the risk then is so serious, you must be cautious in indulging lightly in the society of the untrained, for it is impossible to rub up against one who is covered with soot and not get sooty oneself. What are you going to do, if he talks about gladiators, about horses, about athletes, worse still if he talks about men: 'So-and-so is bad', 'So-and-so is good': 'That was well done', 'That was ill done': again, if he mocks or jeers, or shows a malicious humour? Has any of you the perfect skill of the lyre-player, who takes up his lyre and has only to touch the strings to know which are out of tune and so tune his instrument? Which of you has the faculty that Socrates had, of drawing to his side those who met him in any kind of society?

How could you have? *You* must needs be converted by your un-trained companions.

Why then are they stronger than you? It is because these unsound sayings of theirs are based upon judgements, but your fine words come merely from your lips: that is why they are without life or vigour, that is why a man may well loathe the sound of your exhortations and your wretched 'virtue', which you prate of so glibly. That is how the untrained get the better of you: for judgement is powerful everywhere, judgement suffers no defeat. Therefore, until your fine ideas are firmly fastened in you, and until you acquire some power to secure them, I advise you to be cautious in associating with the untrained: otherwise anything you take note of in the lecture-room will melt away day by day like wax in the sun. Therefore go away somewhere far from the sun, as long as your ideas are in this waxen state. For this reason philosophers even advise us to leave our own countries, because old habits are a drag on us and prevent us from beginning to acquire a new set of habits, and we cannot bear men meeting us and saying, 'Look, So-and-so is turning philosopher, behaving like this and like that.' On the same principle physicians send away patients who are ill for long to a new country and a new climate, and rightly so. Do the same. Adopt new habits: fix your opinions, exercise yourselves in them. No, you leave the lecture-room to go to a show, a gladiatorial display, a colonnade, a circus: then you come back here from them and return there again, and nothing affects you. So you acquire no habit that gives you distinction; you pay no regard or attention to yourself: you do not watch yourself and ask, 'How do I deal with the impressions that meet me? Naturally, or unnaturally? How am I to answer their call? Rightly or wrongly? Do I warn things beyond my will that they have no concern with me?' I say, if you are not yet in this state, then fly from your former habits, fly from the uneducated, if you wish to begin at last to be more than ciphers.

CHAPTER SEVENTEEN
Concerning Providence

WHEN YOU ACCUSE PROVIDENCE, only consider the matter, and you will understand that its action is according to reason.

'But the unjust man', you say, 'is better off.'

In what? In money: for in regard to this he has the advantage over you, because he flatters, is shameless, is vigilant. Is this surprising? But look whether he is better off than you in being trustworthy and self-respecting. You will find that he is not; where you are superior to him, you will find that you are better off. So when some one was indignant once at the prosperity of Philostorgos, I said, 'Would you be willing to share the bed of Suras?' 'May that day never come!' he said. 'Why then are you indignant at his getting a return for what he sells, or how do you come to count him blessed who gets what he has by means that you abhor? Or what is the harm in Providence giving the better lot to those who are better? Is it not better to be self-respecting than to be rich?'

He agreed.

Man, why are you indignant then at having the better lot? Therefore always remember the truth and be ready to apply it–that it is a law of nature for the better to have the advantage of the worse in that in which he is better, and then you will never be indignant.

'But my wife uses me ill.'

Very well: if any one asks you, 'What is the matter?' say, 'My wife uses me ill.'

'Nothing else?'

Nothing.

'My father gives me nothing' ... but need you go further in your own mind and add this lie, that poverty is evil? For this reason it is not poverty that we must cast out, but our judgement about poverty, and so we shall be at peace.

CHAPTER EIGHTEEN

That we must not Allow News to Disturb us

WHEN ANY DISTURBING NEWS is brought you, bear this in mind, that news cannot affect anything within the region of the will. Can any one bring news to you that you are wrong in your thought or wrong in your will? Surely not: but only that some one is dead; what does that concern you? That some one speaks ill of you; what does that concern you? That your father has some design or other. Against whom? Is it against your will? How can he have? No, it is against your wretched body, or your wretched property; you are safe, it is not against you.

But the judge pronounces that you are guilty of impiety. Did not the judges pronounce the same on Socrates? Is it your concern that the judge pronounced on you? No. Why then do you trouble yourself? Your father has a duty of his own, which he must fulfil, or else lose his character as father, affectionate and gentle. Do not try to make him lose anything else for that reason; for a man never suffers harm except in that in which he is at fault.

Again, it is your duty to make your defence with firmness, self-respect, dispassionately: otherwise you lose your character as son, self-respecting and honourable. What then? Is the judge free from danger? No: he too incurs danger just as much. Why then do you still fear what judgement he will give? What have you to do with another's evil? Your evil is to defend yourself badly: that is the only thing you need be careful about. Whether you are condemned or not condemned is an-other's business, and the evil in the same way is another's.

'So-and-so threatens you.'

Threatens me? No.

'He blames you.'
It will be for him to see how he does his own business.
'He is going to condemn you unjustly.'
All the worse for him!

CHAPTER NINETEEN

What is the Difference between the Philosopher and the Uneducated Man

THE FIRST DIFFERENCE BETWEEN the philosopher and the uneducated man is that the latter says, 'Woe is me for my child, for my brother, woe is me for my father', and the other, if he is compelled to speak, considers the matter and says, Woe is me for myself.' For nothing outside the will can hinder or harm the will; it can only harm itself. If then we accept this, and, when things go amiss, are inclined to blame ourselves, remembering that judgement alone can disturb our peace and constancy, I swear to you by all the gods that we have made progress.

Instead of this we have come the wrong way from the beginning. When we were still children, if we stumbled when we were star-gazing, the nurse, instead of rebuking us, struck the stone. What is wrong with the stone? Was it to move out of the way because of your child's folly? Again, if (when children) we do not find something to eat after our bath our attendant does not check our appetite, but flogs the cook. Man, did we appoint you to attend on the cook? No, on our child: correct him, do him good. So even when we are grown up we appear like children: for it is being a child to be unmusical in musical things, ungrammatical in grammar, uneducated in life.

CHAPTER TWENTY

That Benefit may be Derived from All Outward Things

In regard to intellectual impressions it is generally agreed that good and evil depend upon us and not upon external things. No one calls the proposition, 'It is day', good, or 'It is night', bad, or 'Three is four', the greatest of evils. No, they say that knowledge is good and error evil, so that good may arise even in regard to what is false; that is, the knowledge that it is false. The same ought to be true in practical life.

'Is health good, and disease evil?'

No, man.

'What then?'

To use health well is good, to use it ill is evil.

'Do you mean that benefit can be gained even from disease?'

By heaven, can it not be gained even from death, ay or from lameness? Do you think Menoeceus gained but little good by his death? 'Nay, if any one says that sort of thing, I wish him a benefit like that Menoeceus gained!'

Out upon you, man, did he not preserve the patriot, the man of great mind, trustworthy and noble? And if he had lived on, was he not bound to lose all these, and win their very opposite? Would he not in that case have assumed the character of the coward, the ignoble, the hater of his country and lover of his life? Go to, do you think he gained but little good by his death? Well, did Admetus' father gain great good by living on so ignobly and miserably? Did he not die afterwards? I adjure you by the gods, cease to admire material things, cease to make yourselves slaves, first of things, and next, for their sake, of men who can acquire them or take them away.

'Can we then get benefit from these things?'

From all.

'Even from one who reviles us?'

Why, what good does the athlete get from the man who wrestles with him? The greatest. So my reviler helps to train me for the contest: he trains me to be patient, dispassionate, gentle. You deny it? You admit that the man who grips my neck and gets my loins and shoulders into order does me good, and the trainer does well to bid me 'lift the pestle with both hands', and the more severe he is, the more good do I get: and are you going to tell me that he who trains me to be free from anger does me no good? That means that you do not know how to get any good from humankind.

'He is a bad neighbour', you say?

Yes, for himself: but he is good for me; he trains me to be considerate and fair-minded.

'A bad father.'

Yes, for himself, but not for me. This is the magic wand of Hermes. 'Touch what you will', he says, 'and it will turn to gold.' Nay, bring what you will and I will turn it to good. Bring illness, bring death, bring poverty, bring reviling, bring the utmost peril of the law-court: the wand of Hermes will turn them all to good purpose!

'What will you make of death?'

What else but an adornment for you, what else but a means for you to show in deed what man is when he follows the will of nature? 'What will you make of sickness?'

I will show its nature, I will shine in it. I will be firm and tranquil, I will not flatter my physician nor pray for death. What more do you look for? Whatever you give me I will make it a means of blessedness and happiness, make it dignified and admirable.

That is not your way. You say, 'See you do not fall ill, it is an evil.' It is like saying, 'See you do not get an impression that three is four, it is an evil.' Man, how is it an evil? If 'I get a right notion of it, it cannot harm me any more. Will it not rather do me good? If then I have proper notions of poverty, of sickness, of life without office, is not that enough for me? Will they not serve my good? How then should I seek any more for good and evil in things external?

But we do not act on this. We carry these views to the lecture-room door, but no one takes them home: as soon as we leave here we are at war with our slave-boy, with our neighbours, with those who jeer and laugh at us. Good luck to the Lesbian, for he convicts me every day of knowing nothing.

CHAPTER TWENTY ONE

To those who Undertake the Profession of Teacher with a Light Heart

THOSE WHO HAVE LEARNT precepts and nothing more are anxious to give them out at once, just as men with weak stomachs vomit food. First digest your precepts, and then you will not vomit them; undigested, they become vomit indeed, impure and uneatable. Show us that you have digested them to some purpose, and that your Governing Principle is changed, as athletes can show their shoulders, as a result of their training and eating, and as those who have acquired the arts can show the result of their learning. The carpenter does not come and say, 'Hear me discourse on carpentry', but he undertakes a contract and builds a house and so shows that he has acquired the art. Do you likewise: eat as a man, drink as a man, adorn yourself, marry, get children, live a citizen's life; endure revilings, bear with an inconsiderate brother, bear with a father, a son, a travelling companion. Show us that you can do this, and then we shall see that you have in truth learnt something from the philosophers. Not you: you say, 'Come and hear me reading out comments!' Away with you, look for some one to disgorge your vomit on.

'I assure you I will expound Chrysippus' doctrines to you as no one else can. I will break up his language and make it quite clear. I will add, it may be, a touch of Antipater's or Archedemus' verve.'

What! is it for this that young men are to leave their countries and their parents, that they may come and hear you expounding petty points of language? Ought they not to return ready to bear with others and work with them, tranquil and free from tumult, furnished with a provision for life's journey, which will enable them to bear what befalls them well and to adorn themselves thereby? And how are you to impart to them what you do not possess yourself? For your sole occupation from the first has been this–how you are to resolve syllogisms and variable arguments, and arguments concluding with a question.

'But So-and-so gives lectures, why should not I?'

Slave, you cannot do this off-hand, and in a random fashion. It demands mature years, and a certain way of life, and the guidance of God.

You say no: but no one sails from harbour without sacrificing to the gods and invoking their help, and men do not sow at random, but only when they have invoked Demeter; and when a man has laid his hand to a task so momentous as this without the gods' help, will he be secure and will those who come to him be fortunate in their coming? Man, what are you doing but making the Mysteries common? You say, 'There is a shrine at Eleusis, lo, here is one also: there is a hierophant there: I too will make a hierophant: there is a herald there, I too will appoint a herald: there is a torch-bearer there, I too will have a torch-bearer: there are torches there, so there are here: the cries are the same. What difference is there between our doings and the Mysteries?'

Most impious of men, is there no difference? The benefit of the Mysteries depends on proper place and time: one must approach with sacrifice and prayer, with body purified and mind ready and disposed to approach holy rites and ancient sanctities. Only so do the Mysteries bring benefit, only so do we arrive at the belief that all these things were established by those of old for our education and the amendment of our life. But you publish and divulge them out of place and out of season, without sacrifices or purifying: you have not the dress which the hierophant should have, nor the proper hair, nor the fillet: you have not the right voice nor age, you have not lived pure as he has, but you have merely learnt off the words and say, 'The words have a holy power in themselves.'

You must approach the task in another fashion: it is momentous and full of mystery, not a chance gift which any one can command. The care of the young demands, it may be, more than wisdom: yes, by Zeus, one must have a certain readiness and special fitness, and a certain habit of body, and above all the counsel of God advising one to discharge this duty, as He counselled Socrates to examine men, and Diogenes to rebuke men in royal fashion, and Zeno to instruct and lay down precepts. You open a doctor's consulting-room with nothing but some drugs, without ever taking the trouble to acquire a knowledge of when or how they are applied. 'See, that's his remedy, eye-salve' (you say): 'I have that too.' Have you also the faculty of using it? Do you know when and how and to whom it will do good? Why then do you play at hazard with matters of highest moment, why are you reckless, why do you take in hand a task unsuited to your powers? Leave it to those who can do it and do it with distinction.

Do not bring disgrace upon philosophy by your personal act, nor join those who disparage the profession; but if the study of precepts really attracts you, sit quietly and turn them over in your mind, but never call yourself a philosopher nor allow any one else to do so, but say: 'He is in error: I am unchanged; my will, my impulses, my assent, are what they were, and, in a word, I have not advanced from my position, but deal with impressions as before.' So think, so speak about yourself, if you would think aright. But if this is beyond you, then play at hazard and do as you are doing, for you will be acting in character.

CHAPTER TWENTY TWO

On the Calling of the Cynic

WHEN ONE OF HIS acquaintance, who seemed inclined to the Cynic School, asked him what should be the character of the Cynic, and what was the primary conception of the school, he said, We will consider it at leisure: but this much I can tell you, that he who undertakes so great an enterprise without God's help is under God's wrath, and has no other wish but to disgrace himself in the public eye, for in a well-managed house a man does not come forward and say to himself, 'I ought to be steward': for, if he does, the master of the house takes notice, and when he sees him swaggering and ordering people about, he drags him away and gives him the lash. So it happens also in this great City of the Universe. Here, too, there is a Master of the House who assigns each thing its place.

'You are the sun: your faculty is to revolve and make the year and the seasons, to give growth and increase to the fruits, to rouse the winds and bring them to rest and to give temperate warmth to men's bodies; go, travel on your course and so move all things from the greatest to the least.'

'You are a calf: when a lion appears, do your part, or you will suffer for it.' 'You are a bull, come near and fight: for this is your proper portion and lies within your powers.' 'You can lead the army against Ilion: be Agamemnon.' 'You can fight Hector in single combat: be Achilles.' But if Thersites came forward and claimed the command he would not get it, or if he got it he would be shamed before a multitude of witnesses.

You, like the rest, must give the matter careful thought: it is not what you think. 'I wear a coarse cloak now and shall do so then, I sleep hard now and shall still do so, I shall take to myself a wallet and a staff and begin to go about begging and reviling those I meet, and if I see any one using pitch-plasters, or with his hair finely dressed, or walking in scarlet, I shall rebuke him.' If that is your impression of the Cynic's calling, give it a wide berth: do not come near it, for you have no concern with it; but if you have a true impression of it and still deem yourself not unworthy, then consider what a great enterprise you are taking in hand.

First, you must show a complete change in your conduct, and must cease to accuse God or man: you must utterly put away the will to get, and must will to avoid only what lies within the sphere of your will: you must harbour no anger, wrath, envy, pity: a fair maid, a fair name, favourites, or sweet cakes, must mean nothing to you. For you must know that other men, when they indulge in such things, have the protection of their walls and houses and darkness. There are many things to hide them: one, may be, has closed the door, or has set some one to guard his chamber: 'If any one comes, say, "He is out" or "He is busy."' But the Cynic, instead of all these, should have self-respect for his shelter: if he has not that, he will be naked and exposed and put to shame. This is his house, his door, this his chamber-guards, this his darkness: for he must not wish to conceal anything that is his: if he does, he disappears; he loses the true Cynic, the free open-air spirit, he has begun to fear outward things, he has begun to have need of concealment, and when he would hide himself he cannot; for he has no place or means to hide himself. But if by chance the public teacher, the 'pedagogue' is caught erring what must be his feelings! Is it possible with these fears before one to be confident with one's whole mind, and command other men? It is impracticable, impossible.

First then you must make your Governing Principle pure, and hold fast this rule of life, 'Henceforth my mind is the material I have to work on, as the carpenter has his timber and the shoemaker his leather: my business is to deal with my impressions aright. My wretched body is nothing to me, its parts are nothing to me. Death? Let it come when it will, whether to my whole body or to a part of it. Exile? Can one be sent into exile beyond the Universe? One cannot. Wherever I go, there is the sun, there is the moon, there are the stars, dreams, auguries, conversation with the gods.'

The true Cynic when he has ordered himself thus cannot be satisfied with this: he must know that he is sent as a messenger from God to men concerning things good and evil, to show them that they have gone astray and are seeking the true nature of good and evil where it is not to be found, and take no thought where it really is: he must realize, in the words of Diogenes when brought before Philip after the battle of Chaeronea, that he is sent 'to reconnoitre'. For indeed the Cynic has to discover what things are friendly to men and what are hostile: and when he has accurately made his observations he must return and report the truth, not driven by fear to point out enemies where there are none, nor in any other way disturbed or confounded by his impressions.

He must then be able, if chance so offer, to come forward on the tragic stage, and with a loud voice utter the words of Socrates: 'O race of men, whither are ye hurrying? What are you doing, miserable creatures? You wander up and down like blind folk: you have left the true path and go away on a vain errand, you seek peace and happiness elsewhere, where it is not to be found, and believe not when another shows the way.' Why do you seek it outside? Do you seek it in the body? It is not there. If you doubt, look at Myron, look at Ophellius. In property? It is not there. If you disbelieve, look at Croesus, look at the rich men of to-day, and see how full their life is of lamentation. In office? It is not there. If it were, then those who have twice or thrice been consuls should be happy, but they are not. Whom shall we trust on this matter? Shall we trust you who look upon their fortune from outside and are dazzled by the outward show, or the men themselves? What do they say? Listen to them, when they lament and sigh, and think their condition to be more miserable and perilous just because of their consulships and glory and distinction. Shall you find it in royalty? It is not there. If it were, Nero would have been happy, and Sardanapalus. Why, even Agamemnon was not happy, though he was a finer fellow than Sardanapalus and Nero. When the rest were snoring what did he do? *'Many hairs he plucked by the roots from his head'*, and what did he say himself? *'Thus do I wander and am in agony of spirit, and my heart leaps from my breast.'* [Homer, *Iliad*, X. 15, 91, 94, 95]

Miserable man, what is wrong with your affairs? Is it your property? No. Your body? No. You have *'store of gold and copper'*. What is wrong with you then? You have neglected and ruined that in you–whatever it be–wherewith we exercise the will to get and to avoid, the impulse to act and not to act. How have you neglected it? It is ignorant of the true nature of the good to which it is born and of the nature of evil, and of what concerns it and what does not. And so when something that does not concern it is in bad case, it says, 'Woe is me, the Hellenes are in peril!' Oh miserable mind of man, alone neglected and uncared for!

'They are going to perish, slain by the Trojans!'

And if the Trojans slay them not, will they not die?

'Yes, but not all at once.'

What does it matter then? If death is evil; it is equally evil, whether men die alone or together. Will anything else happen, but that body and soul will be separated?

Nothing.

And if the Hellenes perish, is *the door closed* to you? Is not death within your power?

'It is.'

Why do you mourn then? Bravo! a king indeed, and holding the sceptre of Zeus!

A king cannot be miserable any more than God can be. What are you then? A shepherd in very truth, for you weep just like shepherds when a wolf carries off one of their sheep: yes and these whom you rule are sheep too. And why did you come here? Was there any danger to your will to get or your will to avoid, your impulse for action and against action?

'No,' he says, 'but my brother's poor wife was carried off.'

It is a great gain to be robbed of an adulterous wife.

'Are we then to suffer the scorn of the Trojans?'

What are they? Are they wise or foolish? If they are wise, why do you make war on them? If they are foolish, what does it matter to you?

In what then does the good reside, since it is not in these things? Tell us, Sir Messenger and Spy.

It is where you think not, and will not seek for it. For if you had wished you would have found it in yourselves and would not have wandered outside and would not have sought the things of others as your own. Turn again to *yourselves*, learn to understand the primary notions which you have. Of what nature do you imagine the good to be?

'Tranquil, fraught with happiness, unhindered.'

Nay, but do you not imagine it as naturally great? Do you not imagine it as precious? Do you not imagine it as free from harm? I ask you then, in what subject must we seek for that which is tranquil and unhindered? In the slavish or the free?

'In the free.'

Your poor body then, is it slavish or free?

'We know not.'

Do you not know that it is a slave to fever, gout, ophthalmia, dysentery, the tyrant, fire, sword, everything stronger than itself? 'Yes, it is a slave.'

How then can any part of the body be still free from hindrance? How can that which is naturally dead–earth and clay–be great or precious? What then? Have you no element of freedom?

'Perhaps none.'

Why, who can compel you to assent to what appears false? 'No one.'

And who to refuse assent to what appears true?

'No one.'

Here then you see that there is something in you which is naturally free. What man among you can have will to get or to avoid, impulse to act or not to act, or can prepare or put an object before himself, without conceiving an impression of what is profitable or fitting?

'No one.'

Here too then you have free and unhindered action. Miserable men, develop this, set your minds on this, seek your good here.

'Nay, but how is it possible for a man who has nothing, naked, without home or hearth, in squalor, without a slave, without a city, to live a tranquil life?'

Lo, God has sent you one who shall show indeed that it is possible. 'Look at me, I have no house or city, property or slave: I sleep on the ground, I have no wife or children, no miserable palace, but only earth and sky and one poor cloak. Yet what do I lack? Am I not quit of pain and fear, am I not free? When has any of you ever seen me failing to get what I will to get, or falling into what I will to avoid? When did I blame God or man, when did I accuse any? Has any of you seen me with a gloomy face? How do I meet those of whom you stand in fear and awe? Do I not meet them as slaves? Who that sees me but thinks that he sees his king and master?' There you have the true Cynic's words; this is his character, and scheme of life. No, you say, what makes the Cynic is a little wallet, and a staff and a big pair of jaws; to devour or hoard everything you give him or to revile out of season those who meet him, or to make a show of his fine shoulder!

Is this the spirit in which you mean to take in hand so great an enterprise? Take a mirror first, look at your shoulders, take note of your loins and your thighs. Man, it is an Olympic contest you are about to enter your name for, not a miserable, make-believe match. At Olympia you cannot simply be beaten and leave the grounds; in the first place you must be disgraced in the sight of all the world, not before men of Athens only or of Lacedaemon or of Nicopolis; in the next place the man who lightly enters the lists must be flogged, but before he is flogged he must suffer thirst and scorching heat and swallow plenty of dust. Think it over more carefully, know yourself, inquire of heaven, attempt not the task without God. If He advise you, know that He wishes you to become great or to receive many stripes. For this too is a very fine strand woven into the Cynic's lot: he must suffer strokes like an ass and love the very men that strike him as though he were the father or brother of all.

No, no; if a man flogs you, you must stand in the midst and cry aloud, 'Caesar, what pains I suffer under your rule of peace! Let us go to the proconsul.'

What has the Cynic to do with Caesar or proconsul or any one else but Zeus, Who has sent him upon earth, and Whom he serves? Does he call upon any one but Him? Is he not convinced that whatever pains he suffers are God's training of him? Why, Heracles, when he was being trained by Eurystheus, did not count himself wretched, but fulfilled all his commands without shrinking, and shall this man, who is under the training and discipline of Zeus, cry aloud in indignation, if he be worthy to carry the staff of Diogenes? Listen to what Diogenes said when the fever was on him to those who passed by: 'Base creatures,' he said, 'will you not stay? You go all that way to Olympia to see athletes killed or matched in battle, and yet have you no wish to see a battle between fever and a man?' I suppose you think a man like that would have been very likely to accuse God, Who sent him, of using him hardly? Nay, he was proud of his distresses, and was fain to be the spectacle of passers-by. On what ground is he to accuse God? That he is living a seemly life, and that he is displaying his virtue in a clearer light? But what does he say of poverty, of death, of pain? How did he compare his own happiness with that of the Great King? Nay, he did not so much as think it comparable. For where there are tumults, and distresses, and fears, where the will to get is unfulfilled, and the will to avoid is foiled, a world of envies and jealousies, how can happiness find a way there? But wherever there are unsound judgements, there all these passions must be.

And when the young man asked Epictetus, whether, if he fell sick and a friend asked him to come to his house to be tended in his sickness, he was to consent, he said, Where will you find me a Cynic's friend? For he must be another like himself, that he may be worthy to be counted as his friend; he must share with him the sceptre and the kingdom and be a worthy minister, if he is to be deemed worthy of his friendship, as Diogenes was worthy of Antisthenes, and Crates of Diogenes. Or do you think that if he salutes him as he comes near that makes him his friend, and the Cynic will count him worthy to receive him in his house? Wherefore, if this is your opinion and such your thoughts, look round rather for a fine dunghill to have your fever on, one that shelters you from the north wind, to save you from a chill. But you seem to me to want to get away into some one's house for a time and eat your fill. How comes it then that you should take in hand so great a matter?

'Will the Cynic', said his questioner, 'accept marriage and children as matters of prime importance?'

If, he replied, you grant me a city of wise men, it may be that no one will lightly adopt the Cynic's calling. For what reason should he take upon him this manner of life? But if we assume that he does, there will be nothing to prevent him from marrying and getting children; for his wife will be like himself, and his wife's father will be like him, and his children will be brought up on these lines. But in the present constitution of the world–which is that of the battlefield–it is a question whether the Cynic should not be undistracted entirely, devoted to the service of God, able to go to and fro among men; not tied down to acts that befit private occasions, nor involved in personal relations, which if he violates he will cease to keep his character as a good man, and if he maintains them he will destroy the Messenger and Spy and Herald of the gods that is in him. For he must show services to his father-in-law, and render them to his wife's other relations and to herself; and so he is reduced to being a sick nurse or a general provider. Not to speak of other things, he must needs have a saucepan, to make water hot for the baby, to wash him in the bath; when his wife has had a child he must provide wool and oil for her, and a bed and a cup–the vessels mount up at once–not to mention other business and distraction. What becomes now of that king of ours who watches every interest of the public,

> *Trusted with clans and full of many cares,*
> [Homer, *Iliad*, II. 25]

whose duty it is to watch others, those who have married and got children, to see which of them uses his wife well, which ill, who is quarrelsome, which house is prospering and which is not, going about like a physician and feeling men's pulses? 'You have a fever, you a headache, you the gout; I prescribe fasting for you, food for you, no bath for you; you need the surgeon's knife, you the cautery.' How can the man who is involved in the acts appropriate to private life find leisure? Must he not procure clothes for the children? Must he not send them to the schoolmaster with their tablets and note-books, and provide them with beds, for they cannot be Cynics from their mother's womb? If he does not provide for them, it were better to fling them aside as soon as born rather than kill them thus. See to what a pass we bring our Cynic, how we take away his kingdom!

'Yes, but Crates married.'

The case you mention was a special one and a love-match, and you have to assume a wife who was a Crates herself. Our inquiry is concerned with ordinary marriages which are liable to distraction; and from this point of view we do not find that in these circumstances marriage has a primary claim on the Cynic.

'How then', says he, 'will he keep society going?'

By God, do you think that those who bring into the world two or three ugly little squeakers to fill their place do men greater benefit than those who exercise oversight, so far as they can, over all men, to see what they do, how they live, what they attend to, what they undutifully neglect? Do you think the Thebans reaped greater benefit from those who left them children than from Epaminondas who died childless? Did Priam who begat fifty sons, rascals all, or Danaus or Aeolus contribute more to society than Homer? What? Shall a man abstain from marrying or getting children for the sake of acting as general or writing a treatise, and be thought to have got a fair exchange for his childlessness, and shall the kingdom of the Cynic be thought no compensation?

Perhaps we do not realize his greatness nor picture at its true worth the character of Diogenes: we only look at the Cynics of to-day,

Dogs of the table, guardians of the gate,
[Homer, *Iliad*, XXII. 69]

who copy those of old in nothing, except perhaps in dirty habits.

If we knew what a Cynic was we should not be moved or astonished at his not marrying or getting children. Man, he is parent to all men, he has men for his sons, women for his daughters; he approaches all and treats all in the spirit of a father. Do you think he reviles those he meets because he is a busybody? He does it as a father, as a brother, and as servant of Zeus, the Father of all.

Nay, ask me if you think well, whether he will take part in politics.

Fool, do you look for a higher form of politics' than those he handles now? Is he to come forward and address an Athenian assembly on revenues or ways and means, when he ought to be discoursing to all mankind, alike to Athenians, to Corinthians, and to Romans, not about ways and means or revenues or peace and war, but about happiness and unhappiness, good fortune and bad fortune, slavery and freedom. When a man is engaged in politics of such moment, do you ask me if he is to be a politician? Nay, ask me if he is to hold office. Fool, what office is greater than this that he holds?

Yet such an one has need also of a body of a certain quality; for if he come forward with a consumptive figure, thin and pale, his testimony no longer carries the same force. For he must not only display mental qualities to convince the lay mind that it is possible to be good and noble without the things that they set store by, but his body must show that the plain and simple life of the open air does no harm to the body–'Look you, how my body and I bear witness to this.' As indeed Diogenes did; for he went about with the glow of health on his face, and attracted the masses by his bodily presence. But a Cynic who excites pity is like a beggar; every one turns from him and takes Offence at him; for he ought not to appear dirty, lest he should scare men away thereby; nay his very squalor should be cleanly and attractive.

Further, the Cynic ought to have great natural grace and quickness of wit (without this he is a driveller, nothing more) that he may be able to give a ready and apposite answer• to each question that arises: as Diogenes answered him who said, 'Are you the Diogenes who disbelieves in the gods?' by saying, 'How can I be when I think the gods hate you?' or again, when Alexander stood over him as he slept and said:

Sleep all night long becomes not men of counsel,
[Homer, *Iliad*, II. 24]

replied, still in his sleep,

Trusted with clans and full of many cares.
[Homer, *Iliad*, II. 25]

But above all, his Governing Principle must be purer than the sun; otherwise he must needs be a gambler and a reckless person; he will be rebuking others when he is involved in evil himself. See what this means. The kings and tyrants of this world have their armed bodyguard which enables them to rebuke certain persons and to punish those who do wrong even though they are wicked themselves, but the Cynic's conscience takes the place of arms and bodyguard and furnishes him with this authority. When he sees that he has watched and toiled for men, and that his sleep has been pure, and that when sleep leaves him he is purer still, and that all the thoughts of his heart have been those of one

who is a friend and servant of the gods, and who shares the rule of Zeus, and that everywhere he is ready to say:

Lead me, O Zeus, and lead me, Destiny,
[Cleanthes]

and 'If thus the gods would have it, be it so'–then, I ask, why should he not have confidence to speak freely to his brothers, to his children, and in a word to his kinsfolk?

Therefore the man whose mind is thus disposed is not fussy nor impertinent, for when he is inspecting the affairs of men, he is concerned with what is not another's but his own, unless you are to call the general too a busybody, when he inspects and reviews and keeps watch over his soldiers, and punishes those who offend against discipline. But if you rebuke others when you are carrying a nice cake hid under your arm, I shall say to you, 'Would not you rather go off into a corner and eat what you have stolen?' What have you to do with other men's concerns? Who are you? Are you the bull or the queen bee? Show me the tokens of your royalty, like those which nature gives her. But if you are only a drone claiming the kingdom of the bees, do not you think that

your fellow citizens will make an end of you, as the bees do to the drones?

The Cynic must have the spirit of patience in such measure as to seem to the multitude as unfeeling as a stone. Reviling or blows or insults are nothing to him; he has given his bit of a body to any one who will, to treat it as he pleases. For he remembers that the inferior must needs be conquered by the superior, where it is inferior, and the body is inferior to the multitude, the weaker inferior to them that are stronger. He therefore never enters upon this contest, where he may be conquered, but at once resigns what does not belong to him and does not claim power over slaves. But when it comes to the will and the power of dealing with impressions then you will see what eyes he has, so that you will say, 'Argus was blind in comparison.' Is there reckless assent, is there vain impulse, will to get which fails, will to avoid which is foiled, purpose incomplete, blame, disparagement or envy? It is on these he concentrates his attention and energy; for the rest he snores and

takes his ease, and all is peace. No one robs him of his will or masters that.

Do they master his bit of a body?

Yes.

And his bit of property?

Yes.

And offices and honours?

What does he care for these? When any one tries to frighten him with these fears he says to him, 'Get away, look for children to frighten. They think masks fearsome, but I know that they are made of pot, and have nothing inside.'

So momentous is the profession you are thinking of. Before God I beg you to wait if you will, and look first to your equipment; for mark what Hector says to Andromache: 'Go rather to the house', he says, 'and weave':

> *War shall be men's concern,*
> *All men's, and mine in chief.*
> [Homer, *Iliad*]

So truly did he realize his own endowment and her incapacity.

CHAPTER TWENTY THREE
To those who Read and Discourse for Display

FIRST SAY TO YOURSELF, what manner of man you want to be; when you have settled this, act upon it in all you do; for in pretty nearly all pursuits we see that done. Athletes first decide what they want to be, and then they act accordingly. If a man is to be a long-distance runner, he takes the diet, the walking, the rubbing, and the gymnastic suited to that; if he is going in for the short course, he alters all this to suit his aim, if for the pentathlon he alters his training still more. You will find the same done in the arts. If you are a carpenter you will have this kind of work; if a smith, you will have that kind. For in everything we do, if we have no standard to go by, we shall do it ineffectively; if we use the wrong standard, we shall fail completely.

Now we have two standards to go by, one general and one special. The first is that we must act as human beings. What does this include? We must not act like a sheep, at random, nor like a brute, destructively. The special standard is relative to each man's occupation and purpose. The lyre-player must act as a lyre-player, the carpenter as a carpenter, the philosopher as a philosopher, the orator as an orator. When therefore you say, 'Come and hear me lecturing to you', see to it first that you are not acting without aim. Then if you find you have a standard, see to it that it is the right one.

Do you wish to do men good or to receive compliments?

At once you have the answer, 'What account do I take of the praise of the multitude?'

An excellent answer. Nor does the musician heed the multitude, so far as he is a true musician, nor the geometrician. Do you wish then to do good? What are you aiming at? Tell us, that we too may run to your lecture-room. Now can any one do good to others unless he has received good himself? No, no more than the man who is no carpenter can help others in carpentry, or he who is no shoemaker in shoemaking.

Would you really know then whether you have received any good? Produce your judgements, my philosopher. What does the will to get profess? Success in getting. And the will to avoid? Escape from what it avoids. Well, do we fulfil their profession? Tell me the truth, and if you lie, I will tell you myself. When lately your audience were slack in their attendance, and did not applaud you, you went away in low spirits. Again when you were lately praised you went round and said to every one, 'What did you think of me?'

'I thought you wonderful, master, as I live.'

'How did I give that passage?'

'Which do you mean?'

'Where I described Pan and the Nymphs.'

'Superlatively.'

And yet you tell me that in respect to that will to get and will to avoid you behave in a natural way. Go to, get some one else to believe you! Did you not lately praise So-and-so against your real opinion? Did you not flatter So-and-so, the senator's son? Did you want your children to be like that?

'Heaven forbid!'

Why then did you praise him and pay him attention?

'He is a young man of parts, and ready to listen to arguments.'

How do you know that?

'He admires me.'

Now you have stated the true reason. After all, what do you think? Do not these very admirers secretly despise you? When a man who is conscious of no good action or good thought meets a philosopher who says, 'Here is a genius, frank and unspoilt', do not you think he is bound to say to himself, 'This man wants something from me'? Tell me, what sign of genius has he displayed? Why, he has been with you all this long time, he has heard you discoursing, he has heard you lecturing. Has he grown modest? Has he returned to himself? Has he realized what misery he is in? Has he cast away his vanity? Is he looking for some one to teach him?

'He is.'

Some one to teach him how he should live? No, you fool, but how he should speak, for that is what he admires you for. Listen and hear what he says: 'This man is a perfect artist in style, his style is much finer than Dio's.' That's a different thing altogether. Does he say, 'This man has self-respect, he is trustworthy and tranquil-minded'? If he did say so, I should say, 'Since he is trustworthy, tell me what you mean by this "trustworthy" man', and if he could not answer I should add, 'First learn what your words mean, and then speak.'

If you are in this sorry state, gaping for men to praise you, and counting your audience, do you really want to do others good?

'To-day I had a much larger audience.'

'Yes, it was a large one.'

'I suppose five hundred.'

'Nonsense! put them at a thousand.'

'Dio never had so large an audience.'

'How is that?'

'Why, they have a fine turn for understanding arguments.'

'Noble teaching, master, can move even a stone.'

There you have the words of a philosopher! These are the feelings of one who is to benefit mankind, there you have a man who has listened to reason, who has read the teaching of Socrates in the spirit of Socrates, and not as so much Lysias or Isocrates! '"I have often wondered by what arguments"—no, "by what argument"–the singular is smoother than the plural.' Did you ever read the words except as one reads paltry songs? If you had read them properly you would not have dwelt on these points of language, but would rather have studied the passage, 'Anytus and Meletus can kill me, but they cannot harm me', and this, 'My nature is such that I cannot attend to my affairs, but only to the argument which appears best to me when I reflect.' That was why no one ever heard Socrates say, 'I know and teach'; no, he sent one man here, another there; and therefore they used to come to him, asking to be introduced by him to philosophers, and he took and introduced them. No, of course, as he went with them he would say, 'Come and hear me discourse to-day in the house of Quadratus'!

What am I to hear from you? Do you want to display to me your fine composition? Man, you compose well enough, and what good does it do you?

'Do praise me, I beg.'

What do you mean by praise?

'Say "Bravo!" to me, or "Marvellous!"'

Very well, I say it; but if praise is what philosophers put in the category of the good, what praise can I give you? If correct speaking is a good thing, teach me that, and I will praise you.

'What? are you bound to dislike listening to fine oratory?'

Heaven forbid! I do not dislike listening to a harp-player, but am I therefore bound to stand and play the harp? Hear what Socrates says, 'It would not be seemly for me, sir, at this time of life, to come before you like a youth framing fine phrases.' [Plato, *Apology*, 17c] 'Like a youth', he says. Yes, it is indeed a pretty art, to select fine phrases and put them together, and then come forward and read them or recite them with ability, and as one reads to add, 'There are not many that can understand what I say, as sure as you hope to live.'

Does the philosopher invite men to a lecture? Does he not draw to him those who are going to get good from him, as the sun draws sustenance to itself? No physician worth the name invites men to come and be healed by him, though I hear that in Rome to-day physicians do invite them; in my day physicians were called in by their patients.

'I bid you to come and hear that you are in a bad way, that you attend to everything rather than what you should attend to, and that you do not know what is good and what is evil, and are unhappy and miserable.'

A fine invitation!

Surely, unless the philosopher's words force home this lesson, they are dead and so is he. Rufus was wont to say, 'If you find leisure to praise me, my words are spoken in vain.' Wherefore he spoke in such fashion that each of us as he sat there thought he was himself accused: such was his grip of men's doings, so vividly did he set each man's ills before his eyes. The philosopher's school, sirs, is a physician's consulting-room. You must leave it in pain, not in pleasure; for you come to it in disorder, one with a shoulder put out, another with an ulcer, another with fistula, another with headache. And then you would have me sit there and utter fine little thoughts and phrases, that you may leave me with praise on your lips, and carrying away, one his shoulder, one his head, one his ulcer, one his fistula, exactly in the state he brought them to me. Is it for this you say that young men are to go abroad and leave their parents and friends and kinsmen and property, that they may say, 'Ye gods!' to you when you deliver your phrases? Was this what Socrates did, or Zeno, or Cleanthes?

You ask, 'Is there not the hortatory style?'

Yes–no one denies it–just as there is the style for proof and the style for teaching. Who has ever named a fourth style along with them, the ostentatious? What is the hortatory style? The power of showing to one and to many what a sordid struggle they are plunged in, and how they pay regard to everything rather than to what they want. For they want what tends to happiness, but they seek it in the wrong place. Is it for this that you must set up a thousand benches and invite men to come and hear you, and then mount the rostrum in a fine robe or an elegant cloak and describe the death of Achilles? Cease, by all your gods, to dishonour noble words and subjects, so far as in you lies.

Nothing is more effective in exhortation than when the speaker makes plain to his hearers that he has need of them. Tell me, in all your readings or discourses, did you ever make one of your audience anxious about himself or rouse him to a sense of his position? Did you ever send one away saying, 'The philosopher has got a good grip of me: I must act so no more'? Why, even if your fame is at its height, he only says to some one, 'A pretty description that about Xerxes!' while another puts in, 'No, the battle of Thermopylae.' Is this what a philosopher's lecture comes to?

CHAPTER TWENTY FOUR

That we ought not to Spend our Feelings on Things beyond our Power

IF A THING GOES against another's nature, you must not take it as evil for you; for you are born not to share humiliation or evil fortune, but to share good fortune. And if a man is unfortunate, remember that his misfortune is his own fault; for God created all men for happiness and peace of mind. To this end He gave men resources, giving each man some things for his own, and some not for his own, things subject to hindrance and deprivation and compulsion not for his own, but things beyond hindrance for his own. The true nature of good and evil He gave man for his own, as was natural for Him to do, Who cares for us and protects us as a Father.

'Oh, but I have just parted from such an one, and he is distressed!'

Why did he count as his own what was not his? When he rejoiced to look on you why did he not reflect that you are mortal, and that you may go on a journey? Wherefore he pays the penalty for his own foolishness. But why do you bewail yourself, and to what end? Did not you study this distinction either? Did you, as worthless women do, regard all the things in which you took pleasure–places, persons, ways of life –as though they would always be with you? And so now you sit and weep because you do not see the same persons and pass your time in the same place. No doubt you deserve this fate–to be more wretched than rooks and ravens, who may fly where they will and change their nests, and cross the seas, without lamenting or long-ing for their first possessions.

'Yes, but this happens to them because they have no reason.'

Is our reason then given us by the gods for misfortune and misery, that we may continue in wretchedness and mourning? Or would you have all men to be immortal, and no one go abroad? Are we never to go away but all to stay rooted like plants, and if one of our close friends goes abroad are we to sit and weep: and again, if he return, are we to dance and clap like little children?

Shall we not at last give up the milk of babes, and remember what we heard from the philosophers, unless we took what they said for enchanters' tales? 'This world is one city, and the substance of which it is constructed is one; and things must needs move in a cycle, one thing giving way to another, and some things must pass away, and others come into being, some must abide as they are and others must move; and the universe is full of friends–the gods first, and after them men, whom nature has made akin to one another; some of them must be with one another and others must go away, and we should rejoice in those that are with us, yet not be sad at those who go away. And man, besides being born to a high courage, and to despise all that is beyond his will, has this too for his own, that he is not rooted nor attached to the earth, but goes now to one place, now to another, at one time under the pressure of business, at another merely to see the world.' Such indeed was the lot of Odysseus:

Cities of many men he saw, and learnt
Their mind;
[Homer, *Odyssey*, I. 3]

and yet earlier it was the lot of Heracles to go about all the inhabited world,

Beholding laws and insolence of men,
[Homer, *Odyssey*, XVII. 487]

cleansing the world and casting forth the insolent, and bringing "in the rule of law. Yet how many friends, think you, had he in Thebes, how many in Argos, how many in Athens, and how many did he win for himself as he went about, seeing that he married a wife, where he thought fit, and got children, and forsook his children, with no mourning nor longing, nor as one leaving them orphans? For he knew that no man is an orphan, but that all men have always the Father Who cares for them continually; for to him it was no mere tale that he had heard that Zeus is the Father of men, for he believed Him to be his own father and called

Him so, and all that he did he did as looking to Him, wherefore it was in his power to live happily everywhere. But happiness and longing for what is absent can never be united; for that which is happy must needs have all that it will, and be as it were in a state of satisfaction; no thirst or hunger must come near it. But Odysseus, you say, had a sense of longing for his wife, and sat upon a rock and wept. Do you take Homer for your authority in everything, and Homer's stories? If Odysseus really wept, was he not miserable, and what good man is ever miserable? The universe is indeed managed ill if Zeus does not take care of His citizens, that they may be happy as He is. It is not lawful or right even to think of such a thing, and if Odysseus wept and lamented, he was no good man. For how can a man be good, when he knows not who he is, and how can he know this when he has forgotten that all things that have come into being are perishable, and that it is impossible for man to be with man for ever? Now to desire what is impossible is slavish and silly; it is to make oneself a stranger in the world, and to fight against God with one's own judgements, as alone one can.

'But my mother mourns because she does not see me.'

Why does she not take to heart these lessons? Yet I do not say that we must not take pains to prevent her lamenting; but that we must not wish absolutely for what is not ours. Another's sorrow is no concern of mine, my sorrow is my own; and so I shall absolutely check my own sorrow, for it is in my power, but another's I shall try to check only so far as I can, but not absolutely; otherwise I shall fight against God, I shall set myself against Zeus and array myself against His conduct of the universe, and the penalty for this battling with God and this disobedience will be paid not only by 'children's children', but by me in my own person, by day and by night, when I start in my dreams and am disturbed, when I tremble at every message, when my peace of mind hangs upon another's letters.

Some one is come from Rome.

'If only it be no ill news!'

What ill can happen to you in a place where you are not?

From Greece.

'If only it be no ill news!'

On this principle, every place can cause you misery. Is it not enough that you should be miserable where you are yourself? Must you needs be miserable overseas, and by letter? Is this what you mean by being secure?

What happens then if your friends there die?

What else except that mortal men have died? How can you wish at the same time to grow old and not to see the death of any that you love? Do you not know that in the long course of time many events of divers sorts must happen? One man must be overcome by fever, another by a robber, a third by a despot. For such is the nature of the atmosphere about us, and of our companions; cold and heat and unsuitable food, and travel by land, and sea, and winds and manifold perils destroy one man and send another into exile, and another they send on an embassy or as a soldier. Sit still then with your wits dazed at all these things–mourning, unfortunate, miserable, depending on something other than yourself–not one thing or two, but things innumerable.

Is this what your lesson comes to, is this what you learnt in the philosopher's school? Do you not know that life is a soldier's service? One man must keep guard, another go out to reconnoitre, another take the field. It is not possible for all to stay where they are, nor is it better so. But you neglect to fulfil the orders of the general and complain, when some severe order is laid upon you; you do not understand to what a pitiful state you are bringing the army so far as in you lies; you do not see that if all follow your example there will be no one to dig a trench, or raise a palisade, no one to keep night watch or fight in the field, but every one will seem an unserviceable soldier.

Again, if you go as a sailor on shipboard, keep to one place and hold fast to that; if you are called on to climb the mast, refuse, if to run out on the bows, refuse that. Why, what ship's master will put up with you, and not fling you overboard like a useless bit of furniture, a mere

4 hindrance and bad example to the other sailors? So too it is in the world; each man's life is a campaign, and a long and varied one. It is for you to play the soldier's part–do everything at the General's bidding, divining His wishes, if it be possible. For there is no comparison between that General and the ordinary one in power and superiority of character. You are set in an imperial City and not in some humble town; you are always a senator. Do you not know that such an one can attend but little to his own household? He must spend most of his time abroad, in command or under command, or as subordinate to some officer, or as soldier or judge? And yet you tell me you want to be attached like a plant and rooted in the same place?

'Yes, for it is pleasant.'

Who denies it? Dainties are pleasant too, and a beautiful woman is a pleasant thing. Your talk is the talk of those who make pleasure their end.

Do you not realize whose language you are using, the language of Epicureans and abandoned creatures? and yet though your actions and your principles are theirs, you quote to us the words of Zeno and

Socrates? Fling away from you, as far as may be, these alien properties that you adorn yourself with, and that do not fit you! People of
that sort have no wish except to sleep without hindrance or compulsion, and then to get up and yawn at their ease and wash their face,
then to write and read at their pleasure, then to talk nonsense and be
complimented by their friends, whatever they say, then to go out for a
walk and after a little walk to have a bath, then to eat, and then go to
sleep–the sort of sleep men of that kind are likely to indulge in–I need
say no more–you may judge what it is.

Come, now, tell me the way of life your heart is set on–you who profess to admire truth and Socrates and Diogenes. What do you want to
do in Athens? Just what you are doing? Nothing else? Then why do you
call yourself a Stoic? If those who speak falsely of the Roman constitution are seriously punished, are those who speak falsely of so great
and serious a subject and a name to get off scot free? That cannot be;
none may escape this divine and mighty law, which exacts the greatest
punishments from those whose offence is greatest. What does it say?
'He that pretends to qualities that concern him not, let him be given to
vanity and arrogance; let him that disobeys the divine government be
an abject slave, let him be subject to pain, envy, pity, in a word, let him
be miserable and full of lamentations.'

'What is your conclusion? Would you have me court this great man
or that and frequent his doorstep?'

If reason so determine, for country's sake or kindred or mankind,
why should you not go to him? You are not ashamed to go to the shoemaker when you want shoes, nor to the market-gardener when you
want lettuces. Are you ashamed to go to the rich when you want something they can give?

'Yes, but I do not admire the shoemaker.'

Do not admire the rich man either.

'I shall not flatter the market-gardener.'

Do not flatter the rich man either.

'How then am I to get what I want?'

Do I say to you, 'Go, and you will get what you want', or only, 'Go,
and act up to your character'?

'Why do I go then?'

That you may come away feeling that you have fulfilled the acts required of a citizen, a brother, a friend. But remember that you have gone
to a shoemaker, a greengrocer, one who has no authority over great or
high matters, though he sell what he has for a big price. You are going as it
were to fetch lettuces; they are worth an obol, but not a talent.

Apply this principle. The business is worth going to a man's door for. Very well, I will go. It is worth an interview. Very well, I will have an interview with him. But if I must kiss his hand and flatter him with compliments, that is like paying a talent. I will have none of it. It is not to my profit, nor to the profit of the city or my friends to ruin a good citizen and a friend.

'But men will think you took no pains if you fail.'

Have you again forgotten why you went there? Do you not know that a good man does nothing for the sake of what men think, but only for the sake of doing right?

'What does he gain by doing right?'

What does a man gain who writes Dio's name correctly? The gain of writing.

'Is there no further reward?'

Do you look for any greater reward for a good man than to do what is noble and right? At Olympia you do not want anything else; you are content to have been crowned at Olympia. Does it seem to you so small and worthless a thing to be noble and good and happy? Therefore, since the gods have made you a citizen of this city and you are bound to set your hand betimes to a man's work, why hanker after nurses and the breast, and allow silly women to soften you and make you effeminate with their tears? Will you then never cease to be a babe? Do you not know that he who acts like a child is ridiculous in proportion to his years?

Did you not see any one in Athens, or go to any one's house?

'Yes, the man I wanted to see.'

Do the same here; choose to see the man you want, and you will see him; only do it in no abject spirit, without will to get or to avoid, and all will be well with you; but it does not depend on going or standing at the door, but on the judgements that are within you. When you have come to despise things without you and beyond your will's control, and have come to regard none of them as your own, but only this–to be right in judgement, in thought, in impulse, in will to get and to avoid, what room is left for flattery or abjectness of mind? Why do you still long for the peace of your home, and for your familiar haunts? Wait a little and these places will become familiar to you in their turn. Then if your spirit is as degenerate as this, go weep and mourn as soon as you are again parted from these.

'How then am I to prove myself affectionate?'

In a noble and not a miserable spirit. For it is against all reason to be of an abject and broken spirit and to depend on another and to blame God or man. Prove yourself affectionate, but see that you observe these rules; if this affection of yours, or whatever you call it, is going to make you a miserable slave, it is not for your good to be affectionate. Nay, what prevents you loving a man as one who is mortal and bound to leave you? Did not Socrates love his children? Yes, but as one who is free and bears in mind that the love of the gods stands first, and therefore he failed in none of the duties of a good man, either in his defence, or in assessing his penalty, or earlier still as a member of the council or a soldier in the field. But we abound in every kind of excuse for a mean spirit; with some of us it is a child, with others our mother or our brothers. We ought not to let any one make us miserable, but let every one make us happy, and God above all, Who created us for this. Go to, did Diogenes love no one, he who was so gentle and kind-hearted that he cheerfully took upon him all those troubles and distresses of body for the general good of men? But how did he love? As the servant of Zeus should love, caring for his friends, but submitting himself to God. That was why he alone made the whole world his country, and no special land, and when he was made prisoner he did not long for Athens or for his friends and companions there, but made himself at home with the pirates who took him and tried to make them better, and afterwards when he was sold he lived in Corinth just as he lived before in Athens; yes, and if he had gone away to the Perrhaebians it would have been just the same. That is how freedom is achieved. That is why he said, 'Since Antisthenes freed me, I have ceased to be a slave.' How did he free him? Hear what he says: 'He taught me what is mine and what is not mine; property is not mine; kinsfolk, relations, friends, reputation, familiar places, converse with men—none of these is my own.'

What is yours then?

'Power to deal with impressions. He showed me that I possess this beyond all hindrance and compulsion; no one can hamper me, no one can compel me to deal with them otherwise than I will. Who then has authority over me any more? Has Philip, or Alexander, or Perdiccas, or the Great King? How can they? for he who is to be mastered by men, must first—long before—allow himself to be mastered by things. When a man is not overcome by pleasure, or pain, or reputation, or wealth, and, when it seems good to him, can spit his whole body in the tyrant's face, and so leave this world, whose slave can you call him any more? To whom is he subject? But if he had sought his pleasure by living in Athens, and had allowed life in Athens to have the mastery over him, he would have been in every man's control, and any one who was stronger than he would have had power to cause him pain. You can imagine how he would have flattered the pirates to sell him to an Athenian, that he might one day see the beautiful Peiraeus and the Long Walls and the Acropolis.

Slave, who are you that want to see them? If you are servile and abject what good will they do you?

'Nay, I shall be free.'

Show me how you are free. Suppose some one, no matter who, takes you away from your familiar course of life; he has laid hands on you and says, 'You are my slave, for it is in my power to prevent you from living as you will, it rests with me to relax your servitude, or to humiliate you; when I choose you can put on a glad face again and go off in high spirits to Athens.' What do you say to this man who leads you captive? Whom do you produce to set you free from him? Or do you refuse to look him in the face, and cutting arguments short implore him to let you go? Man, you ought to go to prison rejoicing, listening thither before your gaoler can lay hands on you. What! You decline to live in Rome, and long for Hellas? I suppose you will weep in our faces again, when you have to die, because you are not going to see Athens and have a walk in the Lyceum?

Is this what you went abroad for? Is this why you sought converse with a teacher who might do you good? Good forsooth! Was your object to analyse syllogisms more readily or track out hypothetical propositions? Was it for this reason that you left brother, country, friends, relations, that you might learn this lesson and return? It was not then to secure constancy or peace of mind that you went abroad; it was not that you might be set beyond harm's reach and never blame or accuse any one any more, it was not that no one should be able to injure you, and that so you might maintain your life unhindered in all its relations.

A fine traffic this that you have achieved by your travels–syllogisms and shifting terms and hypothetical arguments! Yes, you had better sit in the market if you think fit, and post up a notice like the druggists. Nay! will you not rather deny knowledge of what you learnt, that you may not get your precepts condemned as useless? What harm has philosophy done you, how has Chrysippus wronged you, that you should prove his labours to be useless by your own act? Not content with the ills you had at home, which were enough to cause you pain and sorrow, even if you had not gone abroad, did you acquire new ills besides?

Yes, and if again you have other friends and companions, and if you attach yourself to another country you will only multiply your causes for lamentation. Why then do you live, only to involve yourself in trouble after trouble and make yourself miserable? What, man! You call this 'affection'? Affection indeed! If affection is good, it can cause no evil. If it is evil, I have no concern with it. I am born for what is good for me, not for what is evil.

What then is the proper training for this? In the first place, the principal and most important thing, on the very threshold so to speak, is that when you are attached to a thing, not a thing which cannot be taken away but anything like a ewer, or a crystal cup, you should bear in mind what it is, that you may not be disturbed when it is broken. So should it be with persons; if you kiss your child, or brother, or friend, never allow your imagination to range at large, nor allow your exultation to go as far as it will, but pluck it back, keep it in check like those who stand behind generals driving in triumph and remind them that they are men. In like manner you must remind yourself that you love a mortal, and that nothing that you love is your very own; it is given you for the moment, not for ever nor inseparably, but like a fig or a bunch of grapes at the appointed season of the year, and if you long for it in winter you are a fool. So too if you long for your son or your friend, when it is not given you to have him, know that you are longing for a fig in winter time. For as winter is to the fig, so is the whole pressure of the universe to that which it destroys. And therefore in the very moment that you take pleasure in a thing, set before your mind the opposite impressions. What harm is there in whispering to yourself as you kiss your child, 'To-morrow you will die', and to your friend in like manner, 'To-morrow you or I shall go away, and we shall see one another no more'?

'But such words are of ill omen.'

Yes, and so are some incantations, but because they do good, I do not mind, if only they do good. But do you give the name 'ill-omened' to anything but what signifies evil? Cowardice is an ill-omened thing, and so is a mean spirit, mourning, sorrow, shamelessness; these are ill-omened words, yet even these we must not hesitate to utter, that we may guard against the things themselves. Do you call any word ill-omened that signifies a process of nature? Say that harvesting ears of corn is ill-omened, for it means destruction of the ears; yes, but not the destruction of the world. Say that the fall of the leaf is ill-omened and the change of the fresh fig into the dry and of grapes into raisins; for all these are changes from a previous state into a new one. This is not destruction but an ordered dispensation and government of things. Going abroad is a slight change; death is a greater change–from what now is, not to what is not, but to what is not now.

'Shall I then be no more?'

You will not be, but something else will be, of which the world now has need; for indeed you came into being, not when you willed it, but when the world had need. For this reason the good man, remembering who he is and whence he has come, and by whom he was created, sets his mind on this alone, how he shall fill his place in an orderly fashion with due obedience to God. To God he says, 'Dost Thou want me still to live? I will live as one who is free and noble, in accordance with Thy will; for Thou didst give me freedom from hindrance in what was mine. Hast Thou no more need of me? Then may it be well with Thee; I stayed here until now for Thee and for none other, and so now I obey Thee and depart.'

'How do you depart?'

Again, as Thou willest, as a free man, as Thy servant, as one who has learnt what Thou dost command and forbid. But as long as I continue among Thy creatures, whom wouldst Thou have me be? A magistrate or a private person, a senator or a commoner, a soldier or a general, a teacher or the head of a household? Whatever place or post Thou dost commit to my charge, 'I will die ten thousand times', tg use Socrates' words, 'sooner than abandon it.' Where wouldst Thou have me be? In Rome or Athens or Thebes or Gyara? Only remember me there. If Thou dost send me to a place where men cannot live as their nature requires, I shall go away, not in disobedience but believing that Thou dost sound the note for my retreat. I do not abandon Thee; heaven forbid! but I recognize that Thou hast no need of me. But if it be given me to live in accordance with nature, I shall not seek another place than where I am or other society than that in which I am.

Let these thoughts be at your command by night and day: write them, read them, talk of them, to yourself and to your neighbour. Go first to one and then to another, asking him, 'Can you help me towards this?' Then if some so-called 'undesirable' event befall you, the first immediate relief to you will be, that it was not unexpected. For in all matters it is a great thing to say, 'I knew that I had begotten a mortal.' For this is what you will say, and again, 'I knew that I was mortal. I knew that I might have to go away, that I might be cast into exile. I knew that I might be thrown into prison.' Then if you reflect within yourself and ask from what quarter the event has come, you will at once remember, 'It comes from the region of things outside my will, which are not mine; how then does it concern me?' Then comes the most commanding question of all: 'Who has sent it me?'

The Prince or the General, the City or the Law of the City.

Give it me then, for I must always obey the law in everything.

And further, when your imagination (which is not in your control) bites deep into your soul, struggle against it with your reason, fight it down, suffer it not to grow strong nor to advance the next step, calling up at pleasure what pictures it will. If you are in Gyara do not imagine your way of life in Rome, and the great delights you enjoyed when you lived there and that you would enjoy on your return. No, make your one effort there, to live a brave life in Gyara, as one who lives in Gyara should; and if you are in Rome do not imagine life in Athens, but make life in Rome your one study.

Further, you should put this delight first in place of all others, the delight that comes from understanding that you are obeying God, that not in word but in deed you are fulfilling the part of the good man. What a fine thing it is to be able to say to myself, 'I am now putting into action what other men talk big of in the lecture-room, and win a name for paradox. As they sit there it is my virtues they are expounding, it is about me they are inquiring, it is my praise they are singing. I say, Zeus wished to make my experience prove this truth to me, and He wished to discover for Himself, whether He had a soldier in the true sense, a citizen in the true sense, and to put me forward as a witness to the rest of mankind of what does and does not depend on man's will. "Behold," He says, "your fears are idle and your desires vain. Do not seek good things outside you but within, or you will not find them." It is on these terms that now He brings me here, and again sends me thither; He shows me to men poor, without office, sick, sends me to Gyara, puts me in prison; not that He hates me–heaven forbid! who hates his best servant?–nor that He takes no thought of me, for He takes thought of the lowliest, but because He is training me and using me as a witness to other men. When I am appointed to such a service as this, it is not for me to consider where or in whose company I am or what they say of me, but rather to spend all my effort on God and His commands and ordinances.'

If you always have these thoughts at hand, and make yourself familiar with them and keep them at command, you will never want for one to comfort and strengthen you. For dishonour consists not in having nothing to eat, but in not having reason sufficient to secure you from fear and pain. But if you once win yourself freedom from fear and pain, then tyrants and their guards, and the Emperor's household, will cease to exist for you; you, who have received this high office from Zeus, will not feel the sting of an imperial appointment or of those who offer sacrifice on the Capitol in virtue of their offices.

Only make no display of your office, and boast not yourself in it, but prove it by your conduct; be content, even if no one observes you, to live in true health and happiness.

CHAPTER TWENTY FIVE

To those who Fail to Achieve what they Set before them

CONSIDER WHICH OF THE aims that you set before you at the first you have achieved, and which you have not, and how some things give you pleasure to remember and some give you pain; and if possible, recover what you failed to obtain. For those who are entering on the greatest of all struggles must not shrink, but must be ready to endure stripes; for the struggle they are concerned with is not wrestling or the pancration, in which a man may succeed or fail, and yet be worth little or worth very much–nay more, he may be most fortunate or most miserable; no, his struggle is for good fortune and happiness itself.

What follows? In this competition, even if we give in for the moment, nothing prevents us from returning to the struggle; we have not to wait for another four years for the next Olympic Games to come. At once you may recover yourself, and pull yourself together, and renew the struggle with the same energy as before; and if you grow faint again, you may renew it again, and if you once attain to victory you are as one who has never failed. Only do not begin to take a pleasure in failing from sheer force of habit, and go about as a sorry athlete defeated in the whole round of all the Games, for all the world like quails that have escaped!

'I am overpowered by the impression of a pretty maid. Well! was I not overpowered lately? I am eager to find fault with some one. Did I not do so lately?'

You talk lightly to us, as though you had got off scot-free. It is as though a man, when his doctor forbade him to bathe, should say, 'Why, did not I bathe quite lately?' What if the doctor can answer him, 'Well, what effect did bathing have on you? Did you not fall into a fever? Did you not get a headache?' So when you found fault with some one lately, was it not the act of a bad man, and of a foolish one? Did you not feed this habit, by putting before it acts which were congenial to it? And when the pretty girl was too much for you, did you get away unpunished? What do you mean then by talking of what you did lately? Nay, you ought rather, I think, to have remembered, as slaves remember their floggings, and to have refrained from repeating the same offence. But it is not the same thing: pain makes the memory of the slave, but what pain or penalty attends your offences? When did you acquire the habit of avoiding evil activities?

CHAPTER TWENTY SIX

To those who Fear Want

ARE YOU NOT ASHAMED of being more cowardly and mean-spirited than runaway slaves? How do they leave their masters when they run away? What lands or servants have they to trust to? Do not they steal just a morsel to last them for the first days, and then go on their way over land or it may be sea, contriving one resource after another to keep themselves alive? And when did a runaway slave ever die of hunger? Yet you are all of a flutter and keep awake at nights for fear you should run short of necessaries. Miserable man, are you so blind as not to see the road, to which want of necessaries leads you? Where does it lead? The same way as fever, the same way as a falling stone–to death. Well, and is not this exactly the situation you often described to your companions? Many a passage did you read and write about it. How often did you boast that you could face death at any rate with a quiet mind!

'Yes, but my family will starve.'

What of that? Does their hunger lead in a different direction? Is not the way that leads below the same, and the world it leads to the same? Will you then not have courage to face every form of want and necessity, and to look on that world whither even the richest and those who have held the highest offices must descend, nay even kings and emperors themselves? Only you will descend hungry, if it so chance, and they will burst with over-eating and over-drinking.

Did you ever by chance see a beggar who was not old? They are all far gone in years; yet they bear the pinch of cold night and day, and lie forlorn upon the ground, and their food is what bare necessity demands and no more, but they almost arrive at immortality, and yet you who are sound in hand and foot are so afraid of starving!

Can you not draw water, or write, or take charge of children, or be another man's doorkeeper?

But it is disgraceful, you say, to be reduced to this necessity.

First learn then what is disgraceful, and then tell us that you are a philosopher; but for the present, if another call you so, do not allow him.

When a thing is not your business, when you are not responsible for it, when it has befallen you without your own act, like a headache or a fever, can it disgrace you? If your parents were poor, or if they made others their heirs instead of you, if they give you no help while they are alive, is this any disgrace to you? Is this what you learnt with the philosophers? Did you never hear that what is disgraceful is blameable, and the blameable is what deserves blame, and it is absurd to blame a man for what is not his own act, done by himself? Well, did you make your father what he is, or is it in your power to mend his character? Is this given you? What follows? Ought you to desire what is not given you, or to be ashamed if you do not attain to it? Is this all the habit you acquired when you studied philosophy, to look to others and to hope for nothing from yourself and your own acts? Lament therefore and mourn, and when you eat be fearful that you will have nothing to eat to-morrow. Tremble for your wretched slaves, lest they should steal, or run away, or die. Live in this spirit, and never cease to live so, you who never came near philosophy, except in name, and disgraced its principles so far as in you lies, by showing them to be useless and unprofitable to those who take them up. You never set your will to gain constancy, tranquillity, and peace of mind; you never paid regard to any master for this end, though you attended to many for the sake of syllogisms. You never tested any of these impressions thoroughly for yourself, asking, 'Can I bear it or can I not? What have I to look to?' No, you assumed that all was well with you, and that you were quite secure, and devoted your efforts to the final study of all, how to be immovable. And in what were you to make yourself immovable? Cowardice, a base spirit, admiration of the rich, failure to get what you will, defeat of your will to avoid. It was to secure these results that you spent all your care.

Ought you not to win some possession from philosophy, before you try to make it secure? Did you ever see any one build a coping, unless he had a wall round which to build it? Who ever appoints a doorkeeper where there is no door to guard?

Again, you make it your study to be able to demonstrate. Demonstrate what? You study not to be shaken by fallacies. Shaken from what position? Show me first what you are guarding, what you are measuring, or what you are weighing; then it is time enough to show me the balance or the bushel. How long do you mean to measure dust and ashes? Ought you not to demonstrate those principles which make men happy, which make things prosper as they wish, principles which make them not blame any one or accuse any one, but acquiesce in the government of the universe? Show me these.

'See, I do show them', he says. 'I will analyse syllogisms for you.'

Slave, this is the measuring instrument, not that which is measured. That is why you now pay the penalty for your neglect of philosophy; you tremble, you lie awake, you take counsel with every one, and unless your plans promise to please every one you think you have taken bad counsel.

Then you fear starvation, as you think; but what you really fear is not starvation; you are afraid that you may not have a cook, that you may not have another to cater for you, another to shoe you, another to dress you, others to rub you, others to follow you; when you have stripped in the bath and stretched yourself out like the crucified, you want to be rubbed on this side and that, and then you want the masseur to stand by and say, 'Turn, and give me his side, take his head, hand me his shoulder'; and then when you have left the bath and gone home you expect to cry out, 'Will no one bring me something to eat?' and then, 'Remove the tables, and wipe them.' What you really fear is that you may not be able to live the life of an invalid; for the life of healthy men you have only to see how slaves and labourers and true philosophers live; the life of Socrates, though he had a wife and children to live with, the life of Diogenes, and of Cleanthes, who combined philosophy with drawing water. If this is what you want to have, you will have it everywhere, and will live with confidence. Confidence in what? In that which alone it is possible to confide in, what is trustworthy, and cannot be hindered or taken away, that is, your own will. Why have you made yourself so useless and unprofitable that no one is willing to take you into his house and take care of you? Every one will pick up a vessel that is whole and fit for use if it is flung aside and will count it gain; but every one will count you loss, not gain. Cannot you even serve the purpose of a dog or a cock? Why then do you wish to live any more, if this is your character?

Does a good man ever fear that food may fail him? It does not fail the blind, it does not fail the lame, will it fail the good man? There is no want of some one to give pay to the good soldier, or workman, or shoemaker: will the good man find none? Does God so disregard His own principles, His servants, His witnesses, whom alone He uses as examples to the untaught, to show 'that He exists and orders the universe well, and does not disregard human things, and that for the good man nothing is evil, whether he lives or dies'? [Plato, *Apology*, 41d] What if He does not provide food? It only means that, like a good general, He has given me the signal to retire. I obey, I follow, I praise my Commander, and laud His acts. For I came when He thought fit, and again shall go when He thinks fit; and while I lived this was the work I had to do, to praise God in my own heart, and to others, be it to one or to many. If He does not provide me with much or with abundance, His will is for me to live simply; for He did not give abundance to Heracles, His own son; another than he was king of Argos and Mycenae, and he was subject to him and suffered toils and discipline. Yet Eurystheus was the man he was, no true king of Argos and Mycenae, for he was not king over himself, while Heracles was ruler and commander of all land and sea, cleansing them from lawlessness and wrong, and bringing in justice and righteousness, and this he did unarmed and single-handed.

And when Odysseus was shipwrecked and cast ashore, his necessity never broke his spirit, or made it abject. Nay, how did he approach the maidens to ask of them the necessaries of life, which men think it most shameful to beg from another?

> *Like hill-bred lion, trusting in his might.*
> [Homer, Odyssey]

Trusting in what? Not in reputation, not in money, nor office, but in his own might, that is in judgements on things within our power and beyond it. For it is these alone that make free men, whom nothing can hinder, which lift up the neck of those who are in humiliation, and make them look with unwavering eyes upon rich men and upon despots.

And this was what the philosopher had to give, but you are going to leave him, it seems, not with courage but trembling for your pitiful clothes and plate. Miserable man! have you so wasted your time until now?

'What then, if I fall ill?'

You shall bear illness well.

'Who shall tend me?'

God, and your friends.

'I shall lie on a hard bed.'

But you can do it like a man.

'I shall not have a proper house.'

If you have one, you will be ill all the same.

'Who will give me food?'

Those who find it for others; you will be no worse off than Manes on your sick-bed. And what is the end of the illness? Nothing worse than death. Will you realize once for all that it is not death that is the source of all man's evils, and of a mean and cowardly spirit, but rather the fear of death? Against this fear then I would have you discipline yourself; to this let all your reasonings, your lectures, and your trainings be directed; and then you will know that only so do men achieve their freedom.

Book Four

CHAPTER ONE

On Freedom

THAT MAN IS FREE, who lives as he wishes, who is proof against compulsion and hindrance and violence, whose impulses are untrammelled, who gets what he wills to get and avoids what he wills to avoid.

Who then would live in error?

No one.

Who would live deceived, reckless, unjust, intemperate, querulous, abject?

No one.

No bad man then lives as he would, and so no bad man is free. Who would live in a state of distress, fear, envy, pity, failing in the will to get and in the will to avoid?

No one.

Do we then find any bad man without distress or fear, above circumstance, free from failure?

None. Then we find none free.

If a man who has been twice consul hear this, he will forgive you if you add, 'But you are wise, this does not concern you.' But if you tell him the truth, saying, 'You are just as much a slave yourself as those who have been thrice sold', what can you expect but a flogging?

'How can I be a slave?' he says; 'my father is free, my mother is free, no one has bought me; nay, I am a senator, and a friend of Caesar, I have been consul and have many slaves.'

In the first place, most excellent senator, perhaps your father too was a slave of the same kind as you, yes and your mother and your grandfather and the whole line of your ancestors. And if really they were ever so free, how does that affect you? What does it matter if they had a fine spirit, when you have none, if they were fearless and you are a coward, if they were self-controlled and you are intemperate?

'Nay, what has this to do with being a slave?' he replies.

Does it seem to you slavery to act against your will, under compulsion and with groaning?

'I grant you that,' he says, 'but who can compel me except Caesar, who is lord of all?'

Why, then, your own lips confess that you have one master: you must not comfort yourself with the thought that he is, as you say, the common master of all, but realize that you are a slave in a large household. You are just like the people of Nicopolis, who are wont to cry aloud, 'By Caesar's fortune, we are free.'

However, let us leave Caesar for the moment if you please, but tell me this: Did you never fall in love with any one, with a girl, or a boy, or a slave, or a free man?

'What has that to do with slavery or freedom?'

Were you never commanded by her you loved to do anything you did not wish? Did you never flatter your precious slave-boy? Did you never kiss his feet? Yet if any one compel you to kiss Caesar's, you count it an outrage, the very extravagance of tyranny. What is this if not slavery? Did you never go out at night where you did not wish, and spend more than you wished and utter words of lamentation and groaning? Did you put up with being reviled and shut out? If you are ashamed to confess your own story, see what Thrasonides says and does: he had served in as many campaigns or more perhaps than you and yet, first of all, he has gone out at night, at an hour when Getas does not dare to go, nay, if he were forced by his master to go, he would have made a loud outcry and have gone with lamentations over his cruel slavery, and then, what does he say?

A worthless girl has made a slave of me,
Whom never foe subdued.
           [Menander, Fragment]

Poor wretch, to be slave to a paltry girl and a worthless one too! Why do you call yourself free then any more? Why do you boast of your campaigns? Then he asks for a sword, and is angry with the friend who refuses it out of goodwill, and sends gifts to the girl who hates him, and falls to praying and weeping, and then again when he has a little luck he is exultant. How can we call him free when he has not learnt to give up desire and fear?

Now look at the lower animals and see how we apply the notion of freedom to them. Men put lions in cages and rear them as tame creatures and feed them, and sometimes even take them about with them. Yet who will call a lion like that 'free'? The softer he lives, the worse is his slavery. What lion, if he got sense or reason, would wish to be a lion of that sort? Look at the birds yonder and see what lengths they go in striving to escape, when they are caught and reared in cages; why, some of them actually starve themselves rather than endure that sort of life; and even those that do not die, pine away and barely keep alive, and dash out if they find any chance of an opening. So strong is their desire for natural freedom, an independent and unhindered existence.

Why, what ails you in your cage?

'What a question! I am born to fly where I will, to live in the air, to sing when I will; you take all this away, from me, and say, "What ails you?"'

Therefore we will call only those creatures free, that do not endure captivity, but escape by death as soon as they are caught. So too Diogenes says somewhere, 'A quiet death is the one sure means of freedom', and he writes to the Persian king, 'You cannot enslave the city of the Athenians any more than you can enslave fishes.'

'What! shall I not capture them?'

'If you capture them,' he says, 'they will straightway leave you and be gone, like fishes; for when you take one of them, he dies. So if the Athenians die as soon as you take them, what is the good of your armament?' These are the words of a free man who has seriously examined the question and found the truth, as is reasonable; but if you look for it elsewhere than where it is, what wonder if you never find it?

The slave is anxious to be set free at once. Why? Do you think it is because he is anxious to pay the tax on his manumission? No! the reason is he imagines that up till now he is hampered and ill at ease because he has not got his freedom. 'If I am enfranchised,' he says, 'at once all will be well, I heed nobody, I talk to all men as an equal and one of their quality, I go where I will, I come whence I will and where I will.' Then he is emancipated, and having nothing to eat he straightway looks for some one to flatter and to dine with; then he either has to sell his body to lust and endure the worst, and if he gets a manger to eat at, he has plunged into a slavery much severer than the first; or if perchance he grows rich, being a low-bred fellow he dotes on some paltry girl and gets miserable and bewails himself and longs to be a slave again.

'What ailed me in those days? Another gave me clothes and shoes, another fed me and tended me in sickness, and the service I did him was a small matter. Now, how wretched and miserable I am, with many masters instead of one! Still, if I can get rings on my fingers I shall live happily and prosperously enough.'

And so first, to get them, he puts up with what he deserves, and having got them repeats the process. Next he says, 'If I go on a campaign I am quit of all my troubles.' He turns soldier and endures the lot of a criminal, but all the same he begs for a second campaign and a third. Lastly, when he gets the crown to his career and is made a senator, once more he becomes a slave again as he goes to the senate; then he enjoys the noblest and the sleekest slavery of all.

Let him not be foolish, let him learn, as Socrates said, what is the true nature of everything, and not apply primary conceptions at random to particular facts. For this is the cause of all the miseries of men, that they are not able to apply their common primary conceptions to particular cases. One of us fancies this, another that. One fancies he is ill. Not at all; it is only that he does not apply his primary conceptions. Another fancies that he is poor, that his father or mother is cruel, another that Caesar is not gracious. But really it is one thing, and one thing only; they do not know how to adjust their primary conceptions. For who has not a primary notion of evil—that it is harmful, to be shunned, by every means to be got rid of? One primary notion does not conflict with another, the conflict is in the application.

What then is this evil which is harmful and to be shunned?

'Not to be Caesar's friend', he says.

He has gone out of his way, he has failed to apply his notions, he is in sore distress, he is seeking for what is nothing to the purpose; for when he has got Caesar's friendship he has equally failed of his object. For what is the object of every man's search? To have a quiet mind, to be happy, to do everything as he will, to be free from hindrance and compulsion. Very well: when he becomes Caesar's friend is he relieved from hindrance and compulsion, is he in peace and happiness? Of whom are we to inquire? Whom can we better trust than the very man who has become Caesar's friend?

Come forward and tell us! when was your sleep more tranquil, now or before you became Caesar's friend?

At once the answer comes, 'Cease, by the gods I beg you, to mock at my fortune; you do not know what a miserable state is mine; no sleep comes near to me, but in comes some one to say, "Now he's awake, now he'll be coming out"; then troubles and cares assail me.'

Tell me, when did you dine more agreeably, now or before?

Hear again what he says about this: if he is not invited, he is distressed, and if he is invited he dines as a slave with his lord, anxious all the while for fear he should say or do something foolish. And what do you think he fears? To be flogged like a slave? How should he come off so well? No, so great a man as he, and Caesar's friend, must fear to lose his neck; nought less were fitting. When did you bathe with more peace of mind, or exercise yourself more at your ease? In a word, which life would you rather live, to-day's or the old life? No one, I can swear, is so wanting in sense or feeling, that he does not lament his lot the louder the more he is Caesar's friend.

Inasmuch then as neither those who bear the name of kings nor kings' friends live as they will, what free men are left? Seek, and you shall find, for nature supplies you with means to find the truth. If, with these means and no more to guide you, you cannot find the answer for yourself, then listen to those who have made the search. What do they say? Does freedom seem to you a good thing?

'The greatest good.'

Can any one who attains the greatest good be miserable or fare badly?

'No.'

Whensoever then you see men unhappy, miserable, mourning, you may declare with confidence that they are not free.

'I do declare it.'

Well then, we have got away from buying and selling, and. that kind of disposal of property which they deal with. For if you are right in making these admissions, no one who is miserable can be free, whether he be a great king or a little one, a consular or one who has twice been consul.

'Granted.'

Answer me once more. Does freedom seem to you a great and noble and precious thing?

'Certainly.'

Can then one who possesses so great and precious and noble a thing be of a humble spirit?

'He cannot.'

Therefore when you see a man cringing to another or flattering him against his true opinion, you may say with confidence that he too is not free, and not only if he does it for a paltry dinner, but even if he does it for a province or a consulship. But those who do it for small objects you may call slaves on a small scale, and the others, as they deserve, slaves on a large scale.

'I grant you this too.'

Again, does freedom seem to you' to be something independent, owning no authority but itself?

'Certainly.'

Then whenever a man can be hindered or compelled by another at will, assert with confidence that he is not free. Do not look at his grandfathers and great grandfathers and search whether he was bought or sold, but if you hear him say 'Master' from the heart and with feeling, then call him slave, though twelve fasces go before him; and if you hear him say, 'Wretched am I, that I am so treated', call him slave; in a word, if you see him bewailing himself, complaining, miserable, call him slave, though he wears the purple hem. If, however, he does not behave like this, call him not free yet, but get to know his judgements and see whether they are liable to compulsion or hindrance or unhappiness, and if you find any such, call him a slave on holiday at the Saturnalia; say that his master is away; he will presently return and then you will learn his true condition.

'In what form will he return?'

In the form of every one who has authority over the things that a man wishes for, to get them for him or to take them away.

'Have we then so many masters?'

Yes, for even before these personal masters, we have masters in circumstance, and circumstances are many. It must needs follow then that those who have authority over any of these are our masters. For no one really fears Caesar himself; men fear death, exile, deprivation of property, prison, disfranchisement. Nor does any one love Caesar, unless he has great merit; we love wealth, the tribunate, the praetorship, the consulship. When we love and hate and fear these, the men who have authority over them are bound to be our masters, and that is why we worship them like gods; for we consider that that which has authority over the greatest benefit is divine; and then if we make a false minor premiss, 'this man has control over the greatest benefit', our conclusion is bound to be wrong too.

What is it then which makes man his own master and free from hindrance? Wealth does not make him so, nor a consulship, nor a province, nor a kingdom; we must find something else. Now what is it which makes him unhindered and unfettered in writing?

'Knowledge of how to write.'

What makes him so in flute-playing?

'Knowledge of flute-playing.'

So too in living, it is knowledge of how to live. You have heard this as a general principle; consider it in detail. Is it possible for one who aims at an object which lies in the power of others to be unhindered? Is it possible for him to be untrammelled?

'No.'

It follows that he cannot be free. Consider then: have we nothing which is in our power alone, or have we everything? Or only some things in our power, and some in that of others?

'How do you mean?'

When you wish your body to be whole, is it in your power or not?

'It is not.'

And when you wish it to be healthy?

'That is not in my power.'

And when you wish it to be beautiful?

'That is not in my power.'

And to live or die?

'That is not mine either.'

The body then is something not our own and must give an account to any one who is stronger than ourselves.

'Granted.'

Is it in your power to have land when you will, and as long as you will, and of the quality you will?

'No.'

And slaves?

'No.'

And clothes?

'No.'

And your bit of a house?

'No.'

And horses?

'None of these things.'

And if you wish your children or your wife or your brother or your friends to live, whatever happens, is that in your power?

'No, that is not either.'

Have you nothing then which owns no other authority, nothing which you alone control, or have you something of that sort?

'I do not know.'

Look at the matter thus and consider it. Can any one make you assent to what is false?

'No one.'

Well, then, in the region of assent you are unhindered and unfettered.

'Granted.'

Again, can any one force your impulse towards what you do not wish?

'He can; for when he threatens me with death or bonds, he forces my impulse.'

Well now, if you despise death and bonds, do you heed him any longer?

'No.'

Is it your doing then to despise death, or is it not yours?

'Mine.'

It rests with you then to be impelled to action, does it not?

'I grant it rests with me.'

And impulse not to act, with whom does that rest? It is yours too.

'Supposing that my impulse is to walk, and he hinders me, what then?'

What part of you will he hinder? Your assent?

'No, but my poor body.'

Yes, as a stone is hindered.

'Granted; but I do not walk any more.'

Who told you that it is your business to walk unhindered? The only thing I told you was unhindered was your impulse; as to the service of the body, and its cooperation, you have heard long ago that it is no affair of yours.

'I grant you this too.'

Can any one compel you to will to get what you do not wish?

'No one.'

Or to purpose or to plan, or in a word to deal with the impressions that you meet with?

'No one can do this either; but if I will to get something a man will hinder me from obtaining it.'

How will he hinder you, if you set your will upon things which are your own and beyond hindrance?

'Not at all.'

But no one tells you that he who wills to get what is not his own is unhindered.

'Am I then not to will to get health?'

Certainly not, nor anything else that is not your own. For nothing is your own, that it does not rest with you to procure or to keep when you will. Keep your hands far away from it; above all, keep your will away, or else you surrender yourself into slavery, you put your neck under the yoke, if you admire what is not your own, and set your heart on anything mortal, whatever it be, or anything that depends upon another.

'Is not my hand my own?'

It is a part of you, but by nature a thing of clay, subject to hindrance and compulsion, slave to everything that is stronger than itself. Nay, why do I name you the hand? You must treat your whole body like a poor ass, with its burden on its back, going with you just so far as it may, and so far as it is given you; but if the king's service calls, and a soldier lays hands on it, let it go, do not resist or murmur; if you do, you will only get a flogging and lose your poor ass all the same.

But when this is your proper attitude to your body, consider what is left for you to do with other things that are procured for the body's sake. As the body is the poor ass, other things become the ass's bridle and pack-saddle, shoes and barley and fodder. Give them up too, let them go quicker and with a lighter heart than the ass itself.

And when you have prepared and trained yourself thus to distinguish what is your own from what is not your own, things subject to hindrance from things unhindered, to regard these latter as your concern, and the former as not, to direct your will to gain the latter and to avoid the former, then have you any one to fear any more?

'No one.'

Of course. What should you fear for? Shall you fear for what is your own, that is, for what makes good and evil for you? Nay, who has authority over what is yours? Who can take it away, who can hinder it, any more than they can hinder God? Is it your body and your property that you fear for? Are you afraid for what is not your own, for what does not concern you at all?

Why, what have you been studying all along but to distinguish what it yours from what is not yours, what is in your power from what is not in your power, things subject to hindrance from things unhindered? Why did you go to the philosophers? Was it that you might be just as unfortunate and miserable as ever? I say that so trained you will be free from fear and perturbation. What has pain to do with you now, for it is only things that cause fear in expectation which cause pain when they come? What shall you have desire for any longer, for your will is tranquil and harmonious, set on objects within its compass to obtain, objects that are noble and within your reach, and you have no wish to get what is beyond your will, and you give no scope to that jostling element of unreason which breaks all bounds in its impatience?

When once you adopt this attitude towards things, no man can inspire fear in you any longer. For how can man cause fear in man by his aspect or his talk or by his society generally, any more than fear can be roused by horse or dog or bee in another horse or dog or bee? No, it is things which inspire fear in every man; it is the power of winning things for another or of taking them away from him, that makes a man feared.

How then is the citadel destroyed? Not by fire or sword, but by judgements. For if we pull down the citadel in the city, we have not got rid of the citadel which is held by fever or by fair women, in a word the citadel in ourselves and the tyrants who are within us, who threaten each one of us day by day, now in new forms, now in old. This is the point where we must begin, this is where the citadel must be destroyed, and the tyrants cast forth; we must give up our body, and all that belongs to it –faculties, property, reputation, offices, honours, children, brothers, friends–all these we must regard as having no concern for us.

If the tyrants are cast forth from this, what need is there for me to blockade the outward citadel? What harm does it do to me by standing? Why do I try and cast forth the guards? I feel them no longer; their rods and their spears and swords are pointed against others. I was never hindered in my will or compelled against my wish.

Nay, how can this be?

I have submitted my will to God. He wills that I should have a fever; I will it too. He wills that I should have an impulse. I will it too. He wills that I should will to get a thing. I too will it. He wills that I should get something, and I wish it; He wills that I should not, I wish it no more I am willing then (if He wills it) to die or be put on the rack. Who can hinder me any more against my own judgement or put compulsion on me? I am as safe as Zeus.

I act as the more cautious travellers do. A man has heard that the road is infested by robbers; he does not dare to venture on it alone, but waits for company–a legate, or a quaestor, or a proconsul–and joining him he passes safely on the road. The prudent man does the same in the world; in the world are many haunts of robbers, tyrants, storms, distresses, chances of losing what is dearest. 'Where is a man to escape? How is he to go on his way unrobbed? What company is he to wait for that he may pass through in safety? To whom is he to join himself? To this or that rich man, or consular? What is the good of that? Your great man himself is stripped, and utters mourning and lamentation. What if my fellow traveller turns against me himself to rob me? What am I to do? I will be "a friend of Caesar"; if I am his companion no one will do me wrong. But first, how many things must I endure and undergo, to become a distinguished person! How often must I suffer robbery and from how many! And then, if I rise to distinction, even Caesar is mortal. And if some circumstance lead him to become my enemy, where, I ask, is it better for me to retire? To the wilderness? Why, does not fever come there? What is to become of me then? Is it impossible to find a travelling-companion who is safe, trustworthy, strong, proof against attack?' Thus he reflects and comes to understand that if he attaches himself to God, he will pass through the world in safety.

'What do you mean by "attach" himself?'

That what God wills, he may will too, and what God wills not, he may not will either.

How then is this to be done?

How else, but by examining the purposes of God and His governance of the world. What has He given me to be my own, and independent, what has He reserved for Himself? He has given me all that lies within the sphere of my choice, and has put it in my hands, unfettered, unhindered. How could He make my clay body free from hindrance? My property, my chattels, my honour, my children, my wife, He made subject to the revolution of the universe. Why then do I fight against God? Why do I will what is not for me to will, what is not given me to hold under all conditions, but to hold only as it is given and so far as it is given?

Suppose He that gave takes away. Why then do I resist? I shall not merely be silly, if I try to compel Him that is stronger; first of all I shall be doing wrong. For whence did I bring what I have into the world? My father gave them me. And who gave them him? Who is it that has made the sun, and the fruits of the earth, and the seasons, and the union and fellowship of men with one another?

You have received everything, nay your very self, from Another, and yet you complain and blame the Giver, if He takes anything away from you. Who are you and for what have you come? Did not He bring you into the world? Did not He show you the light? Has He not given you fellow workers? Has He not given you senses too, and reason? And in what character did He bring you into life? Was it not as a mortal, one who should live upon earth with his little portion of flesh and behold God's governance and share for a little while in His pageant and His festival? Will you not then look at the pageant and the festal gathering as long as it is given you, and then, when God leads you forth, go away with an obeisance to Him and thanksgiving for what you have heard and seen?

'No, I wanted to go on feasting.'

Yes, those at the Mysteries too want to go on with the. ceremony, and those at Olympia to see fresh competitors, but the festival is at an end. Leave it and depart, in a thankful and modest spirit; make room for others. Others must come into being, even as you did, and being born must have room and dwellings and necessaries. But if the first corners do not retire, what is left for them? Why will nothing satisfy or content you? Why do you crowd the world's room?

'Yes, but I want my wife and my children to be with me.'

Are they yours? Are they not His who gave them? Are they not His who has made you? Will you not give up what it not yours, and give way to Him who is stronger than you?

'Why then did He bring me into the world on these terms?'

Depart, if it does not suit you. God has no need of a querulous spectator. He needs men who join in the feast and in the dance, ready to applaud and glorify and praise the festival. But the impatient and miserable He will gladly see left outside the festival: for even when they were there they did not behave as at a festival nor fill the place appropriate to them, but were peevish and complained of fate and fortune and their company: insensible to fortune's gifts and to their own faculties, which they have received for just the opposite–a great heart, a noble spirit, and the very freedom we are now in search of.

'For what then have I received these gifts?'

To use them.

'For how long?'

Just so long as He who lent them wills.

'But what if they are necessary for me?'

Do not set your heart on them, and they will not be. Do not tell yourself that they are necessary, and they are not.

This is what you ought to practise from sunrise to sunset, beginning with the meanest things and those most subject to injury–a jug or a cup. From this go on to a tunic, a dog, a horse, a field; and from that to yourself, your body and its members, your children, your wife, your brothers. Look carefully on all sides and fling them away from you. Purify your judgements, and see that nothing that is not your own is attached to you or clings to you, that nothing shall give you pain if it is torn from you. And as you train yourself day by day, as in the lecture-room, say not that you are a philosopher (I grant you that would be arrogant)., but that you are providing for your enfranchisement; for this is freedom indeed. This was the freedom which Diogenes won from Antisthenes, and said that no one could enslave him any more. That explains his bearing as a captive, and his behaviour to the pirates: did he call any of them master? I do not mean the mere name (I have no fear of that), but the state of mind, of which it is the expression. Think how he rebukes them for feeding their prisoners badly. Think how he was sold: did he look for a master? No, for a slave. And when he was sold, think how he bore himself towards his master: he began talking to him at once, telling him that he ought not to dress as he did, or shave as he did, and what life his sons ought to lead. What wonder in that? For if he had bought a slave skilled in gymnastic would he have used him as a servant in the palaestra or as a master? As a master; and in the same way if he had bought a man skilled in medicine or in architecture. And on this principle the man with skill is bound in every subject to be superior to the man without skill. Whoever then possesses knowledge of life in general must be master. For who is master on shipboard?

'The helmsman.'

Why? Is it because any one who disobeys him is punished? No! but because he possesses skill in steering.

'But my master can flog me.'

Can he do it with impunity?

'So I thought.'

But as he cannot do it with impunity, therefore he has no authority to do it. No one can do wrong acts with impunity.

'What penalty falls on the man who imprisons his own slave, if he think fit?'

The very act of imprisoning him is his penalty, and this you will admit yourself, if you will hold fast the principle that man is not a brute but a civilized creature. For when does a vine do badly? When it acts against its nature. When does a cock do badly? In the same conditions. The same is true of a man. What is his nature then? Is it to bite and kick and cast into prison and behead? No, but to do good, to work with others and pray for them. Therefore, whether you will or no, man does badly when he acts without sense.

'Did not Socrates then do badly?'

No, but his judges and accusers did.

'Did not Helvidius in Rome do badly?'

No, but his murderer did.

'What do you mean?'

Just as you do not say the fighting-cock has done badly when it has won and been wounded, but when it has been beaten without a scratch, and you do not count a hound happy when he does not strain in the pursuit, but when you see him sweating, in distress, his flanks bursting with the chase. What is there incredible in the statement that every man's evil is that which contradicts his nature? Is this incredible? Is it not what you say in every other sphere? Why then do you take another line only when man is in question? Is our other statement then incredible–that man's nature is civilized and affectionate and trustworthy?

'No, this is not, either.'

How comes it then, further, that he suffers no harm though he be flogged or imprisoned or beheaded? Is not it true that, if he suffer these things in a noble spirit, he goes away the gainer, and is profited, whereas he who suffers harm is the man who undergoes the most pitiful and shameful fate, the man who changes from a man into a wolf or a serpent or a wasp?

Come now and let us review the conclusions we have agreed to. He is free, whom none can hinder, the man who can deal with things as he wishes. But the man who can be hindered or compelled or fettered or driven into anything against his will, is a slave. And who is he whom none can hinder? The man who fixes his aim on nothing that is not his own. And what does 'not his own' mean? All that it does not lie in our power to have or not to have, or to have of a particular quality or under particular conditions. The body then does not belong to us, its parts do not belong to us, our property does not belong to us. If then you set your heart on one of these as though it were your own, you will pay the penalty deserved by him who desires what does not belong to him. The road that leads to freedom, the only release from slavery is this, to be able to say with your whole soul:

Lead me, O Zeus, and lead me, Destiny,
Whither ordainèd is by your decree.
[Cleanthes]

But, what say you, my philosopher, suppose the tyrant call on you to say something unworthy of you? Do you assent or refuse? Tell me. 'Let me think it over.'

You will think it over now, will you? And what, pray, did you think over when you were at lecture? Did you not study what things are good and what are evil, and what are neither?

'Yes, I did.'

What conclusion did you approve then?

'That things right and noble were good, things wrong and shameful bad.'

Is life a good thing?

'No.'

Is death evil?

'No.'

Is prison?

'No.'

And what did you think of ignoble and faithless speech, and treachery to a friend and flattery of a tyrant?

'We thought them evil.'

Why do you ask the question now, then? You should have asked it and made up your mind long ago. It is nonsense to question now whether, when I can win the greatest goods, it is fitting for me not to win the greatest evils? A fine and necessary question forsooth, needing a deal of thought! Man, why do you mock us?

That is not the sort of thing that men 'question'. If you really imagined shameful acts to be bad, and noble acts good, and all else to be indifferent, you would not have proceeded to raise this question: not at all: you would at once have been able to decide the question by intuition, as an act of sight. For when do you question whether black things are white, or heavy things light, instead of following the obvious conclusions of your senses? Why then do you talk now of considering whether things indifferent are more to be shunned than things evil? These are not your judgements: prison and death do not seem to you indifferent, but the greatest evils, nor do base words and acts seem evil, they seem not to matter for us.

This is the habit to which you have trained yourself from the first. 'Where am I? In the lecture-room. And who are listening to me? I am talking to philosophers. But now I have left the lecture-room. Away with those sayings of pedants and fools!' That is how a philosopher gives witness against a friend, that is how a philosopher turns parasite: that is how he hires himself out at a price, and speaks against his real opinion in the Senate, while in his heart his judgement cries aloud, not a flat and miserable apology for an opinion, hanging to idle discussions as by a hair-thread, but a judgement strong and serviceable, trained by actions, which is the true initiation. Watch yourself and see how you take the news, I do not say that your child is dead (how should that befall you?), but that your oil is spilt, or your wine drunk up: well may one who stands by, as your temper rises high, say just this to you, 'Philosopher, you use different language in the lecture-room: why do you deceive us? Why, worm that you are, do you call yourself a man?' I would fain stand by one of these men when he is indulging his lust, that I might see howeager he is, and what words he utters, and whether he remembers his own name, or the discourses which he hears or delivers or reads.

'Yes, but what has this to do with freedom?'

Nay! what else but this has to do with it, whether you rich people agree, or not?

'And who is your witness to this?'

Why, it is none other than your very selves. You who own that great master, and live at his nod and motion, and your blood runs cold if he so much as look at one of you with a sour face: you who pay court to old women and old men, and say, 'I cannot do that, I am not allowed.' Why are you not allowed? Did you not just now contend with me and assert you were free?

'Yes, but Aprulla has forbidden me.'

Tell the truth then, slave that you are, and do not run away from your masters, nor disown your slavery, nor dare to claim your enfranchisement, when you have so many proofs of slavery against you. I declare that the man who is compelled by love to act against his opinion, seeing the better course all the time, but wanting the strength to follow it, one might be more inclined to think deserving pardon, as overpowered by an influence violent and in a way divine. But who can bear with you, whose love is all for old women and old men, wiping their faces clean and washing them and giving them presents, and tending them like a slave in their illness, while all the time you are praying for them to die, and questioning the doctors, whether they are sick unto death at last? Or again, when you kiss the hands of other people's slaves in order to get those great and splendid offices and honours, becoming the slave of men who are not even free? Then, if you please, you walk in splendour as praetor or consul. Do I not know how you became praetor, where you got the consulship, who gave it you? For my part I would not wish to live, if I had to owe my life to Felicio, and put up with his contempt and slavish arrogance; for I know what a slave is who is prosperous as the world thinks and puffed up with vanity.

'Are you then free?' says one.

By the gods, I wish to be and pray to be, but I cannot yet look in the face of my masters, I still set store by my poor body, I count it of great moment to keep it sound, yes though I have not a sound body to begin with. But I can show you one who is free, that you may not have to look for your example. Diogenes was free. How came he by this? Not because he was of free parents (he was not), but because he was free himself, had cast away all the weakness that might give slavery a hold on him, and so no one could approach or lay hold on him to enslave him.

Everything he had he was ready to let go, it was loosely attached to him. If you had laid hold on his property, he would have let it go rather than have followed you for it; if you seized his leg, he would have let that go; if his whole poor body, he would have let his whole body go; and the same with kinsfolk, friends, and country. For he knew whence he had them and from whom, and on what conditions he received them. His true ancestors, the gods, and his true Country he would never have deserted, nor have suffered another to yield them more obedience or attention, nor would another have died for his Country more cheerfully. For he never sought to get the reputation of acting for the universe, but he remembered that everything that comes to pass has its source there and is done for that true Country's sake and is entrusted to us by Him that governs it. Wherefore look what he says and writes himself: 'Therefore, Diogenes,' he says, 'you have power to converse as you will with the king of the Persians and with Archidamus, king of the Lacedaemonians.' Was it because he was the son of free parents? When all the men of Athens and Lacedaemon and Corinth were unable to converse with them as they wished, and feared and flattered them instead, was it because they were sons of slaves? 'Why have I the power to do it then?' he says. 'Because I count my poor body not my own, because I need nothing, because law and nothing else is all in all to me.' These were the things which left him free.

And that you may not think that I point you to the example of a man alone in the world, with no wife or children or country or friends or kindred, who might have bent his will and drawn him from his purpose, take Socrates and look at him: he had wife and children, but regarded them as not his own; a country, in such manner and so far as duty allowed: friends, kinsmen, all these things he had made subject to law and obedience to law. For this reason, when duty called him to take the field, he was the first to leave Athens and ran all risks of battle most ungrudgingly, but when he was sent by the Tyrants to fetch Leon, he never entertained the idea, because he thought it shameful, though he knew that he would have to die, if it so chanced. And what did it matter to him? Why, he wanted to preserve something else–not his poor flesh, but his honour and self-respect. These are things which cannot be trusted to another or made subject to another. Afterwards when he had to plead for his life, did he behave as one who had children or as one who had a wife? No, but as one alone in the world. And again, when he had to drink the poison, how did he behave? When he might have saved himself, and when Crito said to him, 'Escape, for the sake of your children', what did he say? Did he think the chance a godsend? No, he looked at what was fitting, and had no eye, no thought for anything besides. For he wished to save not his poor body, but 'that which right increases and preserves, and wrong diminishes and makes to wither'. Socrates refuses to save himself with dishonour: he who would not put the question to the vote, when the Athenians bade him, who despised the Tyrants, who held such noble discourse on virtue and goodness–it is impossible to save him with dishonour: his safety is secured by death, not by flight. For the good actor too, if he stops when he ought, has more chance of safety than one who acts out of season.

What will your children do then?

'If I had gone away to Thessaly you would have looked after them: and when I have gone away to Hades, will there be no one to look after them?' [Plato, *Crito*, 54a]

See how he calls death by smooth names and scoffs at it. But if you and I had been in his place, we should at once have argued that we ought to repay injury with injury: and we should have added, 'I shall be useful to many men if I keep alive, but to no one if I die.' Nay, had it been necessary to creep out through a hole in the rock to escape, we should have done so. And yet how could we have been of use to any one? For those we were trying to help would not have stood fast. Or again, if we did good by living, should we not have done much more good to men by dying when and as we ought? Even so now that Socrates is dead, the memory of what he did or said in his lifetime is no less useful to men, or it may be even more useful than before.

Make this your study, study these judgements, and these sayings: fix your eyes on these examples, if you wish to be free, if you set your desires on freedom as it deserves. It is no wonder that you pay this great, this heavy price for so vast an object. Men hang themselves, or cast themselves down headlong, nay sometimes whole cities perish for the sake of what the world calls 'freedom', and will you not repay to God what He has given, when He asks it, for the sake of true freedom, the freedom which stands secure against all attack? Shall you not practise, as Plato says, not death only, but torture and exile and flogging, in a word practise giving back all that is not yours? If not, you will be a slave among slaves, even if you are consul ten thousand times, and no less, if you go up into Caesar's Palace; and you will discover that 'what philosophers say may be contrary to opinion', as Cleanthes said, 'but not contrary to reason'. For you will really get to know that what they say is true, and that none of these objects that men admire and set their hearts on is of any use to those who get them, though those who have never chanced to have them get the impression, that if only these things were theirs their cup of blessings would be full, and then, when they get them, the sun scorches them and the sea tosses them no less, and they feel the same boredom and the same desire for what they have not got. For freedom is secured not by the fulfilling of men's desires, but by the removal of desire. To learn the truth of what I say, you must spend your pains on these new studies instead of your studies in the past: sit up late that you may acquire a judgement that makes you free: pay your attentions not to a rich old man, but to a philosopher, and be seen about his doors: to be so seen will not do you discredit: you will not depart empty or without profit, if you approach in the right spirit. If you doubt my word, do but try: there is no disgrace in trying.

CHAPTER TWO

On Intercourse with Men

THE ONE THING TO be careful about beyond all others is this–not to get so involved with any of your former companions or friends, as to compromise your character for his sake, for if you do this you will destroy yourself. If the thought slips in, 'I shall seem rude to him, and he will not be the same to me as before', remember that nothing is done without paying for it, and that it is not possible to be the same man that you once were, unless you do as you did before. Choose then which you will –to be like your former self and be loved as before by those who loved you, or to be better than before, and so miss what they once gave you. For if this is the better choice, then incline to this, and let no irrelevant arguments distract you, for no one can make progress by facing both ways. No; if you have chosen this course before all, if you wish to devote yourself to this and nothing else, and to spend all your labour on this, then dismiss all other thoughts, or else this facing both ways will produce a double result–you will not make progress as you ought, and you will fail to get what you got before; for before, when you frankly set your desires on worthless objects, you were agreeable to your companions. You cannot excel both ways; in proportion as you succeed on the one side, you must needs fall short on the other. When you do not drink with those whom you used to drink with, you cannot seem as agreeable to them as of old; choose then, whether you wish to be a drinker and gratify them, or sober and displease them. If you do not sing with those that you sang with, you cannot win their affection as before: here too then you must choose which you prefer. For if it is better to have self-respect and self-control, than to have it said of one, 'What a charming fellow!', then give up all other considerations, put them from you, turn away from them, and have nothing to do with them. But if this is not going to satisfy you, then turn round completely, and practise the very opposite–unnatural lust, adultery, and all that is in keeping with them, and you shall get what you want. Yes, jump up and shriek applause over your dancer.

But characters so opposite do not mix: you cannot act both Thersites and Agamemnon. If you want to be Thersites you must be humpbacked and bald, if Agamemnon, you must be handsome and tall, and love your subjects.

CHAPTER THREE

What to Aim at in Exchange

IF YOU GIVE UP any external possession, mind you see what you are to get in exchange for it: and if it is worth more, then never say, 'I have been a loser.' You will not lose if you get a horse for an ass, an ox for a sheep, a noble action for a piece of money, true peace instead of pedantry, self-respect instead of foul language. If you remember this you will everywhere preserve your character as it ought to be: if you do not remember it, I warn you that your time perishes for nought, and you will waste and overthrow all the pains that you now spend upon yourself. It needs but a little to overthrow and destroy everything–just a slight aberration from reason. For the helmsman to wreck his vessel, he does not need the same resources, as he needs to save it: if he turn it but a little too far to the wind, he is lost; yes, and if he do it not deliberately but from mere want of attention, he is lost all the same. It is very much the same in life: if you doze but a little, all that you have amassed up till now leaves you. Keep awake then and watch your impressions: it is no trifle you have in keeping, but self-respect, honour, constancy, a quiet mind, untouched by distress, or fear, or agitation–in a word, freedom.

What are you going to sell all this for? Look and see what your purchase is worth.

'But I am not going to sell my freedom for anything of that kind.'

Well, suppose you waive external gain, consider what the exchange is that you are making. It is yours to say, 'Self-control for me, a tribunate for him: a praetorship for him, self-respect for me. I do not clamour, when to do so is unseemly, I will not jump from my seat, when I ought not, for I am free and God's friend, to obey Him of my own free will. I must not lay claim to anything else–body, property, office, reputation, anything in short, for He does not wish me to lay claim to them:

had He wished it, He would have made them good for me, but He has not done so, and therefore I cannot transgress any of His commands.' In everything you do, guard what is your own good: for the rest, be content just to take anything that is given you, so far as you may use it rationally. Otherwise you will be wretched and miserable, hampered and hindered. These are the laws that are sent you from God, these are His ordinances. These you must expound, and these obey, not those of Masurius and Cassius.

CHAPTER FOUR

To those whose Heart is Set on a Quiet Life

REMEMBER THAT IT IS not only desire of office and of wealth that makes men abject and subservient to others, but also desire of peace and leisure and travel and learning. Regard for any external thing, whatever it be, makes you subservient to another. What difference does it make then whether you desire to be a senator, or not to be a senator, to be in office, or to be out of office? What difference is there between saying, 'I am miserable, I don't know what to do, I am tied to my books like a corpse', and saying, 'I am miserable, I have no leisure to read'? For books, like salutations and office, belong to the outer world which is beyond your own control. If you deny it, tell me why do you want to read? If you are drawn by the mere pleasure of reading, or by curiosity, you are a trifler, without perseverance: but if you judge it by the true standard, what is that but peace of mind? If reading does not win you peace of mind, what is the good of it?

'Nay,' he says, 'it does, and that is just why I am vexed at being deprived of it.'

And what, pray, is this peace of mind, which any one can hinder–I do not mean Caesar, or Caesar's friend, but a raven, a flute-player, a fever, countless other things? Nothing is so characteristic of peace of mind as that it is continuous and unhindered. Suppose now I am called away to do something: I shall go and attend to the limits which one must observe–acting with self-respect and security, with no will to get or to avoid external things, watching men also to see what they say and how they move, and that not from ill nature, nor to blame or mock at them, but looking at myself all the time to see if I am making the same mistakes too.

'How then shall I cease to err?' you ask.

Time was when I made the same mistakes as others, but I do so no more, thanks be to God. If you have acted thus and devoted yourself to this, have you done worse than if you had read a thousand lines or written as many? When you eat, are you vexed that you are not reading? Are you not content with eating as your reading bids you? And the same when you wash and take exercise? Why, then, do you not keep an equable tenor always, even when you approach Caesar or this or that great man? What do you lack, if you keep yourself free from passion, undismayed, modest, if you are rather a 'spectator of events than a spectacle to others, if you do not envy those preferred to you, if you are not dazzled by material things?

You say you lack books? How, or to what end? Books are, no doubt, a preparation for life, but life itself is made up of things different from hooks. To ask for books is as though an athlete should complain, as he enters the arena, that he is not training outside. Life is what you were training for all along, this is what the leaping-weights, and the sawdust, and the young men you wrestled with were leading up to. What? Are you hankering after them, when the time for action is come? It is as if in the sphere of assent, when impressions are presented to us, some which are 'apprehensive', and some which have no such power, we should refuse to distinguish between them and should prefer to read the theory of apprehensive impressions.

What, then, is the reason of our failure?

The reason is that we never directed our reading or our writing to the right object–that is, to dealing naturally with the impressions that come upon us, when we have to act. We are content to go thus far and no farther–to understand what is said, and to be able to explain it to another, to analyse the syllogism and trace out the hypothetical argument. Therefore hindrance besets us in the sphere where our pains are spent.

Do you want things which are not always in your power?

Be condemned, then, to hindrance, obstruction, failure. But if we were to study the doctrine of impulse, not to see what is said about impulse but to make our own impulses good, if we were to study the will to get and the will to avoid to the end that we may never fail to get what we will nor fall into what we avoid, and study the doctrine of what is fitting that we may remember our true relations and may do nothing irrationally or contrary to what is fitting–then we should not have to suffer vexation at being hindered in regard to the principles we have studied, but should find contentment in acting in accordance with them, and we should cease to calculate as we have been wont to do till to-day, 'To-day I read so many lines, wrote so many', and should reckon thus, 'To-day I governed my impulse by the precepts of the philosophers, I did not entertain desire, I avoided only things within the compass of my will, I was not awed by this man, or over-persuaded by that man, but trained my faculty of patience, of absti-nence, of co-operation': and then we should give thanks to God, for the gifts for which our thanks are due.

As it is, we do not realize that we too, with a difference, behave like the multitude. Another man fears that he may not become a magistrate, you fear that you may be one. Man, act not so. Nay, just as you laugh at him who fears he may not hold office, so laugh at yourself too. There is nothing to choose between being thirsty with fever, and shunning water like a madman. If you act thus; how shall you be able to say, as Socrates did, 'If God so wills, so be it'? Do you think that, if Socrates had set his desire on a life of leisure and daily conversation with young men in the Lyceum or the Academy, he would have cheerfully gone on all the campaigns in which he served? Would he not have groaned and lamented, 'Unhappy that I am, wretched and miserable in the field, when I might be sunning myself in the Lyceum.' What? Was this your task in life, to sun your-self? Was it not to have a mind at peace, to be free from hindrance and encumbrance? Nay, how would he have been Socrates any more, if he had lamented like that? How could he have written songs of triumph in prison?

In a word, then, remember this, that, whenever you pay regard to anything outside your will's control, you so far destroy your will. And freedom from office lies outside your will just as much as office, leisure just much as business.

'Am I, then, to pass my life amid this tumult?'

What do you mean by 'tumult'?

'Amid a multitude of men.'

Well, and what is there hard in that? Imagine you are at Olympia, make up your mind that it is a festival. There, too, one cries this, an-other that, one does this, another that, and one man jostles another. The public baths, too, are thronged, yet which of us does not enjoy this assemblage, and leave it with pain? Be not dissatisfied nor pee-vish at what happens. 'Vinegar disgusts me, for it is acid; honey dis-gusts me, for it upsets my tone; I dislike green stuff.' In the same way you say, 'I dislike retirement, it means solitude; I dislike a crowd, it means disturbance.'

Say not so, but, if things so turn out, that you live alone or in a small company, call it 'peace' and make a proper use of it: converse with yourself, train your impressions, develop your primary notions. If you chance on a crowd, call it 'games', 'assembly', 'festival', and try to share the feast with your fellow men. For what sight is pleasanter for the man who loves his kind than a multitude of men? We are pleased to see troops of horses or oxen, we delight to see a multitude of ships: does the sight of a multitude of men vex us?

'Nay, but their clamour overwhelms me.'

Well, that is only a hindrance to your hearing: how does it affect you? Does it affect your faculty of dealing with your impressions? Who can hinder you from dealing naturally with the will to get and the will to avoid, the impulse to act and not to act? What tumult can avail to touch these?

Only remember these general principles: 'What is mine, what is not mine? What is given me? What does God wish me to do now? What does He not wish?' A little while ago His will was that you should live a quiet life in converse with yourself, and write on these matters, read, listen, prepare yourself: you had sufficient time for this. Now He says to you, 'Now come into the conflict, show us what you have learnt, how you have trained. How long are you going to exercise yourself in solitude? The time has now come for you to discover whether you are an athlete worthy of victory, or one of those who go about the world suffering continual defeat.' Why, then, are you vexed? There is no conflict without a crowd: there must be many to train beforehand, many to cry applause, many stewards, many spectators.

'Yes, but I wanted to live a quiet life.'

Lament and mourn, then, as you deserve: for what greater penalty than this can fall on him who is uninstructed and disobedient to the ordinances of God than to be distressed, to mourn, to envy, in a word, to be unhappy and miserable? Have you no wish to free yourself from these ills?

'And how shall I free myself?'

Have you not often heard, that you must get rid of the will to get altogether, and must will to avoid only those things which are within your control? That you must give up everything–body, property, reputation, books, the throng, office, private life? For if once you swerve from this path you become a slave and a subject, you are liable to hindrance and compulsion, and completely at the mercy of others. But the saying of Cleanthes is ready to our need,

Lead me, O Zeus, and lead me, Destiny.

Will you have me go to Rome? To Rome then. To Gyara? I will go to Gyara. To Athens? I will go to Athens. To prison? I will go to prison. If once you say, 'When are we to get away to Athens?' you are lost. That wish, if unfulfilled, must make you miserable, and, if fulfilled, it must make you puffed up, elated on false grounds: again, if you are hindered. it must make you unhappy, at the conflict between circumstances and your will. Give up all these things then.

'Athens is beautiful.'

Yes, but happiness is far more beautiful–freedom from passion and disturbance, the sense that your affairs depend on no one.

'In Rome there is crowd and salutations.'

Yes, but peace of mind outweighs all discomforts. If, then, the time for these has come, why do you not get rid of your will to avoid them? Why must you bear your burden like a cudgelled ass? If you do this, you must needs (look you) be the perpetual slave of him who has power to accomplish your departure, or him who can in any way hinder it, and you are bound to pay respect to him as to an Evil Genius.

There is but one way to peace of mind (keep this thought by you at dawn and in the day-time and at night)–to give up what is beyond your control, to count nothing your own, to surrender everything to heaven and fortune, to lehve everything to be managed by those to whom Zeus has given control, and to devote yourself to one object only, that which is your own beyond all hindrance, and in all that you read and write and hear to make this your aim. Therefore I cannot call a man industrious, if I am merely told that he reads or writes, no, not even if one adds 'he is at work all night', unless I know what he is working for. You do not call a man industrious who keeps late hours for the sake of a mistress: neither do I. But if he does it for glory, I call him ambitious; if for money, I call him fond of money, not fond of work. But if the object of his work is his own Governing Principle, if he is working to make this live a natural life, then and then only I call him industrious. You must never praise or blame men for qualities that are indifferent, but for their judgements. For it is these which are each man's property, these which make their actions base or noble. Bear this in mind and rejoice in what is at hand and be content with what the moment brings. If you see any of the principles that you have learnt and thought over being realized by you in action, rejoice over them. If you have put away bad nature, and evil-speaking, or made them less, if you have got rid of wantonness, foul speaking, recklessness, slackness, if you are not excited by things that once excited you, or at least not as before, then you can keep festival day by day, to-day because you behaved well in this action, to-morrow because you did well in another. How much greater cause is this for offering sacrifice than if you were made consul or prefect! These things come to you from your own self and from the gods. Remember Who is the Giver, and to whom He gives and why. If you are brought up to reason thus, you need no longer raise the question, 'Where shall I be happy?' and 'Where shall I please God?' Do not men have their equal portion in all places? Do they not everywhere alike behold what comes to pass?

CHAPTER FIVE

To those that are Contentious and Brutal

THE GOOD AND NOBLE man does not contend with any one, and to the best of his power does not suffer others to contend. We have an illustration of this, as of other qualities, set out for us in the life of Socrates, who not only avoided contention himself on all occasions, but tried to prevent the contentions of others. Look at the *Symposium* of Xenophon and see how many contentions he has reconciled, and again how patient he was with Thrasymachus, with Polus, with Callicles, and how patient always with his wife, and with his son, when his son tried to convict him of fallacious arguments. For he remembered to hold fast the truth that no man is master of another's Governing Principle. Therefore he wished to do nothing that was not his own. What does that mean? Not to move other people to act naturally, for that is not his to do: but to let others act for themselves, as they think fit, and himself none the less to live and spend his days in accord with nature, only doing his own business in such a way that they, too, should follow nature. For this is the conduct which the good and noble man always has set before him.

Is it his will to become praetor?

No, but if this is given him, to keep his own Governing Principle in these circumstances.

To marry?

No, but if marriage is given him, to keep himself in a natural state in those circumstances. But if he wills that his son or his wife should not go wrong, then he wills to make his own what is not his own. In fact education is this, to learn what is one's own and what is not.

Where, then, is there any room for contention if a man bears himself thus? Is he amazed at anything that happens? Does anything take him by surprise? Does he not expect the wicked to deal worse and more severely with him than the event turns out? Does he not count everything gain in which they fall short of the worst?

'Such a one reviled you.'

Many thanks to him for not striking.

'But he did strike too.'

Many thanks to him for not wounding.

'But he did wound.'

Many thanks to him for not killing. For when, or in whose school, did he learn 'that man is a gentle and sociable creature and that wrong-doing in itself does great harm to the wrongdoer'?

If, then, he has not learnt this or been convinced of it, why should he not follow what appears to be his interest?

'My neighbour has thrown stones.'

Is that any offence on your part?

'But my crockery is broken.'

You are no piece of crockery: you are a rational will. You ask what is given you to meet this attack? If you want to act the wolf, you may bite back, and throw more stones at him than he threw: but if you seek to act as a man, then examine your store and see what faculties you have brought into the world with you. Have you brought the faculty of a brute, the faculty of revenging wrongs? When is a horse miserable? When it is deprived of its natural faculties, not when it is unable to crow like a cock, but when it is unable to run. And the dog? Not when it cannot fly, but when it cannot follow a trail. On the same principle a man is wretched, not when he cannot throttle lions or embrace statues (for he has not been endowed by nature with faculties for this), but when he has lost his rational and trustworthy faculty. This is he for whom men

> *should meet and mourn*
> *The miseries he has come to,*

not, by Zeus, the man who is born or dies, but he whose lot it is to lose while he lives what is his own–not his patrimony, his paltry field or house or inn or slaves (for none of these is man's own, but all are alien to him, all are subject and subservient to their Masters, who give them now to one now to another)–to lose the qualities that make him man, the distinctive stamp impressed upon his mind: like the stamp we look for on coins, which if we find we pass them, and if we do not, fling them away.

Whose imprint does this sesterce bear?

'Trajan's.'

Here with it.

'Nero's.'

Fling it away, it will not pass, it is good for nothing.

So, too, it is with man. What stamp have his judgements? 'Gentle, sociable, patient, affectionate.' Good, I accept him, I make him a citizen, I accept him as a neighbour and fellow voyager. Only beware that he has not the stamp of Nero. Is he hot-tempered, is he wrathful, is he querulous? 'If it takes his fancy, he cuffs the heads of those he meets.' Why, then, did you say that he is a man? Is everything judged by its outward form alone? On that principle you must call your waxen apple an apple. No, it must smell and taste like an apple: the outward semblance is not enough. So, when you judge man, nose and eyes are not sufficient, you must see if he has the judgements of a man. Here is one who does not listen to reason, does not understand when his fallacies are exposed; he is an ass. Here is one whose self-respect is deadened: he is useless, anything rather than a man. Here is one looking to find some one he can kick or bite; it follows he is not even a sheep or an ass, but some savage beast or other.

'What then? Do you want me to be despised?'

By whom? By those who know? Nay, how will those who know despise one who is gentle and self-respecting? By those who do not know? What do you care for them? No craftsman cares for those who have no skill!

'Yes, but they will attack me much more.'

What do you mean by 'me'? Can any one injure your will or hinder you from dealing with the impressions you meet with in a natural way? 'No.'

Why, then, do you persist in being troubled and want to show yourself a man of fears? Why do you not come forward and openly proclaim that you are at peace with all men, whatever they do, and that you laugh above all at those who think that they are harming you? saying, 'These slaves do not know who I am, nor where to find what is good or bad for me, for they have no way of getting at my position.' In the same way those who inhabit a strong city laugh at those who besiege it. 'Why are these men troubling themselves for nothing? Our wall is secure, we have food for a long time, and all other supplies.' These are the things that make a city secure against capture; the soul of man is made secure by judgements alone. For what wall is so strong, or what substance so impenetrable, or what property so secure against robbery, or what reputation so unassailable? When the objects that a man sets his mind on are bound to bring him trouble of mind, sick hopes, fear, mourning, disappointment of the will to get, failure of the will to avoid, they are always subject to death and to capture.

If this be so, are we not willing to make the one means of safety which is given us secure, and, abandoning what is mortal and slavish, to spend our efforts on what is immortal and free by nature? Do we not remember that one man does not harm nor benefit another? It is man's judgement on each situation that harms him. It is this which overthrows him, this is contention, this is faction, this is war. The conflict of Eteocles and Polynices was caused by nothing else but this judgement, the judgement on kingship, the judgement on exile–that exile is the worst of evils, kingship the greatest good: and the nature of every man is this–to pursue the good, to avoid the evil, to consider him who takes away from one's good and who involves one in evil as an enemy and aggressor, even though he be a brother, a son, a father, for no kinship is closer than that of the good. Wherefore, if these outward things are reckoned good and evil, there is no love between father and sons or between brother and brother, but the whole world is full of enemies, aggressors, malicious persons. But if a right will is the only good thing, and a wrong will the only evil, what becomes of conflict and reviling? How can it arise? Over things that do not concern us? With whom should we contend? With the ignorant, the miserable, with those who are deluded in regard to the highest matters?

Socrates remembered this when he lived in his own house and bore with a most shrewish wife and an unfeeling son. For what did her shrewishness mean? Pouring water at will over his head, and trampling on his cake. What is that to me, if I make up my mind that it is nothing to me? This is what I have to do, and no king nor master shall hinder me against my will, the many shall not prevail against the one, nor the stronger against the weaker: for God has given each man his reason to use unhindered. These judgements make affection in a household, concord in a city, peace among nations; they make a man grateful towards God, confident in all places, for he looks on outward things as alien to him and as worth nothing. But though we are capable of writing and reading these sentiments, though we can praise them as we read, yet they do not bring conviction to us, nor anything like it. Wherefore the proverb about the Lacedaemonians,

> *Lions at home, foxes at Ephesus,*
> [Author unknown]

will fit us too. In the lecture-room we are lions, and foxes in the world outside!

CHAPTER SIX

To those who are Distressed at Being Pitied

'I AM VEXED', he says, 'at being pitied.'

Is it your doing that you are pitied, or the doing of those who pity you? Or again, does it rest with you to stop their pity?

'Yes, if I show them that I do not deserve their pity.'

But is it in your power, or is it not, not to deserve pity? 'I think that it is in my power.'

But these men do not pity you for what would deserve pity, if anything did–I mean for your errors–but for poverty and lack of office and diseases and death and other things of this sort. Are you, then, prepared to persuade the multitude that none of these things, after all, is evil, but that it is possible for a man who is poor, and without office or honour, to be happy, or do you try to show off to them as a man of wealth and office? The second course stamps you as a braggart without taste or worth. And consider by what means you would achieve your pretence: you will have to borrow some wretched slaves and possess a few pieces of plate, and show them many times over, if you can, and try not to let men know that they are the same; and you must display gay apparel and other splendours and show yourself off as one who is honoured by eminent persons and must try to dine at their table, or at least be thought to do so; and you must use base arts on your person, to make yourself seem handsomer and better made than you really are: these are the contrivances you must adopt, if you wish to take the second way of avoiding pity.

But the first way is a long, nay an endless, one–to attempt the very task which Zeus could not accomplish–to convince all men of what is good and what is evil. Is this given to you? No! This only is given you –to convince yourself: you have not yet done that: and yet you are already attempting–are you?–to convince others. Why! Who has been your companion so long as you have been yourself, and who can exercise such persuasion on you as you can on yourself, and who is more kindly and friendly disposed to you than you are? How is it, then, that you have not yet persuaded yourself to learn? Are not your thoughts turned upside down? Have you set your mind on this, and not on learning how to be quit of pain and trouble and humiliation, and so to be free? Have you not heard, then, that there is but one way which leads to this–to give up all that lies beyond the will, to abandon it and confess that it is not yours?

To what class of things does another man's opinion about you belong? 'To what is outside the will.'

Then it concerns you not at all?

'Not at all.'

While, then, you still allow yourself to be vexed and troubled at men's opinion, do you imagine that you have attained conviction as to what is good and evil?

Will you not, then, let other men alone and become your own master and pupil? 'Other men shall see for themselves whether it is to their advantage to be in an unnatural state and live their lives so, but no man is nearer me than I am myself. Why is it, then, that though I have heard the arguments of philosophers and assent to them, they have not lightened my burden? Am I so wanting in ability? Why, in all the other things I chose to undertake, I was not found to be duller than most. I was quick at learning letters and wrestling and geometry and the analysis of syllogisms. Is it, then, that reason has failed to convince me? Why, there is nothing which I have so stamped with my approval and choice from the first–and even now these principles are the subject of my reading, I hear and write of nothing else: up till to-day we have found no argument to prevail against this. What then do I lack? Is it that the contrary judgements have not been removed from my mind? Is it that my own convictions are untrained and unaccustomed to confront facts, like arms put away in a cupboard and grown rusty, that cannot be fitted to my body? Yes, of course! In wrestling or writing or reading I am not content with merely learning; I twist the arguments put before me to and fro and construct new ones, and I deal with variable premises in like manner. But when I have to deal with those necessary principles, which enable a man, if he grounds himself on them, to escape pain, fear, passion, hindrance–to be free,

I do not exercise myself in them nor devote to them the practice that is proper for them. And then, am I concerned by what the multitude will say of me, and whether in their eyes I shall appear a happy or important personage?'

Miserable man, will you not see what opinion you pronounce on yourself? How do you appear to yourself? What manner of man in thought, in will to get and will to avoid: what manner of man in impulse, preparation, design, and the other activities of man? Yet you are concerned whether other men pity you?

'Yes, but they pity me when I do not deserve it.'

Is this what pains you? and is the man who is pained to be pitied?

'Yes.'

Then you are not pitied without deserving it after all. By the very feelings you entertain in regard to pity you make yourself worthy of pity. What does Antisthenes say? Did you never hear? 'It is the part of a king, Cyrus, to do well and be ill-spoken of.' My head is sound and all think that I have a headache. What do I care? I am free from fever, and men sympathize with me as though I had fever: 'Unhappy man, this long time you have had fever without ceasing.' I put on a gloomy face and assent: 'It is quite true I have been ill for a long time.' 'What is to happen then?' 'What God wills': and as I say it I laugh in my sleeve at those who pity me.

What prevents me, then, from doing the same here too? I am poor, but I hold a right judgement on poverty: what do I care then, whether they pity me for poverty? I am not in office and others are; but I hold the right opinion as to being in office and out of it. Those who pity me shall take their own views: I have neither hunger nor thirst nor cold, but their own hunger or thirst makes them imagine the same of me. What am I to do for them then? I go about proclaiming and saying, 'Sirs, be not deluded, all is well with me, I take no heed of poverty, or want of office, or, in a word, of anything at all except right judgements: these I hold free from hindrance, I have paid regard to nothing besides.' Yet what nonsense am I talking? How do I hold right judgements any longer if I am not content with being what I am, and am excited over other men's opinion of me?

'But others will get more than I do, and will be preferred to me.'

Well, what is more reasonable than that those who have spent their pains on any object should have the advantage in that on which they have spent their pains? They have spent their pains on office, you on judgements, they on wealth, you on the way to deal with impressions. See whether they have the advantage of you in that on which you have spent pains and which they neglect: whether in assent they keep more to natural standards, whether they are more successful in getting what they will to get, and in avoiding what they will to avoid, whether in design, in purpose, in impulse they aim better than you, whether they do what is fitting for them as men, as sons, and as parents, and in each relation that you name in turn. But if they hold office and you do not, will you not tell yourself the truth–that you do nothing to gain office, and they do everything, and it is most unreasonable that one who pays attention to a thing should have less success in it than one who does not?

'Nay, but I pay regard to right judgements and therefore it is more reasonable that I should rule.'

Yes, in judgements, for you have devoted yourself to them: but you must give place to others in that to which they have devoted themselves. You might as well claim to be a better shot with the bow than regular bowmen because you have right judgements, or to be better at smith's work than the professional smith. Give up your devotion to judgements then and busy yourself with the objects you wish to obtain, and then complain if you do not succeed, for you have a right to complain. But, as it is, you say you are bent on other things, and attending to other things, and the proverb of the people is a good one: 'One business has nothing in common with another.' One man rises at dawn and tries to find whom he can salute as he leaves home, or to whom he can make a pleasant speech, or send a gift, how he can please the dancer, how he can deal maliciously with one man to gratify another. When he prays, his prayers are for this object; when he sacrifices, his sacrifice is for this; the prayer of Pythagoras

That sleep fall not upon his tender eyes–
[Ascribed to Pythagoras]

he has turned to this end. 'How went I wrong?' Was it in matters of flattery? 'What wrought I?' Have I acted as a free man and a gentleman? And if he finds himself acting so he blames and accuses himself and says, 'Whatever should you say this for? Might you not have told a lie? Even philosophers say, "There is nothing to hinder one's telling a lie."'

But if you have really given your mind to nothing but how to deal properly with impressions, then as soon as you get up in the morning you must consider, 'What do I lack to secure freedom from passion? What do I lack to be unperturbed? What am I? Am I a mere body, or property, or reputation?'

None of these.

What then?

A rational creature.

What then are the demands upon me?

Reflect upon your actions. 'Where have I gone wrong' in regard to peace of mind? 'What have I done' unfriendly, or unsociable, or heartless? What did I fail to accomplish in this regard that I ought to have done?

Seeing then that there is this great difference in men's desires and acts and prayers, do you still wish to be equal with them in matters to which they have given their minds and you have not? And, that being so, are you surprised and annoyed if they pity you? They are not annoyed if you pity them. Why? Because they are convinced that their lot is a good one, and you are not convinced. That is why you are not content with your portion, but hanker after theirs, and they are content with their portion and do not hanker after yours. For, if you were really convinced that you are right in regard to what is good and that they are far away from the truth, you would never have taken any account of what they say of you.

CHAPTER SEVEN

On Freedom from Fear

WHAT MAKES THE EMPEROR an object of fear?

The guards, one says, with their swords, and the chamberlains and those who close the door against those who enter.

Why is it then that, if you bring a child to him when his guards are with him, the child is not afraid? Is it because the child is not aware of them? Now if a man is aware of the guards and their swords, but comes for that very purpose, because his misfortunes make him wish to die and he is anxious to die easily by some one else's hand, does he fear the guards?

'No, for he wishes for the very thing which makes men fear them.'

If then a man whose will is not set on dying or living, but who is content with what is given him, comes before the Tyrant, what prevents him from coming without fear?

'Nothing.'

Now suppose a man is of the same mind in regard to property as this man in regard to his body: suppose he feels the same about wife and children: suppose, in a word, he is so distracted and desperate that he regards it as indifferent whether he has these things or not: just as children playing with potsherds are anxious about the game, but do not care for the potsherds in themselves, so he has not set his heart on material things, but accepts the game cheerfully, and enjoys handling them–how can any tyrant, how can any guards or swords inspire fear in such a one?

Yet if madness can produce this attitude of mind, if even habit can produce it in the Galilaeans, can reason and demonstration teach no one that God has made all things in the world, and the world itself as a whole to have its own end without hindrance, but its individual parts to subserve the whole? Now all other things are without the capacity of understanding His governance, but the rational creature has faculties that enable him to reflect on all these things, to realize that he is a part, and what part he is, and that it is well for the parts to give way to the whole. And further, being by nature noble and generous and free, he sees that he has some of the things about him unhindered and in his own control, and some again subject to hindrance and dependent on others, the acts of his will unhindered, and things beyond his will subject to hindrance. And therefore if he makes up his mind that his good and his interest lie in the former alone, in things that are unhindered and depend upon himself, he will be free, tranquil, happy, unharmed, high-minded, reverent, giving thanks for everything to God, on no occasion blaming or accusing any one for what happens; but if he finds his good in things outside and beyond his will, he is bound to be hindered and hampered, and to be the slave of those who have authority over those things on which his admiration and his fear are centred, he is bound to be irreverent because he thinks that God is injuring him, and unfair, always seeking to win for himself more than his share; he is bound to be of a mean and paltry spirit.

If a man understands this, there is nothing to prevent him from living with an easy and obedient spirit, content with his past lot and awaiting with a gentle spirit all that may yet befall him.

'Would you give me poverty?' Give it me and you shall learn what poverty is when a good actor plays the part. 'Would you give me office?' Give it me, and troubles with it. 'Exile?' Wherever I go, it will be well with me: for even here it was not the place that made me well off, but my judgements, and these I shall carry away with me, for no one can rob me of them; these alone are my own and cannot be taken away, with these I am content wherever I am and whatever I do. 'But now the time is come to die.' What do you mean by 'die'? Do not use fine words, but state the facts as they are. 'Now is the time for your material part to be restored to the elements of which it was composed.' What is there dreadful in that? What loss to the universe will this mean, what strange or irrational event? Is this a thing to make one fear the tyrant? Is this what makes the swords of the guards seem long and sharp? Let others look to that; I have considered the whole matter, and no one has authority over me. God has set me free, I have learnt to understand His commands, no one can make a slave of me any more, my judges and he who claims my freedom are as they should be.

'Am I not master of your body?'

What does that concern *me*?

'Am I not master of your property?'

Well, how does that concern me?

'Am I not master of exile and imprisonment?'

Again, I resign all, yes, and my body itself for you to deal with, when you will. Only try your authority and you will learn how far it extends. What then can I fear any more? The chamberlains? What should I fear their doing? Fear their shutting me out? If they find me wanting to en-ter, let them shut me out!

'Why then do you come to the king's door?'

Because I think it is fitting for me to join in the game while it lasts.

'How then do you escape being shut out?'

If I am not received, it is not my will to enter; my will is always to prefer what comes to pass, for I consider what God wills better than what I will. I will attach myself to Him as His minister and servant, my impulses and my wishes are one with His, in a word my will is His will. There can be no exclusion for me, but only for those who try to press in.

Why then do I not press in?

Because I know that nothing good is given within to those who have entered. But when I hear a man called happy because he is honoured by Caesar I say, 'What is his portion?' 'A province or a procuratorship.' Does he also get a judgement, such as a governor should have? Does he get the skill to use a procuratorship? Why should I push my way in any more? Some one flings a shower of figs and nuts: the children try to seize them, and fight with one another for them; grown men do not, for they count it a small matter. If one fling potsherds even children do not try to catch them. Governorships are being given to this man and that: the children shall see to them! A praetorship, a consulship: let the children scramble for them: let them be shut out and beaten, let them kiss the hands of the giver and his slaves; for me they are figs and nuts. But what if a fig chance to fall into my lap when he is throwing? Take and eat it, for one may value a fig so far. But if I stoop for it and upset my neighbour or am upset by him, if I flatter those who enter, the fig is not worth while, nor is any other of the good things which the philosophers have persuaded me not to believe to be good.

Show me the swords of the guards.

'See how large and how sharp they are.'

Well, what do these large, sharp swords do?

'They kill.'

What does fever do?

'The same.'

What does a tile do?

'The same.'

Would you have me then stand in awe of all these things, and pay them reverence, and go about as the slave of all?

God forbid! No, if I have once learnt that what is born must needs also be destroyed in order that the world may not stand still or be hindered, it makes no difference to me whether a fever is to destroy it or a falling tile or a soldier, but if I must compare them I know that the soldier will do the thing quicker and with less pain. Seeing then that I neither fear anything that he can do to me nor desire anything that he can provide, why do I stand in awe and amazement before him any more? Why do I fear the guards? Why do I rejoice if he speaks to me in a friendly way and gives me a welcome? Why do I tell other people how he talked to me? Is he a Socrates or a Diogenes, that his praise of me should be a proof of what I am? Do I admire his character? No, it is to keep up the game that I come to him and serve him, so long as he commands me to do nothing stupid or unseemly. But if he says to me, 'Go and fetch Leon of Salamis', I say to him, 'Look for some one else, I will play no longer.'

'Away with him.'

I follow; it is in the game.

'But you lose your neck.'

Well! does the Emperor himself, and you who obey him, keep his neck for ever?

'But you will be flung abroad unburied.'

I shall be, if I and the dead body are one, but if I am not the same as the dead body, state the facts with more discrimination, and do not try to frighten me. These are things to frighten children and fools. But if a man has once entered a philosopher's lecture-room and does not know what his true self is, he deserves to fear and to flatter what he flattered afterwards: I mean, if he has not yet learnt that he is not flesh or bones or sinews, but the faculty which uses them, and which also governs the impressions and understands them.

'Yes, but these arguments make men despise the laws.'

'Nay, these arguments of all others make those who adopt them obedient to the laws. Law is not what any fool can do. Yet see how these arguments make us behave rightly even towards our critics, since they teach us to claim nothing against them, in which they can surpass us. They teach us to give way in regard to our poor body, to give way in regard to property, children, parents, brothers, to give up everything, resign everything: only our judgements they reserve, and these Zeus willed should be each man's special property. How can you call this lawlessness, how can you call it stupidity? I give way to you in that wherein you are better and stronger than I: where, on the other hand, I am the better man, it is for you to give way to me, for I have made this my concern, and you have not. You make it your concern, how to live in a palace, how slaves and freedmen are to serve you, how you are to wear conspicuous raiment, how you are to have a multitude of huntsmen, minstrels, players. Do I lay claim to any of these? But you, for your part, have you concerned yourself with judgements? Have you concerned yourself with your own rational self? Do you know what are its constituents, what is its principle of union, how it is articulated, what are its faculties and of what nature? Why are you vexed then, if another who has made these things his study has the advantage of you here?

'But these are the greatest matters of all.'

Who, I ask, prevents you from busying yourself with these and devoting your attention to these? Who has a larger equipment of books, of leisure, of masters who will do you good? Only incline your mind to these things, bestow a little time, if no more, on your own Governing Principle, consider what this possession is and whence it has come to you, this faculty which uses all the rest, which proves all the rest, selecting and rejecting. So long as you busy yourself with external things, no one will succeed with them so well as you, but this faculty of reason will be, what your own choice makes it, mouldy and neglected.

CHAPTER EIGHT

To those who Hastily Assume the Character of Philosophers

NEVER BESTOW PRAISE OR blame on any one for qualities which are indifferent, nor credit them with skill or want of skill; then you will escape at once from recklessness and malice. 'This man washes hastily.' Does he do evil then? Not at all. What is it he does then? He washes hastily. Do you mean that everything is well done? By no means: but acts based on right judgements are done well and those based on bad judgements are done badly. Until you have learnt from what judgement each of a man's acts proceeds, do not praise or blame him. But a judgement is not easily determined by externals. 'This man is a carpenter.' Why? 'He uses an adze.' What has that to do with it? 'This man is a musician, for he sings.' What does that matter? 'This man is a philosopher.' Why? 'He wears a cloak and long hair.' But what do mountebanks wear? Therefore, if a man sees one of them misbehaving, he says at once, 'Look what the philosopher is doing.' But his misconduct should rather have led him to say that he was no philosopher. For, if this is the primary conception and profession of a philosopher, to wear a cloak and long hair, they would be right: but if it is rather this–to be free from error–why do they not deprive him of the name 'philosopher' because he does not fulfil the philosopher's profession? For this is what happens in other arts. When one sees a man planing badly, one does not say, 'What is the good of the carpenter's art, see what bad work carpenters do', but one says quite the contrary, 'This man is not a carpenter, for he planes badly.' In like manner if one hears a man singing badly, one does not say, 'See how badly musicians sing', but rather, 'This man is no musician.' It is only in regard to philosophy that men behave so: when they see any one acting contrary to the philosopher's profession, instead of refusing him the name, they assume that he is a philosopher, and then finding from the facts that he is misbehaving, they infer that there is no use in being a philosopher. What is the reason for this? The reason is that we pay regard to the primary notion of the carpenter, and to that of the musician, and to that of other craftsmen in like manner, but pay no regard to the notion of the philosopher, but as it is indistinct and inarticulate in our minds we judge it by externals only. Can you name any other art that is acquired by dress and hair, and is destitute of principles and subject-matter and end?

What then is the subject-matter of the philosopher? Is it a cloak? No, it is reason.

What is his end? Is it to wear a cloak?

No, but to keep his reason right.

What are his principles? Are they concerned with how to grow a long beard or thick hair?

No, but rather, as Zeno says, to understand the elements of reason, the true nature of each, and how they are duly related to one another, and all that is consequential on this. Will you not, then, first see whether he fulfils his profession by behaving unseemly, and only then, if it be so, accuse his calling? As it is, when you think that he is behaving ill, when your own conduct is discreet, you say, 'Look at the philosopher', as though it were fitting to call the man who acts so a philosopher, and again, 'There's your philosopher!' But you do not say, 'Look at the carpenter', or 'Look at the musician', when you discover one of that class in adultery or see him eating greedily. So true it is that you realize the philosopher's profession to a certain extent, but you fall away from it and are confounded by sheer want of practice.

But even those who are called philosophers use vulgar means to pursue their calling: they just put on a cloak and let their beard grow and say, 'I am a philosopher.' But no one if he merely buys a harp and a plectrum will say, 'I am a musician', nor if he puts on a smith's cap and apron will say, 'I am a smith': no doubt they fit the dress to the art, but they take their name from the art and not from the dress. For this reason Euphrates was right in saying, 'For a long time I tried not to be known for a philosopher and this was useful to me. For, in the first place, I knew that what I did rightly was done for my own sake and not for the spectators: it was for myself that I ate rightly and was modest in my aspect and my gait: all was for myself and God. Secondly, as the performance was mine only, so also was the risk: if I did anything shameful or unseemly the cause of philosophy was not endangered, nor did I injure the public by going wrong as a philosopher. For this reason those who did not know my design wondered how it was that, though I was familiar and conversant with all philosophers, I was not a philosopher myself. What harm is there in the philosopher being discovered by my acts, and not by outward signs?'

See how I eat, how I drink, how I sleep, how I bear and forbear, how I work for others, how I exercise the will to get and the will to avoid, how I observe my relationships, natural and acquired, without confusion and without hindrance. Judge me by this, if you can. But if you are so deaf and blind, that you do not consider Hephaestus a good smith unless you see him with his smith's cap on his head, what harm is there in being unrecognized by so foolish a judge?

So it was that most men did not recognize Socrates for a philosopher, and they came to him and asked him to introduce them to philosophers. Well, was he annoyed with them, as we should be? Did he say, 'Do not you think me a philosopher?' No, he took them and introduced them, and was content with this one thing, that he was a philosopher, and was glad that he was not vexed at being not taken for one: for he remembered his proper business.

What is the business of a good and true man? To have many pupils? Certainly not: those who have set their heart on that shall look to that. Is it then to take difficult principles and define them precisely? Others there will be who will look to this.

Where then was it that Socrates asserted himself and wished to assert himself?

In the region of injury and benefit. 'If any one', said he, 'can injure me, I am of no good; if I wait for some one to benefit me, I am naught. If I will, and my will is not done, I am miserable.' This was the great field of conflict to which he challenged every man, and in which I think he would have given way to none. But how, think you? Was it by proclaiming aloud, 'This is the man I am'? Never! but by being the man he was. For, again, it is a fool's and a braggart's part to say, 'I am free from passion and tumult. Men, I would have you know, that, while you are in turmoil and disturbance about worthless matters, I alone am relieved from all perturbation.' What, are you not content to be free from pain, without proclaiming, 'Come, all ye who suffer from gout, headache, fever, come ye lame and blind and behold how I am untouched by any sickness'? That is a vain and vulgar boast, unless, like Asclepius, you can at once show them by what treatment they too can be relieved of disease, and for this purpose produce your own good health as an example.

Such is the character of the Cynic whom Zeus has deemed worthy of crown and sceptre. He says, 'Men, you are looking for happiness and peace not where it is but where it is not, and, that you may see this, behold I have been sent to you by God as an example, having neither property nor house nor wife nor children–no, not even a bed or a tunic or a piece of furniture. See how healthy I am. Try me, and if you see that I am at peace in my mind, hear my remedies and the treatment which cured me.' This indeed is a humane and noble saying. But notice whose work it is: the work of Zeus or whomsoever He thinks worthy of this service–never to lay bare before the multitude any weakness whereby he should make of none effect the witness which he bears to virtue, and bears against outward things.

> *His noble face ne'er paled, nor from his cheeks*
> *Wiped he a tear.*
> [Homer, Odyssey, XI. 529]

Not only so, he must not long for anything or hanker after anything– human being or place or way of life–as children hanker after sweet grapes or holidays: he must be adorned with self-respect on every side, as others find their adornment in walls and doors and door-keepers.

Instead of that your would-be philosophers just take a start towards philosophy, and, like dyspeptics rushing to some dainty food, of which they are bound soon to grow sick, they claim at once the sceptre and the kingdom. He lets his hair grow, assumes a cloak, bares his shoulder for all to see, fights with those that meet him, and, if he sees any one in a fine cloak, quarrels with him. Man, discipline yourself first: watch your own impulse, to see that it is not like the sickly craving of a woman with child. Study first not to let men know what you are: keep your philosophy to yourself for a little. That is how fruit is produced. The seed must needs be buried first, and be hidden, and increase by slow degrees, that it may come to fullness. But if it bear the ear before it grows the stalk, it is like a plant from the garden of Adonis and comes to no good. That is the sort of plant you are: you have blossomed sooner than you ought, and will wither away when the storm comes.

Look what farmers say about seeds, when the hot weather comes before its time. They are all anxiety for fear that the seeds should grow insolent and then a single frost seize them and expose their weakness. You, too, man, must beware: you have grown insolent and have leapt to an opinion before the time: you think yourself a somebody, fool that you are among fools; you will be frost-bitten, nay you are frost-bitten already down at the root, though above you still blossom for a little and therefore think you are still alive and flourishing. Leave us at least to ripen in the natural course. Why do you expose us to the air, why do you force us? We cannot bear the air yet. Let the root grow, and then produce the stem, first one joint, then the second, then the third: then in that way the fruit will force its way naturally, whether I will or no.

For who that has conceived and travailed with such great judgements does not become aware of his own gifts and hasten to act in accordance with them? Why, a bull is not ignorant of his own nature and endowment when he catches sight of a wild beast, nor does he wait for some one to encourage him; and so with a dog, when he sees a wild animal. If then I have the equipment of a good man, am I to wait for you to equip me to do my proper work? But as yet I have not the equipment, believe me. Why then would you make me wither away before the time, just as you have withered away yourself?

CHAPTER NINE

To One who was Modest and has Become Shameless

WHEN YOU SEE ANOTHER man in office, set against his office the fact that you have no need of office: when you see another rich, look what you have instead. If you have nothing instead, you are miserable, but if you have this–that you have no need of wealth–know that you are better off and have something much more valuable. Another has a beautiful wife, you have freedom from desire for a beautiful wife. Do these seem to you small matters? Nay, what a price the rich themselves, and those who hold office, and who live with beautiful wives, would give to despise wealth and office and the very women whom they love and win! Do you not know what the thirst of a man in a fever is like, how different from the thirst of a man in health? The healthy man drinks and his thirst is gone: the other is delighted for a moment and then grows giddy, the water turns to gall, and he vomits and has colic, and is more exceeding thirsty. Such is the condition of the man who is haunted by desire in wealth or in office, and in wedlock with a lovely woman: jealousy clings to him, fear of loss, shameful words, shameful thoughts, unseemly deeds.

'Nay, but what do I lose?' he says.

Man, you were self-respecting and are so no more; have you lost nothing? Instead of Chrysippus and Zeno you read Aristides and Evenus; have you lost nothing? Instead of Socrates and Diogenes you admire the man who can cajole and corrupt most women. You want to be handsome and you make yourself up as what you are not; you want to show off glittering clothes, that you may attract women's eyes, and you count yourself lucky if you light on some precious cosmetic. Before, you thought of none of these things; your only concern was to find seemly discourse, a man of worth, a noble thought; and therefore you slept like a man, you walked like a man, you dressed like a man, your conversation was what a good man's should be. Can you say then, 'I have lost nothing'? Do you mean that men lose nothing but mere money? Is there no loss of self-respect, no loss of decency? Does the loss of these count for nothing? To you perhaps the loss of these qualities seems as nothing: there was a time when you counted this the only loss and the only harm, and when your one anxiety was that no one should dislodge you from these views and these acts.

And lo! you have been dislodged from them, but by none other than yourself. Fight against yourself, deliver yourself, that you may be modest, self-respecting, free. If any one ever told you that some one was compelling me to be a profligate, to dress like a profligate, to scent myself, would you not go and murder the man who so abused me? Will you not help yourself then? And how much easier this help is to give! There is no need to kill or to imprison or to assault any one, no need to come out into the market-place: you have only to talk to yourself, to the man who is most likely to be persuaded, and whom no one can persuade better than yourself. Therefore, first realize what is happening to you, and having done so, do not be faint-hearted or behave as men of a mean spirit do, who when once they have given in surrender completely and are swept away, so to speak, by the stream: no, learn a lesson from the trainers. The boy has fallen, suppose. 'Get up', says the trainer, 'and wrestle again, until you are made strong.' Let this be your attitude; for know that nothing is more amenable than the mind of man. You have but to will a thing and it is done, and all is right; on the other hand you have but to relax your effort and all is lost. For destruction and deliverance lie within you.

'What good do I get then?'

What greater good do you look for than this? You were shameless and shall be self-respecting, you were undisciplined and shall be disciplined, untrustworthy and you shall be trusted, dissolute and you shall be self-controlled. If you look for greater things than these, go on doing as you do now: not even a god can save you.

CHAPTER TEN

What Things we should Despise, and What we should Deem Important

ALL MEN'S DIFFICULTIES AND perplexities are concerned with external things. 'What am I to do?' 'How is it to be done?' 'How is it to turn out?' 'I fear this or that may befall me.' All these phrases are used by persons occupied with matters outside their will. For who says, 'How am I to refuse assent to the false?' 'How am I to refuse to swerve from the true?' If a man is so gifted by nature as to be anxious about these things, I will remind him: 'Why are you anxious? It rests with you: be not troubled. Be not overhasty in assent, before you have applied the rule of nature.'

Again, if he is anxious about his will to get, lest it should fail of its object and miss the mark, and about his will to avoid, lest it should fall into what it avoids, first of all I will salute him, because he has got rid of the excitements and fears of other men, and has turned his thoughts to his own business where his true self lies. Then I shall say to him: 'If you would not fail to get what you will, nor fall into what you will to avoid, do not will to get what is not your own, nor to avoid what is not in your control: otherwise you are bound to fail and to fall into disaster. Where is the difficulty if you do as I say? What room is there for phrases like, "How am I to get it?" "How is it to turn out?" "I fear this or that may befall me."'

Is not the issue of the future outside our will?

'Yes.'

And the essence of good and evil is in the region of the will?

'Yes.'

Is it in your power then to make a natural use of every event that happens? Can any one hinder you from that?

'No one.'

Say no more then, 'What is to happen?' For whatever happens, you will turn it to good purpose, and the issue will be your good fortune. What would Heracles have been if he had said, 'How am I to prevent a big lion from appearing, or a big boar, or brutal men?' What care you, I say? If a big boar appears, you will have a greater struggle to engage in; if evil men appear, you will free the world from evil men.

'But if I die thus?'

You will die a good man, fulfilling a noble action. For since you must die in any case, you must be found doing something–whatever it be– farming or digging or trading or holding the counsulship or suffering indigestion or diarrhoea. What then would you have death find you doing? For my part I would be found busy with some humane task, whatever it be–something noble, beneficent, advancing the common weal. And if I cannot be found doing great things like these, I would do what none can hinder, what is given me to do, setting myself right, bringing to perfection the faculty that deals with impressions, working to achieve freedom from passion, rendering what is due to each relation in life; nay, if I am so fortunate, attaining to the third sphere of activity, that concerned with certainty of judgements.

If death finds me thus occupied, I am content if I can lift up my hands to God and say, 'I have not neglected the faculties which I received from Thee, to enable me to understand Thy governance and follow it, I have not dishonoured Thee so far as in me lay. See how I have dealt with my senses, see how I have dealt with my primary notions. Did I ever complain of Thee, did I ever show discontent with anything that happened to any one, or wish it to happen otherwise, did I offend in my relations towards others? In that Thou didst beget me I am grateful for Thy gifts: in so far as I have used what Thou gayest me I am satisfied. Take Thy gifts back again and place them where Thou wilt: for they were all Thine, Thou hast given them to me.' Are you not content to leave the world in this state of mind? Nay, what life is better or more seemly than his who is so minded, and what end can be more happy?

But to achieve this, you must put up with great troubles and great losses. You cannot have this and wish to get a consulship, you cannot have this and set your heart on owning lands, you cannot take thought for yourself and for wretched slaves at the same time. No, if you wish for what is not your own, you lose what is yours. This is in the nature of things: nothing is done but at a price. And what need for wonder? If you wish to become consul, you must keep late hours, run to and fro, kiss people's hands, lie perishing at other men's doors, say and do many things unfit for a free man, send gifts to many, and presents every day to some. And what do you get for it? Twelve bundles of rods, the privilege of sitting three or four times on the tribunal and of giving games in the Circus, and doles in baskets. If it be not so, let any one show me what there is besides. Will you then spend nothing, and use no effort to secure release from passion and perturbation, that sleeping you may sleep and waking you may wake, that you may fear nothing and be anxious for nothing? But if while you are thus engaged you have losses or spend money amiss, or if another gets what you ought to have got, are you going to be vexed all at once at what happens? Will you not weigh what the exchange is and how precious your gain, instead of wishing to obtain this great prize for nothing? Nay, how can you? 'One business interferes with another.'

You cannot combine attention to outward possessions with attention to your own Governing Principle. If you want outward things, let your reason go, or you will have neither the one nor the other, being pulled both ways. If you wish for reason, you must let outward things go. The oil will be spilt, my poor furniture will perish, but I shall be free from passion. Say a fire shall arise when I am away and my books perish, yet I shall deal with my impressions in accord with nature.

'But I shall have nothing to eat.'

If I am so miserable, death is my harbour. Death: this is the harbour, this the refuge from all things, therefore nothing in life is difficult. When you wish, you leave, and no smoke annoys you. Why then are you anxious, why keep late hours? Why do you not reckon up at once where your good and your evil lie, and say, 'Both are in my power: no one can deprive me of my good, and no one can plunge me in evil against my will. Why then do I not snore at my ease? I am secure in what is mine: what is not mine will be the concern of any one who gets it as a gift from Him who has authority to give it. Who am I to will that what is not mine should be thus or thus? Is it given to me to choose? Has any one set me to administer it? I am content with the things over which I have authority. These I must make as beautiful as possible; the rest must be as their master wills.'

If a man has this before his eyes he is no longer wakeful, 'hither and thither tossed'. [Homer, *Iliad*, XXIV. 5] What would he have, or what does he long for? Does he long for Patroclus or Antilochus or Menelaus? When did he think any of his friends was immortal? When had he not before his eyes the fact that to-morrow or the day after he or his friend must die?

'Yes,' he says, 'but I thought he would outlive me and enrich my son.'

Yes, for you were a fool, and set your thoughts on uncertainties. Why not then accuse yourself, instead of sitting crying like young girls? 'Nay, but he set food for me to eat.'

Yes, fool, for he was alive: now he cannot. But Automedon will set meat for you, and if he dies you will find another. If the pot in which your meat was boiling is broken, must you needs die of hunger, because you have lost the pot you are used to? Do not you send and buy another?

'Nay,' he says,

'No worse ill could befall me.'
[Homer, *Iliad*, XIX. 321]

What! Is this what you call ill? And yet you forbear to remove it and blame your mother for not warning you, that you might spend your days lamenting ever since. What think you? Did not Homer compose these lines on purpose that we might see that there is nothing to prevent the noblest, the strongest, the richest, the most handsome, from being most wretched and most miserable when they have not the judgements they should have?

CHAPTER ELEVEN

On Cleanliness

S OME MEN RAISE THE question whether the social faculty is a necessary element in man's nature: nevertheless even they, I think, would
not question that cleanliness at any rate is essential to it, and that this,
if anything, divides him from the lower animals. So when we see one of
the other animals cleaning itself, we are wont to say in our surprise, 'He
does it like a man.' And again, if some one finds fault with an animal
for being dirty we are wont to say at once, as if in defence, 'Of course
he is not a man.' So true is it that we think the quality to be distinctive
of man, deriving it first from the gods. For since the gods are by nature
pure and unalloyed, just in so far as men have approached them by virtue of reason, they have a tendency to purity and cleanliness. But since
it is impossible for their nature to be entirely pure, being composed of
such stuff as it is, the reason which they have received endeavours, so
far as in it lies, to make this stuff clean.

The primary and fundamental purity is that of the soul, and so with
impurity. You cannot find the same impurity in a soul as in a body:
the soul's impurity you will find to be just this–that which renders it
unclean for its own functions; and the functions of a soul are: impulse
to act and not to act, will to get and will to avoid, preparation, design, assent. What is it then which renders the soul foul and unclean
in these functions? It is nothing but its evil judgements. And so the
soul's impurity consists in bad judgements, and purification consists
in producing in it right judgements, and the pure soul is one which
has right judgements, for this alone is proof against confusion and
pollution in its functions.

And one ought to endeavour, as far as may be, to achieve a simi-
lar cleanliness in one's body too. Man's temperament is such that there

must needs be mucous discharge: for this reason nature made hands, and the nostrils themselves like channels to cleanse his humours. If he swallows them I say that he does not act as a man should. It was impossible for men's feet not to be made muddy and dirty when they pass through mud and dirt; for this reason nature provided water and hands to wash with. It was impossible that some impurity should not stick to the teeth from eating. Therefore we are bidden to wash our teeth. Why? That you may be a man and not a beast or a pig. It was impossible that sweat and the pressure of our clothes should not leave some defilement clinging to the body, and needing to be cleansed. Therefore we have water, olive-oil, hands, towel, strigils, soap, and on occasion every other sort of apparatus, to make the body clean.

'Not for me', you say.

What! The smith will clean his iron tool of rust, and will have instruments made for the purpose, and even you will wash your plate when you are going to eat, unless you are absolutely foul and dirty, and yet you will not wash nor make clean your poor body? 'Why should I?' says he. I will tell you again: first, that you may act like a man, next, that you may not annoy those you meet. You are doing something very like it even here, though you are not aware of it. You think you deserve to have a scent of your own. Very well, deserve it: but do you think those who sit by you deserve it too, and those who recline by you, and those who kiss you? Go away then into a wilderness, where you deserve to go, and live by yourself, and have your smell to yourself, for it is right that you should enjoy your uncleanness by yourself. But if you are in a city, what sort of man are you making yourself, to behave so thoughtlessly and inconsiderately? If nature had trusted a horse to your care, would you have left it uncared for? Imagine that your body has been committed to you as a horse: wash it, rub it down well, make it such that no one will shun it or turn from it. But who does not turn from a man who is dirty, odorous, foul-complexioned, more than from one who is be-spattered with muck? The smell of the latter is external and accidental, that of the former comes from want of tendance; it is from within, and shows a sort of inward rottenness.

'But Socrates rarely washed.'

Why, his body was clean and bright, nay, it was so gracious and agreeable that the handsomest and noblest were in love with him, and desired to recline by him rather than by those who were perfect in beauty. He might have never washed or bathed, if he had liked: I tell you his ablutions, if rare, were powerful. If you will not wash in hot water, wash in cold.

But Aristophanes says:

I mean the pallid folk, that shoeless go.
[Aristophanes, Clouds]

True, but he also says he trod the air and stole clothes from the Gymnasium. The fact is, that all who have written about Socrates bear witness to just the opposite: he was not only pleasant to hear, but pleasant to look upon. They write the same again about Diogenes.

You must not scare away the masses from philosophy by your bodily appearance, but show yourself cheerful and unruffled in the body as in other things. 'Men, look at me, I have nothing, I need nothing; without house, without city, an exile, if it so chance, and without a hearth, behold how I live a life more tranquil and happy than all the noble and the rich: but you see also that my poor body is not disfigured by my hard living!' But if a man says this to me, and wears the face and figure of one condemned, no god will ever persuade me to come near philosophy, if that is the sort of men she makes. Far be it from me: though it were to make me wise, I would not.

By the gods, when the young man feels the first stirrings of philosophy I would rather he came to me with his hair sleek than dishevelled and dirty: for that shows a sort of reflection of the beautiful, and a longing for the comely, and where he imagines these to be, there he spends his effort. It only remains then to point him the way and say, 'Young man, you are in search of the beautiful, and you do well. Know then, that it is to be found where your reason is. Seek for it in the region of impulses to act and not to act, in the region of the will to get and the will to avoid. This is your distinctive possession, your body is born to be but clay. Why do you toil for it in vain? Time, if nothing else, will teach you that it is nothing.' But if he comes to me befouled, dirty, with a beard trailing to his knees, what can I say to him, what similitude can I use to attract him? To what is he devoted that has any likeness to the beautiful, that I may change his direction and say, 'The beautiful is not here, but here'? Would you have me say to him, 'The beautiful is to be found not in filthiness but in reason'? Does he want the beautiful? Does he show any sign of it? Go and reason with a pig, that he wallow no more in the mire! That was why Xenocrates' discourses laid hold on Polemo, for he was a young man of taste; he had come with glimmerings of devotion to the beautiful, though he sought it elsewhere.

Why, nature did not make even those lower animals dirty who associate with men. Does a horse or a well-bred dog wallow in mire? No, it is only the pig, and greasy geese, and worms and spiders, creatures the furthest removed from human society. Do you then, being a man, choose to be a wretched worm or spider, lower even than the animals that associate with men? Will you never wash, be it how you will? Will you not cleanse yourself? Will you not come clean among us that you may give pleasure to your companions? What! do you enter our temples, where custom forbids spitting or wiping the nose, in this condition, a man of filth and drivel?

'What?' you ask. 'Do you call on us to adorn ourselves?'

Far from it, if it be not with our natural adornment of reason, judgements, activities, and the body only so far as to be cleanly and give no offence. If you hear that you must not wear scarlet, must you needs go off and spread filth on your cloak, or tear it in half?

'But how am I to have a beautiful cloak?'

Man, you have water, wash it. Here is a young man worthy to be loved, here is an old man worthy to love and to be loved, one to whom a man is to hand over his son to be instructed: daughters and young men will come to him, if it so chance, and for what? That he may discourse to them on a dunghill? God forbid. All eccentricity springs from some human source, but this comes near to being inhuman altogether.

CHAPTER TWELVE

On Attention

WHEN YOU RELAX YOUR attention for a little, do not imagine that you will recover it wherever you wish, but bear this well in mind, that your error of to-day must of necessity put you in a worse position for other occasions. For in the first place–and this is the most serious thing–a habit of inattention is formed, and next a habit of deferring attention: and you get into the way of putting off from one time to another the tranquil and becoming life, the state and behaviour which nature prescribes. Now if such postponement of attention is profitable, it would be still more profitable to abandon it altogether: but if it is not profitable, why do you not keep up your attention continuously?

'I want to play to-day.'

What prevents you, if you attend?

'I want to sing.'

What prevents you, if you attend? Is any part of life excluded, on which attention has no bearing, any that you will make worse by attention, and better by inattention? Nay, is there anything in life generally which is done better by those who do not attend? Does the carpenter by inattention do his work better? Does the helmsman by inattention steer more safely? and is any of the minor duties of life fulfilled better by inattention? Do you not realize, that when once you have let your mind go wandering, you lose the power to recall it, to bring it to bear on what is seemly, self-respecting, and modest: you do anything that occurs to you and follow your inclinations?

To what then must I attend? First to those universal principles I have spoken of: these you must keep at command, and without them neither sleep nor rise, drink nor eat nor deal with men: the principle that no one can control another's will, and that the will alone is the sphere of good and evil. No one then has power to procure me good or to involve me in evil, but I myself alone have authority over myself in these matters. So, when I have made these secure, what need have I to be disturbed about outward things? What need have I to fear tyrant, or disease, or poverty, or disaster?

'But I do not please So-and-so.'

Well, is he my doing? Is he my judgement?

'No.'

What concern is it of mine then?

'Nay, but he is highly thought of.'

That will be for him to consider, and for those who think much of him: I have One Whom I must please, One to Whom I must submit myself and obey–God and those who come next to God. He commended me to myself, and made my will subject to me alone, and gave me rules for the right use of it; and if I follow these in syllogisms I pay no heed to any one who contradicts me, if I follow them in dealing with variable premisses I pay regard to no one. Why then am I annoyed by those who criticize me in greater matters? What is the reason for this perturbation? It is none other than that I have had no training in this sphere. For every science is entitled to despise ignorance and the ignorant, and this is true of arts as well as of sciences. Take any shoemaker, any carpenter you like, and you find he laughs the multitude to scorn when his own craft is in question.

First then we must have these principles ready to our hand. Without them we must do nothing. We must set our mind on this object: pursue nothing that is outside us, nothing that is not our own, even as He that is mighty has ordained: pursuing what lies within our will, and all else only so far as it is given us to do so. Further, we must remember who we are, and by what name we are called, and must try to direct our acts to fit each situation and its possibilities.

We must consider what is the time for singing, what the time for play, and in whose presence: what will be unsuited to the occasion; whether our companions are to despise us, or we to despise ourselves: when to jest, and whom to mock at: and on what occasion to be conciliatory and to whom: in a word, how one ought to maintain one's character in society. Wherever you swerve from any of these principles, you suffer loss at once; not loss from without, but issuing from the very act itself.

What then? Is it possible to escape error altogether? No, it is impossible: but it is possible to set one's mind continuously on avoiding error. For it is well worth while to persist in this endeavour, if in the end we escape a few errors, and no more. As it is, you say, 'I will fix my attention to-morrow': which means, let me tell you, 'To-day I will be shameless, inopportune, abject: others shall have power to vex me: to-day I will harbour anger and envy.' Look what evils you allow yourself. Nay, if it is well to fix my attention to-morrow, how much better to do so to-day! If it is profitable to-morrow, much more so is it to-day: that you may be able to do the same to-morrow, and not put off again to the day after.

CHAPTER THIRTEEN

To those who Lightly Communicate their Secrets

WHEN A MAN SEEMS to have talked frankly to us about his own affairs,. how we are drawn to communicate our own secrets to him and think this is frankness! First because it seems unfair to have heard our neighbour's affairs and yet not give him a share of our own in turn: next because we think we shall not give the impression of being frank if we are silent about our own affairs. In fact we often find men in the habit of saying, 'I've told you all my affairs, won't you tell me any of yours? How it that?' Besides we think we may safely confide in one who has already confided his affairs to us: for we have a sort of feeling that he would never talk of our affairs for fear that we should talk of his. This is exactly the way in which reckless persons are caught by soldiers in Rome. A soldier sits by you in civilian dress, and begins to speak ill of the Emperor: then, as you have, so to speak, taken security from him for his good faith in the fact that he began the abuse, you are led to speak your own mind and so are arrested and imprisoned. The same sort of thing happens to us in ordinary life. Still, though he has confided his affairs to me with security, am I to do the same to the first man I meet? No, I hear and hold my tongue, if I am that sort of man, but he goes off and tells every one. Then, if I hear what he has done, if I am like him, I go and tell his secrets, because I want to have my revenge, and so I bring confusion to others and myself. But if I bear in mind, that one man does not harm another, but that it is his own acts which help or harm a man, I achieve this conquest–that I abstain from doing the same as he did, but still my own babbling has put me in the position I am in.

'Yes,' you say; 'but it is unfair to hear your neighbour's secrets, and give him no share of your own in return.'

Man, did I invite your confidences? Did you tell me your secrets on conditions, that you might hear mine in return? If you are a babbler and think every one you meet is a friend, do you want me to be like yourself? What! if you have done well to confide in me, but it is not possible to confide in you and do well, do you still want me to unbosom myself? That is just as though I had a sound cask and you an unsound one, and you came and handed over your wine to me to put it into my cask, and then were vexed that I did not trust my wine to you, because your cask had a hole in it.

What becomes of your equality now? You trusted to one who is trustworthy, self-respecting, who believes that good and harm depend on his own activities and on nothing outside: would you have me confide in you, you who have made light of your own will and want to get pelf or office or advancement at court, even at the cost of slaying your children like Medea? Where is the equality in that?

No, show yourself to me as one who is trustworthy, self-respecting, safe, show that your judgements are those of a friend, show that your vessel is not unsound, and then you will see that I will not wait for you to confide your affairs to me, but will come to you myself and ask you to hear mine. For who is there that will not use a goodly vessel, who that despises a loyal and faithful counsellor, who that will not gladly welcome one who is ready to share the burden of his distresses and to relieve him by the very fact of sharing in them?

'Yes; but I trust you, and you do not trust me.'

In the first place you do not trust me; you are only garrulous and therefore cannot keep anything back. For if what you say is true, trust your secrets to me and no one else: instead of which, whenever you see any one at leisure, you sit down by him and say, 'My brother, you are the dearest friend I have; I beg you to listen to my story'. And you do this to those you have not known even for a short while. If you really trust me, you trust me, of course, because I am trustworthy and self-respecting, not because I told you my secrets. Let me too then be allowed to think as you do. Prove to me that if a man tells his secrets to another, he is therefore trustworthy and self-respecting. If that were so, I should have gone about the world telling every man my affairs, if that were going to make me trustworthy and self-respecting. It is not really so. No, to be trustworthy a man needs judgements beyond the ordinary. If you see that a man is devoted to things outside his own will and has made his will subject to these, be sure that he has countless persons who hinder and constrain him. He has no need of a pitch-plaster or a rack to make him reveal what he knows, but the nod of a pretty maid, if it so chance, will shake his principles, a kindness from one of Caesar's officers, a lust for office or inheritance, and countless other motives such as these. You must therefore remember generally, that confidences require trust and trustworthy principles: and where can you easily find these nowadays? Let me be shown a man who is so minded as to say, 'I have no concern except with what is my own, with what is beyond hindrance and by nature free. This is the true good, and it is mine: all else I leave to the Giver of events to decide, and raise no question.'

Fragments[1]

FROM ARRIAN THE PUPIL OF EPICTETUS. TO ONE

DISCOURSING ON SUBSTANCE

WHAT MATTERS IT WHETHER the world is composed of atoms or of infinite parts or of fire and earth? Is it not enough to know the true nature of good and evil, and the limits of the will to get and the will to avoid, and again of impulses for action and against it, and using these as rules so to order our life, and dismiss those things that are beyond us. It may be that the human mind cannot comprehend them, and even if one should assume that it can, of what use is it to comprehend them? Should we not say that those who lay down that these things are necessary for the philosopher trouble themselves in vain? Is then the command at Delphi also superfluous: 'Know thyself'?

'No,' he replies.

What then is its meaning? If one ordered a chorus-singer to know himself, would he not attend to the order by paying heed to his fellows in the chorus so as to sing in harmony with them?

---

1   Most of these fragments come from two selections from Greek writers, made by Stobaeus, John of Stobi in Macedonia (sixth century A.D.). Those marked Ecl. are from his Eclogues, and those marked Flor. from his Anthology. Fragments 9 and 10 are from the Noctes Atticae of Aulus Gellius, a Latin grammarian of the second century A.D.; 26, 27, 28 from the Meditations of the Emperor Marcus Aurelius Antoninus; 10a from the Against the Heathen of Arnobius, an African Latin writer (ca. A.D. 300); 36 from Antonius Melissa ('The Bee'), a Greek monk of uncertain date. The reference to Musonius Rufus in the headings of 4-8 is not clear; the natural meaning would be that they are sayings of Rufus, incorporated by Epictetus in his discourses on Friendship.' (Matheson)

'Yes.'

And the same with a sailor and a soldier. Do you think then that man is a creature made to live by himself or for society?

'For society.'

By whom?

'By Nature.'

What Nature is and how it administers the universe and whether it is or no–these are matters it is not necessary to trouble ourselves with. Stob. *Flor.* 80. 14; *Ecl.* ii. 1. 18a.

2

FROM ARRIAN

HE WHO IS DISCONTENTED with what he has and with what is given him by fortune is an ignoramus in life, and he who bears it in a noble spirit and makes reasonable use of it deserves to be considered a good man. *Flor.* 108. 65.

3

FROM THE SAME

ALL THINGS OBEY AND serve the Universe[2] –earth and sea and sun and the other stars and the plants and animals of the earth; and our body too obeys it, enjoying sickness or health, and passing through youth and old age and other changes when the Universe wills. Is it not reasonable then that what is in our power, that is our judgement, should not be the only thing to strive against it? For the Universe is strong and superior to us and has provided for us better than we can, ordering our goings along with all things. And, besides, to act against it is to side with unreason, and brings nothing with it but vain struggle, involving us in miseries and pains. *Flor.* 108. 66.

2   The ordered universe, which is sometimes identified with its Creator, God.' (Matheson)

4

RUFUS: FROM THE SAYINGS OF EPICTETUS ON

FRIENDSHIP

GOD HAS DIVIDED ALL things into those that He put in our power, and those that are not in our power. He put in our power that which is noblest and highest, that which in fact constitutes His own happiness, the power to deal with impressions. For this faculty when rightly exercised is freedom, peace, courage, steadfastness, and this too is justice and law and self-control and all virtue. All else He put beyond our power. We ought then to will what God wills and, adopting His division, hold fast by all means to what is in our power and leave what is not in our power to the world's order, and gladly resign to it children, or country, or body, or anything else it may ask of us. *Ecl.* ii. 7. 30.

5

RUFUS: FROM EPICTETUS ON FRIENDSHIP

WHICH OF US DOES not admire that saying of Lycurgus the Lacedaemonian? For when one of his young fellow citizens had blinded him in one eye and was handed over to Lycurgus by the people to be punished as he chose, he did not punish him but educated him and made a good man of him, and brought him before the Lacedaemonians in the theatre, and when they wondered he said, 'This man, when you gave him me, was insolent and violent; I give him back to you a free and reasonable citizen'. *Flor.* 19. 13.

6

FROM THE SAME

BUT THIS ABOVE ALL things is the function of Nature, to associate in close harmony the impulse that springs from the impression of what is fitting and that which springs from the impression of what is serviceable. *Flor,* 20. 60.

7

FROM THE SAME

It is a sure work of folly and want of breeding to think that we shall be contemptible if we do not take every means to injure the first enemies we meet; for we say that a man is perceived to be contemptible by his incapacity of doing harm, whereas really it is much more by his incapacity to do good. *Flor.* 20. 61.

8

RUFUS: FROM EPICTETUS ON FRIENDSHIP

Such was and is and shall be the nature of the universe, and it is impossible that what happens should be other than it is. And this process of revolution and change is shared not only by mankind and the other living creatures upon earth, but also by things divine; yes, and even by the four elements themselves, which turn and change upwards and downwards, earth turning into water and water into air, and this again into ether; and similarly the elements change from above downwards. If a man endeavours to adjust his mind to this and to persuade himself to accept necessity with a good will, he will live out his life very reasonably and harmoniously. *Flor.* 108. 60.

9

FROM THE SAME

A philosopher famous in the Stoic school . . . brought out of his satchel the fifth book of Epictetus the philosopher's Discourses, which were arranged by Arrian, and no doubt are in agreement with the writings of Zeno and Chrysippus. In this book, written of course in Greek, we read this sentence: 'Impressions (which philosophers call φαντασίαι), by which man's mind is struck at first sight of anything that reaches his intellect, are not under his will or control, but thrust themselves on the recognition of men by a certain force of their own; but the assents (which they call συγκαταθέσεις) by which these impressions are recognized are voluntary and depend on man's control.

Therefore when some fearful sound of thunder or a falling house or sudden news of some danger or other, or something else of this sort happens, even the wise man is bound to be moved for a while and shrink and grow pale, not from anticipation of any evil, but from rapid and unconsidered movements forestalling the action of the rational mind. Presently, however, the wise man does not assent to such impressions (that is, these appearances which terrify his mind), he does not approve or confirm them by his opinion, but rejects and repels them and does not think that there is anything formidable in them; and this they say is the difference between the wise man and the fool, that the fool thinks that the impressions which at first strike him as harsh and cruel are really such, and as they go on approves them with his own assent and confirms them by his opinion as if they were really formidable (προσεπιδοξάζει is the phrase the Stoics use in discussing this), while the wise man, after showing emotion in colour and complexion for a brief moment, does not give his assent, but keeps the opinions which he has always held about such impressions, firm and strong, as of things which do not really deserve to be feared at all, but only inspire an empty and fictitious terror.'

These opinions and words of Epictetus the philosopher, derived from the judgements of the Stoics, we read, in the book I have mentioned, that he held and expressed. Aul. Gell. *N. A.* 19. I.

10

I HAVE HEARD FAVORINUS say that Epictetus the philosopher said that most of those who seemed to philosophize were philosophers only with their lips and without action. There is a still stronger saying which Arrian in the books that he composed on his lectures has recorded that he constantly used. For, said he, when he noticed a man lost to shame, of misdirected energy and debased morals, bold and confident in speech and devoting attention to all else but his soul, when he saw a man of this sort meddling with the pursuits and studies of philosophy, venturing into Physics and studying Dialectic, and initiating many inquiries of this sort, he would appeal to gods and men, and so appealing would chide the man in these words: 'Man, where are you putting them? Look and see whether your vessel is made clean. For if you put them into the vessel of fancy (οἴησις) they are lost; if they turn bad, they might as well be vinegar or urine or worse.' Nothing surely could be truer or weightier than these words, in which the greatest of philosophers asserted that the written doctrines of philosophy, if poured into the dirty and defiled vessel of a false and debased mind, are altered, changed and spoilt, and (to use his Cynic phrase) turn to urine or anything fouler than that. Moreover Epictetus also, as we heard from the same Favorinus, used to say that there were two faults far more serious and vile than any others, want of endurance and want of self-control, the failure to bear and endure the wrongs we have to bear, and the failure to forbear the pleasures and other things that we ought to forbear. And so, he said, if a man should take to heart these two words, and watch and command himself to keep them, he will be free for the most part from error and will live a most peaceful life. And the words he said were these two: 'Bear' and 'Forbear'. Aul. Gell. *N. A.* 17. 19.

10A

WHEN THE SAFETY OF our souls and regard for our true selves is in question, one may have to act at times without reason: this is a saying of Epictetus quoted with approval by Arrian. Arnobius, *Against the Heathen*, 2. 78.

11

FROM THE DISCOURSES OF ARRIAN, EXHORTING

TO VIRTUE

BUT WHEN ARCHELAUS SENT for Socrates and said he would make him rich, he bade the messenger take back word to him, 'At Athens one can buy four quarts of barleymeal for an obol, and there are running springs of water'. For if what I have is not sufficient for me, yet I am sufficient for it, and so it is sufficient for me. Do you not see that Polus did not act Oedipus the king in better voice or with greater pleasure than he acted Oedipus the poor beggar at Colonus? What! is the good man and true to show himself inferior to Polus, instead of playing any part well that Providence puts upon him? Will he not rather make Odysseus his pattern, who was just as remarkable in his rags as in his rich cloak of purple? *Flor.* 97. 28.

1 2

FROM ARRIAN

THERE ARE CERTAIN PERSONS who indulge their anger gently, and who do all that the most passionate do, but in a quiet passionless way. Now we must guard against their error as a much worse fault than passionate anger. For the passionate are soon sated with their revenge, but the colder spirits persist for a long period like men who take a fever lightly. *Flor.* 20. 48.

1 3

FROM THE MEMORABILIA OF EPICTETUS

'BUT', ONE SAYS, 'I see the noble and good perishing of hunger and cold.' Well, and do you not see those who are not noble and good perishing of luxury and ostentation and vulgarity?

'Yes; but it is base to be maintained by another.'

Miserable man, is there any one that maintains himself? Only the Universe does that. The man who accuses Providence because the wicked are not punished, but are strong and rich, is acting just as absurdly as if, when they had lost their eyes, he said that they had not been punished, because their nails were sound. For my part I hold that there is a much greater difference between virtue and vice than between eyes and nails. *Ecl.* i. 3. 50.

1 4

FROM THE MEMORABILIA OF EPICTETUS

... BRINGING FORWARD THE peevish philosophers, who hold that pleasure is not natural, but accompanies things which are natural–justice, self-control, freedom. Why then does the soul take a calm delight, as Epicurus says, in the lesser goods, those of the body, and does not take pleasure in her own good things, which are the greatest? I tell you that nature has given me a sense of self-respect, and I often blush when I think I am saying something shameful. It is this emotion which prevents me from regarding pleasure as a good thing and as the end of life. *Flor.* 6. 50.

15

FROM THE SAME

In Rome women make a study of Plato's Republic, because he enacts community of wives; for they only attend to the man's words and not to his spirit, not noticing that he does not first enact the marriage of one man and one woman and then wish wives to be common, but removes the first kind of marriage and introduces another kind in its place. And in general men are fond of finding justifications for their own faults; for philosophy says that one ought not even *to hold out one's finger at random*. *Flor.* 6. 58.

16

FROM THE MEMORABILIA OF EPICTETUS

You must know that it is not easy for a man to arrive at a judgement, unless he should state and hear the same principles every day and apply them all the time to his life. *Flor.* 29. 84.

17

FROM EPICTETUS

When we are invited to a drinking-party we enjoy what is before us, and if one should bid his entertainer to serve him fish or cakes one would be thought eccentric. Yet in the world we ask the gods for what they do not give us, and that although there are many gifts which they have given us. *Flor.* 4. 92.

18

FROM THE SAME

Fine fellows, he said, are they who pride themselves on those things which are beyond our control. 'I am better than you,' says one, 'for I have abundance of lands, and you are prostrate with hunger.' Another says, 'I am a consular'; another, 'I am a procurator'; another, 'I have curly hair.'

A horse does not say to a horse, 'I am better than you, for I have plenty of fodder and plenty of barley, and I have bridles of gold and saddles of inlaid work', but 'for I am swifter than you'. And every creature is better or worse according as its own virtue or vice makes it so. Is man then the only creature that has no virtue of his own, that we should have to look at his hair and his clothes and his ancestors? *Flor.* 4. 93.

19

SICK MEN ARE ANGRY with their physician when he gives them no advice, and think that he has given them up. Why should one not adopt the same attitude to the philosopher and conclude that he has given up hope of one's wisdom, if he tells one nothing that is of use? *Flor.* 4. 94.

20

FROM EPICTETUS

THOSE WHOSE BODIES ARE in good condition can endure heat and cold; so those whose souls are in good condition can bear anger and pain and exultation and other emotions. *Flor.* 4. 95.

21

FROM THE SAME

IT IS RIGHT TO praise Agrippinus for this reason, that having shown himself a man of the highest worth, he never praised himself, but blushed if any one else praised him. His character was such that when any distress befell him he wrote a eulogy of it; if fever was his portion he praised fever; if disrepute, he praised disrepute; and if exile, he praised exile. And one day, when he was about to breakfast, a messenger interrupted him to say that Nero ordered him into exile. 'Well then,' said he, 'we will breakfast at Aricia.' *Flor.* 7. 17.

22

FROM AGRIPPINUS

Agrippinus, when governor, tried to convince those whom he sentenced that it was proper for them to be sentenced. 'It is not as their enemy', he said, 'or as a robber that I give sentence against them, but as their guardian and kinsman, just as the physician encourages the man on whom he is operating and persuades him to submit his body.' *Flor.* 48. 44.

23

FROM EPICTETUS

Wondrous is Nature, and 'fond of her creatures', as Xenophon says. At any rate, we love and tend the body, the least agreeable and most vile of all things! For if we had to tend our neighbour's body for ten days only we could not bear it. Consider what it would be to get up in the morning and clean some one else's teeth, and then to perform some other necessary office for him. Truly it is wondrous that we should love that for which we do such mean services day by day. I stuff this bag; then I empty it; what could be more tiresome? But I am bound to serve God. That is why I stay here and put up with washing this miserable body of mine, and giving it fodder and shelter; and when I was younger, it laid other commands on me as well, and yet I bore with it. Why then, when Nature, who gave you your body, takes it away, can you not bear it? 'I love it', he says. Well, but is it not Nature, as I said just now, that has given you this very love of it? And yet Nature too says, 'Let it go now, and trouble no more'. *Flor.* 121. 29.

24

FROM THE SAME

If a man dies young he accuses the gods, and an old man sometimes accuses them because he still is put to trouble when the time for rest has fully come, and yet, when death comes near, he is fain to live and sends to his doctor and bids him spare no pains or effort. Wondrous, he said, are men, for they are unwilling to live or to die. *Flor.* 121. 30.

25

FROM THE SAME

WHEN YOU ATTACK A man with threats and show of violence, remember to warn yourself that you are not a wild beast; then you will do nothing savage, and will live your life through without having to repent or be called to account. *Flor.* 20. 67.

26

YOU ARE A LITTLE soul, carrying a corpse, as Epictetus used to say. M. Aurelius, iv. 41.

27

EPICTETUS SAID THAT WE must discover the art of assent, and use careful attention in the sphere of the will; our impulses must be 'with qualification', and social and according to desert: we must abstain altogether from the will to get, and not attempt to avoid any of those things that are not in our power. M. Aurelius, xi. 37.

28

IT IS NO ORDINARY matter that is at stake, he said; the question is between sanity and madness. M. Aurelius, xi. 38.

29 [3]

ALWAYS TAKE THOUGHT FOR nothing so much as what is safe; silence is safer than speech; refrain from saying what shall be void of sense and open to blame. *Flor.* 35. 10.

---

3   The genuineness of the remaining fragments has been suspected.

30

We must not fasten our ship to one small anchor nor our life to one hope. *Flor.* 110. 22.

31

We must not stretch our hopes too wide, any more than our stride. *Flor.* 110. 23.

32

It is more needful to heal soul than body; for death is better than living ill. *Flor.* 121. 27.

33

The rarest pleasures give most delight. *Flor.* 6. 59

34

If a man should go beyond the mean, the most joyous things would turn to utter joylessness. *Flor.* 6. 60.

35

No one is free that is not his own master. *Flor.* 6. 59.

36

Truth is a thing immortal and eternal; it gives us not a beauty that fades with time; nor does it take away the confident speech that is based on justice, but confirms things just and lawful, distinguishing things unjust from them and showing their falsehood. Antonius, i. 21.

The Manual [Enchiridion] of Epictetus[4]

1

OF ALL EXISTING THINGS some are in our power, and others are not in our power. In our power are thought, impulse, will to get and will to avoid, and, in a word, everything which is our own doing. Things not in our power include the body, property, reputation, office, and, in a word, everything which is not our own doing. Things in our power are by nature free, unhindered, untrammelled; things not in our power are weak, servile, subject to hindrance, dependent on others. Remember then that if you imagine that what is naturally slavish is free, and what is naturally another's is your own, you will be hampered, you will mourn, you will be put to confusion, you will blame gods and men; but if you think that only your own belongs to you, and that what is another's is indeed another's, no one will ever put compulsion or hindrance on you, you will blame none, you will accuse none, you will do nothing against your will, no one will harm you, you will have no enemy, for no harm can touch you.

Aiming then at these high matters, you must remember that to attain them requires more than ordinary effort; you will have to give up some things entirely, and put off others for the moment. And if you would have these also–office and wealth–it may be that you will fail to get them, just because your desire is set on the former, and you will certainly fail to attain those things which alone bring freedom and happiness.

---

4   This 'hand-book' of Epictetus' principles was probably compiled by Arrian, and contains an excellent summary of the master's thought.

Make it your study then to confront every harsh impression with the words, 'You are but an impression, and not at all what you seem to be'. Then test it by those rules that you possess; and first by this–the chief test of all–'Is it concerned with what is in our power or with what is not in our power?' And if it is concerned with what is not in our power, be ready with the answer that it is nothing to you.

2

REMEMBER THAT THE WILL to get promises attainment of what you will, and the will to avoid promises escape from what you avoid; and he who fails to get what he wills is unfortunate, and he who does not escape what he wills to avoid is miserable. If then you try to avoid only what is unnatural in the region within your control, you will escape from all that you avoid; but if you try to avoid disease or death or poverty you will be miserable.

Therefore let your will to avoid have no concern with what is not in man's power; direct it only to things in man's power that are contrary to nature. But for the moment you must utterly remove the will to get; for if you will to get something not in man's power you are bound to be unfortunate; while none of the things in man's power that you could honourably will to get is yet within your reach. Impulse to act and not to act, these are your concern; yet exercise them gently and without strain, and provisionally.

3

WHEN ANYTHING, FROM the meanest thing upwards, is attractive or serviceable or an object of affection, remember always to say to yourself, 'What is its nature?' If you are fond of a jug, say you are fond of a jug; then you will not be disturbed if it be broken. If you kiss your child or your wife, say to yourself that you are kissing a human being, for then if death strikes it you will not be disturbed.

4

WHEN YOU ARE ABOUT to take something in hand, remind yourself what manner of thing it is. If you are going to bathe put before your mind what happens in the bath–water pouring over some, others being jostled,. some reviling, others stealing; and you will set to work more securely if you say to yourself at once: 'I want to bathe, and I want to keep my will in harmony with nature,' and so in each thing you do; for in this way, if anything turns up to hinder you in your bathing, you will be ready to say, 'I did not want only to bathe, but to keep my will in harmony with nature, and I shall not so keep it, if I lose my temper at what happens'.

5

WHAT DISTURBS MEN'S MINDS is not events but their judgements on events: For instance, death is nothing dreadful, or else Socrates would have thought it so. No, the only dreadful thing about it is men's judgement that it is dreadful. And so when we are hindered, or disturbed, or distressed, let us never lay the blame on others, but on ourselves, that is, on our own judgements. To accuse others for one's own misfortunes is a sign of want of education; to accuse oneself shows that one's education has begun; to accuse neither oneself nor others shows that one's education is complete.

6

BE NOT ELATED AT an excellence which is not your own. If the horse in his pride were to say, 'I am handsome', we could bear with it. But when you say with pride, 'I have a handsome horse', know that the good horse is the ground of your pride. You ask then what you can call your own. The answer is–the way you deal with your impressions. Therefore when you deal with your impressions in accord with nature, then you may be proud indeed, for your pride will be in a good which is your own.

7

WHEN YOU ARE ON a voyage, and your ship is at anchorage, and you disembark to get fresh water, you may pick up a small shellfish or a truffle by the way, but you must keep your attention fixed on the ship, and keep looking towards it constantly, to see if the Helmsman calls you; and if he does, you have to leave everything, or be bundled on board with your legs tied like a sheep. So it is in life. If you have a dear wife or child given you, they are like the shellfish or the truffle, they are very well in their way. Only, if the Helmsman call, run back to your ship, leave all else, and do not look behind you. And if you are old, never go far from the ship, so that when you are called you may not fail to appear.

8

ASK NOT THAT EVENTS should happen as you will, but let your will be that events should happen as they do, and you shall have peace.

9

SICKNESS IS A HINDRANCE to the body, but not to the will, unless the will consent. Lameness is a hindrance to the leg, but not to the will. Say this to yourself at each event that happens, for you shall find that though it hinders something else it will not hinder you.

10

WHEN ANYTHING HAPPENS TO you, always remember to turn to yourself and ask what faculty you have to deal with it. If you see a beautiful boy or a beautiful woman, you will find continence the faculty to exercise there; if trouble is laid on you, you will find endurance; if ribaldry, you will find patience. And if you train yourself in this habit your impressions will not carry you away.

11

NEVER SAY OF ANYTHING, 'I lost it', but say, 'I gave it back'. Has your child died? It was given back. Has your wife died? She was given back. Has your estate been taken from you? Was not this also given back? But you say, 'He who took it from me is wicked'. What does it matter to you through whom the Giver asked it back? As long as He gives it you, take care of it, but not as your own; treat it as passers-by treat an inn.

12

IF YOU WISH TO make progress, abandon reasonings of this sort: 'If I neglect my affairs I shall have nothing to live on'; 'If I do not punish my son, he will be wicked.' For it is better to die of hunger, so that you be free from pain and free from fear, than to live in plenty and be troubled in mind. It is better for your son to be wicked than for you to be miserable.[5] Wherefore begin with little things. Is your drop of oil spilt? Is your sup of wine stolen? Say to yourself, 'This is the price paid for freedom from passion, this is the price of a quiet mind.' Nothing can be had without a price. When you call your slave-boy, reflect that he may not be able to hear you, and if he hears you, he may not be able to do anything you want. But he is not so well off that it rests with him to give you peace of mind.

13

IF YOU WISH TO make progress, you must be content in external matters to seem a fool and a simpleton; do not wish men to think you know anything, and if any should think you to be somebody, distrust yourself. For know that it is not easy to keep your will in accord with nature and at the same time keep outward things; if you attend to one you must needs neglect the other.

14

IT IS SILLY TO want your children and your wife and your friends to live for ever, for that means that you want what is not in your control to be in your control, and what is not your own to be yours. In the same way if you want your servant to make no mistakes, you are a fool, for you want vice not to be vice but something different. But if you want not to be disappointed in your will to get, you can attain to that.

Exercise yourself then in what lies in your power. Each man's master is the man who has authority over what he wishes or does not wish, to secure the one or to take away the other. Let him then who wishes to be

5   Matheson's translation of παῖδα as 'son' here and at the beginning of chapter 12 can hardly be correct. Throughout the whole section it should be rendered as 'slave-boy'. The reading 'son' imposes unnecessarily upon Stoicism a brutality and lack of normal human sympathy and affection which it can ill afford to carry.

free not wish for anything or avoid anything that depends on others; or else he is bound to be a slave.

15

REMEMBER THAT YOU MUST behave in life as you would at a banquet. A dish is handed round and comes to you; put out your hand and take it politely. It passes you; do not stop it. It has not reached you; do not be impatient to get it, but wait till your turn comes. Bear yourself thus towards children, wife, office, wealth, and one day you will be worthy to banquet with the gods. But if when they are set before you, you do not take them but despise them, then you shall not only share the gods' banquet, but shall share their rule. For by so doing Diogenes and Heraclitus and men like them were called divine and deserved the name.

16

WHEN YOU SEE A man shedding tears in sorrow for a child abroad or dead, or for loss of property, beware that you are not carried away by the impression that it is outward ills that make him miserable. Keep this thought by you: 'What distresses him is not the event, for that does not distress another, but his judgement on the event.' Therefore do not hesitate to sympathize with him so far as words go, and if it so chance, even to groan with him; but take heed that you do not also groan in your inner being.

17

REMEMBER THAT YOU ARE an actor in a play, and the Playwright chooses the manner of it: if he wants it short, it is short; if long, it is long. If he wants you to act a poor man you must act the part with all your powers; and so if your part be a cripple or a magistrate or a plain man. For your business is to act the character that is given you and act it well; the choice of the cast is Another's.

18

WHEN A RAVEN CROAKS with evil omen, let not the impression carry you away, but straightway distinguish in your own mind and say, 'These portents mean nothing to me; but only to my bit of a body or my bit of property or name, or my children or my wife. But for me all omens are favourable if I will, for, whatever the issue may be, it is in my power to pt benefit therefrom.'

19

YOU CAN BE INVINCIBLE, if you never enter on a contest where victory is not in your power. Beware then that when you see a man raised to honour or great power or high repute you do not let your impression carry you away. For if the reality of good lies in what is in our power, there is no room for envy or jealousy. And you will not wish to be praetor, or prefect or consul, but to be free; and there is but one way to freedom–to despise what is not in our power.

20

REMEMBER THAT FOUL WORDS or blows in themselves are no outrage, but your judgement that they are so. So when any one makes you angry, know that it is your own thought that has angered you. Wherefore make it your first endeavour not to let your impressions carry you away. For if once you gain time and delay, you will find it easier to control yourself.

21

KEEP BEFORE YOUR EYES from day to day death and exile and all things that seem terrible, but death most of all, and then you will never set your thoughts on what is low and will never desire anything beyond measure.

2 2

IF YOU SET YOUR desire on philosophy you must at once prepare to meet with ridicule and the jeers of many who will say, 'Here he is again, turned philosopher. Where has he got these proud looks?' Nay, put on no proud looks, but hold fast to what seems best to you, in confidence that God has set you at this post. And remember that if you abide where you are, those who first laugh at you will one day admire you, and that if you give way to them, you will get doubly laughed at.

2 3

IF IT EVER HAPPEN to you to be diverted to things outside, so that you desire to please another, know that you have lost your life's plan. Be content then always to be a philosopher; if you wish to be regarded as one too, show yourself that you are one and you will be able to achieve it.

2 4

LET NOT REFLECTIONS SUCH as these afflict you: 'I shall live without honour, and never be of any account'; for if lack of honour is an evil, no one but yourself can involve you in evil any more than in shame. Is it your business to get office or to be invited to an entertainment?

Certainly not.

Where then is the dishonour you talk of? How can you be 'of no account anywhere', when you ought to count for something in those matters only which are in your power, where you may achieve the highest worth? 'But my friends,' you say, 'will lack assistance.'

What do you mean by 'lack assistance'? They will not have cash from you and you will not make them Roman citizens. Who told you that to do these things is in our power, and not dependent upon others? Who can give to another what is not his to give?

'Get them then,' says he, 'that we may have them.'

If I can get them and keep my self-respect, honour, magnanimity, show the way and I will get them. But if you call on me to lose the good things that are mine, in order that you may win things that are not good, look how unfair and thoughtless you are. And which do you really prefer? Money, or a faithful, modest friend? Therefore help me rather to keep these qualities, and do not expect from me actions which will make me lose them.

'But my country,' says he, 'will lack assistance, so far as lies in me.'

Once more I ask, What assistance do you mean? It will not owe colonnades or baths to you. What of that? It does not owe shoes to the blacksmith or arms to the shoemaker; it is sufficient if each man fulfils his own function. Would you do it no good if you secured to it another faithful and modest citizen?

'Yes.'

Well, then, you would not be useless to it.

'What place then shall I have in the city?'

Whatever place you can hold while you keep your character for honour and self-respect. But if you are going to lose these qualities in trying to benefit your city, what benefit, I ask, would you have done her when you attain to the perfection of being lost to shame and honour?

25

HAS SOME ONE HAD precedence of you at an entertainment or a levée or been called in before you to give advice? If these things are good you ought to be glad that he got them; if they are evil, do not be angry that you did not get them yourself. Remember that if you want to get what is not in your power, you cannot earn the same reward as others unless you act as they do. How is it possible for one who does not haunt the great man's door to have equal shares with one who does, or one who does not go in his train equality with one who does; or one who does not praise him with one who does? You will be unjust then and insatiable if you wish to get these privileges for nothing, without paying their price. What is the price of a lettuce? An obol perhaps. If then a man pays his obol and gets his lettuces, and you do not pay and do not get them, do not think you are defrauded. For as he has the lettuces so you have the obol you did not give. The same principle holds good too in conduct. You were not invited to some one's entertainment? Because you did not give the host the price for which he sells his dinner. He sells it for compliments, he sells it for attentions. Pay him the price then, if it is to your profit. But if you wish to get the one and yet not give up the other, nothing can satisfy you in your folly.

What! you say, you have nothing instead of the dinner?

Nay, you have this, you have not praised the man you did not want to praise, you have not had to bear with the insults of his doorstep.

26

IT IS IN OUR power to discover the will of Nature from those matters on which we have no difference of opinion. For instance, when another man's slave has broken the wine-cup we are very ready to say at once, 'Such things must happen'. Know then that when your own cup is broken, you ought to behave in the same way as when your neighbour's was broken. Apply the same principle to higher matters. Is another's child or wife dead? Not one of us but would say, 'Such is the lot of man'; but when one's own dies, straightway one cries, 'Alas! miserable am I'. But we ought to remember what our feelings are when we hear it of another.

27

AS A MARK IS not set up for men to miss it, so there is nothing intrinsically evil in the world.

28

IF ANY ONE TRUSTED your body to the first man he met, you would be indignant, but yet you trust your mind to the chance corner, and allow it to be disturbed and confounded if he revile you; are you not ashamed to do so?

29

IN EVERYTHING YOU DO consider what comes first and what follows, and so approach it. Otherwise you will come to it with a good heart at first because you have not reflected on any of the consequences, and afterwards, when difficulties have appeared, you will desist to your shame. Do you wish to win at Olympia? So do I, by the gods, for it is a fine thing. But consider the first steps to it, and the consequences, and so lay your hand to the work. You must submit to discipline, eat to order, touch no sweets, train under compulsion, at a fixed hour, in heat and cold, drink no cold water, nor wine, except by order; you must hand yourself over completely to your trainer as you would to a physician, and then when the contest comes you must risk getting hacked, and sometimes dislocate your hand, twist your ankle, swallow plenty of sand, sometimes get a flogging, and with all this suffer defeat. When you have considered all this well, then enter on the athlete's course, if you still wish it. If you act without thought you will be behaving like children, who one day play at wrestlers, another day at gladiators, now sound the trumpet, and next strut the stage. Like them you will be now an athlete, now a gladiator, then orator, then philosopher, but nothing with all your soul. Like an ape, you imitate every sight you see, and one thing after another takes your fancy. When you undertake a thing you do it casually and halfheartedly, instead of considering it and looking at it all round. In the same way some people, when they see a philosopher and hear a man speaking like Euphrates (and indeed who can speak as he can?), wish to be philosophers themselves.

Man, consider first what it is you are undertaking; then look at your own powers and see if you can bear it. Do you want to compete in the pentathlon or in wrestling? Look to your arms, your thighs, see what your loins are like. For different men are born for different tasks. Do you suppose that if you do this you can live as you do now–eat and drink as you do now, indulge desire and discontent just as before? Nay, you must sit up late, work hard, abandon your own people, be looked down on by a mere slave, be ridiculed by those who meet you, get the worst of it in everything–in honour, in office, in justice, in every possible thing. This is what you have to consider: whether you are willing to pay this price for peace of mind, freedom, tranquillity. If not, do not come near; do not be, like the children, first a philosopher, then a tax-collector, then an orator, then one of Caesar's procurators. These callings do not agree. You must be one man, good or bad; you must develop either your Governing Principle, or your outward endowments; you must study either your inner man, or outward things–in a word, you must choose between the position of a philosopher and that of a mere outsider.

30

APPROPRIATE ACTS ARE IN general measured by the relations they are concerned with. 'He is your father.' This means you are called on to take care of him, give way to him in all things, bear with him if he reviles or strikes you.

'But he is a bad father.'

Well, have you any natural claim to a good father? No, only to a father.

'My brother wrongs me.'

Be careful then to maintain the relation you hold to him, and do not consider what he does, but what you must do if your purpose is to keep in accord with nature. For no one shall harm you, without your consent; you will only be harmed, when you think you are harmed. You will only discover what is proper to expect from neighbour, citizen, or praetor, if you get into the habit of looking at the relations implied by each.

31

FOR PIETY TOWARDS THE gods know that the most important thing is this: to have right opinions about them–that they exist, and that they govern the universe well and justly–and to have set yourself to obey them, and to give way to all that happens, following events with a free will, in the belief that they are fulfilled by the highest mind. For thus you will never blame the gods, nor accuse them of neglecting you. But this you cannot achieve, unless you apply your conception of good and evil to those things only which are in our power, and not to those which are out of our power. For if you apply your notion of good or evil to the latter, then, as soon as you fail to get what you will to get or fail to avoid what you will to avoid, you will be bound to blame and hate those you hold responsible. For every living creature has a natural tendency to avoid and shun what seems harmful and all that causes it, and to pursue and admire what is helpful and all that causes it. It is not possible then for one who thinks he is harmed to take pleasure in what he thinks is the author of the harm, any more than to take pleasure in the harm itself. That is why a father is reviled by his son, when he does not give his son a share of what the son regards as good things; thus Polynices and Eteocles were set at enmity with one another by thinking that a king's throne was a good thing. That is why the farmer, and the sailor, and the merchant, and those who lose wife or children revile the gods. For men's religion is bound up with their interest. Therefore he who makes it his concern rightly to direct his will to get and his will to avoid, is thereby making piety his concern. But it is proper on each occasion to make libation and sacrifice and to offer first-fruits according to the custom of our fathers, with purity and not in slovenly or careless fashion, without meanness and without extravagance.

32

WHEN YOU MAKE USE of prophecy remember that while you know not what the issue will be, but are come to learn it from the prophet, you do know before you come what manner of thing it is, if you are really a philosopher. For if the event is not in our control, it cannot be either good or evil. Therefore do not bring with you to the prophet the will to get or the will to avoid, and do not approach him with trembling, but with your mind made up, that the whole issue is indifferent and does not affect you and that, whatever it be, it will be in your power to make good use of it, and no one shall hinder this. With confidence then approach the gods as counsellors, and further, when the counsel is given you, remember whose counsel it is, and whom you will be disregarding if you disobey. And consult the oracle, as Socrates thought men should, only when the whole question turns upon the issue of events, and neither reason nor any art of man provides opportunities for discovering what lies before you. Therefore, when it is your duty to risk your life with friend or country, do not ask the oracle whether you should risk your life. For if the prophet warns you that the sacrifice is unfavourable, though it is plain that this means death or exile or injury to some part of your body, yet reason requires that even at this cost you must stand by your friend and share your country's danger. Wherefore pay heed to the greater prophet, Pythian Apollo, who cast out of his temple the man who did not help his friend when he was being killed.[6]

33

LAY DOWN FOR YOURSELF from the first a definite stamp and style of conduct, which you will maintain when you are alone and also in the society of men. Be silent for the most part, or, if you speak, say only what is necessary and in a few words. Talk, but rarely, if occasion calls you, but do not talk of ordinary things–of gladiators, or horse-races, or athletes, or of meats or drinks–these are topics that arise everywhere– but above all do not talk about men in blame or compliment or comparison. If you can, turn the conversation of your company by your talk to some fitting subject; but if you should chance to be isolated among

---

6   'Aelian, Var. Hist., tells how three men sent to Delphi had an encounter with robbers. One ran away, another accidentally killed the third in trying to defend him. The Oracle would have nothing to say to the runaway, and absolved the homicide.' (Matheson)

strangers, be silent. Do not laugh much, nor at many things, nor without restraint.

Refuse to take oaths, altogether if that be possible, but if not, as far as circumstances allow.

Refuse the entertainments of strangers and the vulgar.[7] But if occasion arise to accept them, then strain every nerve to avoid lapsing into the state of the vulgar. For know that, if your comrade have a stain on him, he that associates with him must needs share the stain, even though he be clean in himself.

For your body take just so much as your bare need requires, such as food, drink, clothing, house, servants, but cut down all that tends to luxury and outward show.

Avoid impurity to the utmost of your power before marriage, and if you indulge your passion, let it be done lawfully. But do not be offensive or censorious to those who indulge it, and do not be always bringing up your own chastity. If some one tells you that so and so speaks ill of you, do not defend yourself against what he says, but answer, 'He did not know my other faults, or he would not have mentioned these alone.'

It is not necessary for the most part to go to the games; but if you should have occasion to go, show that your first concern is for yourself; that is, wish that only to happen which does happen, and him only to win who does win, for so you will suffer no hindrance. But refrain entirely from applause, or ridicule, or prolonged excitement. And when you go away do not talk much of what happened there, except so far as it tends to your improvement. For to talk about it implies that the spectacle excited your wonder.

Do not go lightly or casually to hear lectures; but if you do go, maintain your gravity and dignity and do not make yourself offensive. When you are going to meet any one, and particularly some man of reputed eminence, set before your mind the thought, 'What would Socrates or Zeno have done?' and you will not fail to make proper use of the occasion.

When you go to visit some great man, prepare your mind by thinking that you will not find him in, that you will be shut out, that the doors will be slammed in your face, that he will pay no heed to you. And if in spite of all this you find it fitting for you to go, go and bear what happens and never say to yourself, 'It was not worth all this'; for that shows a vulgar mind and one at odds with outward things.

---

7   I.e., those untrained in philosophy.

In your conversation avoid frequent and disproportionate mention of your own doings or adventures; for other people do not take the same pleasure in hearing what has happened to you as you take in recounting your adventures.

Avoid raising men's laughter; for it is a habit that easily slips into vulgarity, and it may well suffice to lessen your neighbour's respect.

It is dangerous too to lapse into foul language; when anything of the kind occurs, rebuke the offender, if the occasion allow, and if not, make it plain to him by your silence, or a blush or a frown, that you are angry at his words.

34

WHEN YOU IMAGINE SOME pleasure, beware that it does not carry you away, like other imaginations. Wait a while, and give yourself pause. Next remember two things: how long you will enjoy the pleasure, and also how long you will afterwards repent and revile yourself. And set on the other side the joy and self-satisfaction you will feel if you refrain. And if the moment seems come to realize it, take heed that you be not overcome by the winning sweetness and attraction of it; set in the other scale the thought how much better is the consciousness of having vanquished it.

35

WHEN YOU DO A thing because you have determined that it ought to be done, never avoid being seen doing it, even if the opinion of the multitude is going to condemn you. For if your action is wrong, then avoid doing it altogether, but if it is right, why do you fear those who will rebuke you wrongly?

36

THE PHRASES, 'It is day' and 'It is night', mean a great deal if taken separately, but have no meaning if combined. In the same way, to choose the larger portion at a banquet may be worth while for your body, but if you want to maintain social decencies it is worthless. Therefore, when you are at meat with another, remember not only to consider the value of what is set before you for the body, but also to maintain your self-respect before your host.

37

IF YOU TRY TO act a part beyond your powers, you not only disgrace yourself in it, but you neglect the part which you could have filled with success.

38

AS IN WALKING YOU take care not to tread on a nail or to twist your foot, so take care that you do not harm your Governing Principle. And if we guard this in everything we do, we shall set to work more securely.

39

EVERY MAN'S BODY IS a measure for his property, as the foot is the measure for his shoe. If you stick to this limit, you will keep the right measure; if you go beyond it, you are bound to be carried away down a precipice in the end; just as with the shoe, if you once go beyond the foot, your shoe puts on gilding, and soon purple and embroidery. For when once you go beyond the measure there is no limit.

40

WOMEN FROM FOURTEEN YEARS upwards are called 'madam' by men. Wherefore, when they see that the only advantage they have got is to be marriageable, they begin to make themselves smart and to set all their hopes on this. We must take pains then to make them understand that they are really honoured for nothing but a modest and decorous life.

41

IT IS A SIGN OF a dull mind to dwell upon the cares of the body, to prolong exercise, eating, drinking, and other bodily functions. These things are to be done by the way; all your attention must be given to the mind.

4 2

WHEN A MAN SPEAKS evil or does evil to you, remember that he does or says it because he thinks it is fitting for him. It is not possible for him to follow what seems good to you, but only what seems good to him, so that, if his opinion is wrong, he suffers, in that he is the victim of deception. In the same way, if a composite judgement which is true is thought to be false, it is not the judgement that suffers, but the man who is deluded about it. If you act on this principle you will be gentle to him who reviles you, saying to yourself on each occasion, 'He thought it right.'

4 3

EVERYTHING HAS TWO HANDLES, one by which you can carry it, the other by which you cannot. If your brother wrongs you, do not take it by that handle, the handle of his wrong, for you cannot carry it by that, but rather by the other handle–that he is a brother, brought up with you, and then you will take it by the handle that you can carry by.

4 4

IT IS ILLOGICAL TO reason thus, 'I am richer than you, therefore I am superior to you', 'I am more eloquent than you, therefore I am superior to you.' It is more logical to reason, 'I am richer than you, therefore my property is superior to yours', 'I am more eloquent than you, therefore my speech is superior to yours.' You are something more than property or speech.

4 5

IF A MAN WASH quickly, do not say that he washes badly, but that he washes quickly. If a man drink much wine, do not say that he drinks badly, but that he drinks much. For till you have decided what judgement prompts him, how do you know that he acts badly? If you do as I say, you will assent to your apprehensive impressions and to none other.

46

ON NO OCCASION CALL yourself a philosopher, nor talk at large of your principles among the multitude, but act on your principles. For instance, at a banquet do not say how one ought to eat, but eat as you ought. Remember that Socrates had so completely got rid of the thought of display that when men came and wanted an introduction to philosophers he took them to be introduced; so patient of neglect was he. And if a discussion arise among the multitude on some principle, keep silent for the most part; for you are in great danger of blurting out some undigested thought. And when some one says to you, 'You know nothing', and you do not let it provoke you, then know that you are really on the right road. For sheep do not bring grass to their shepherds and show them how much they have eaten, but they digest their fodder and then produce it in the form of wool and milk. Do the same yourself; instead of displaying your principles to the multitude, show them the results of the principles you have digested.

47

WHEN YOU HAVE ADOPTED the simple life, do not pride yourself upon it, and if you are a water-drinker do not say on every occasion, 'I am a water-drinker.' And if you ever want to train laboriously, keep it to yourself and do not make a show of it. Do not embrace statues. If you are very thirsty take a good draught of cold water, and rinse you mouth and tell no one.

48

THE IGNORANT MAN'S POSITION and character is this: he never looks to himself for benefit or harm, but to the world outside him. The philosopher's position and character is that he always look to himself for benefit and harm.

The signs of one who is making progress are: he blames none, praises none, complains of none, accuses none, never speaks of himself as if he were somebody, or as if he knew anything. And if any one compliments him he laughs in himself at his compliment; and if one blames him, he makes no defence. He goes about like a convalescent, careful not to disturb his constitution on its road to recovery, until it has got firm hold. He has got rid of the will to get, and his will to avoid is directed no longer to what is beyond our power but only to what is in our power and contrary to nature. In all things he exercises his will without strain. If men regard him as foolish or ignorant he pays no heed. In one word, he keeps watch and guard on himself as his own enemy, lying in wait for him.

49

WHEN A MAN PRIDES himself on being able to understand and interpret the books of Chrysippus, say to yourself, 'If Chrysippus had not written obscurely this man would have had nothing on which to pride himself.'

What is my object? To understand Nature and follow her. I look then for some one who interprets her, and having heard that Chrysippus does

I come to him. But I do not understand his writings, so I seek an interpreter. So far there is nothing to be proud of. But when I have found the interpreter it remains for me to act on his precepts; that and that alone is a thing to be proud of. But if I admire the mere power of exposition, it comes to this–that I am turned into a grammarian instead of a philosopher, except that I interpret Chrysippus in place of Homer. Therefore, when some one says to me, 'Read me Chrysippus', when I cannot point to actions which are in harmony and correspondence with his teaching, I am rather inclined to blush.

50

WHATEVER PRINCIPLES YOU put before you, hold fast to them as laws which it will be impious to transgress. But pay no heed to what any one says of you; for this is something beyond your own control.

51

How long will you wait to think yourself worthy of the highest and transgress in nothing the clear pronouncement of reason? You have received the precepts which you ought to accept, and you have accepted them. Why then do you still wait for a master, that you may delay the amendment of yourself till he comes? You are a youth no longer, you are now a full-grown man. If now you are careless and indolent and are always putting off, fixing one day after another as the limit when you mean to begin attending to yourself, then, living or dying, you will make no progress but will continue unawares in ignorance. Therefore make up your mind before it is too late to live as one who is mature and proficient, and let all that seems best to you be a law that you cannot transgress. And if you encounter anything troublesome or pleasant or glorious or inglorious, remember that the hour of struggle is come, the Olympic contest is here and you may put off no longer, and that one day and one action determines whether the progress you have achieved is lost or maintained.

This was how Socrates attained perfection, paying heed to nothing but reason, in all that he encountered. And if you are not yet Socrates, yet ought you to live as one who would wish to be a Socrates.

52

The first and most necessary department of philosophy deals with the application of principles; for instance, 'not to lie'. The second deals with demonstrations; for instance, 'How comes it that one ought not to lie?' The third is concerned with establishing and analysing these processes; for instance, 'How comes it that this is a demonstration? What is demonstration, what is consequence, what is contradiction, what is true, what is false?' It follows then that the third department is necessary because of the second, and the second because of the first. The first is the most necessary part, and that in which we must rest. But we reverse the order: we occupy ourselves with the third, and make that our whole concern, and the first we completely neglect. Wherefore we lie, but are ready enough with the demonstration that lying is wrong.

53

ON EVERY OCCASION WE must have these thoughts at hand,

'Lead me, O Zeus, and lead me, Destiny,
Whither ordainèd is by your decree.
I'll follow, doubting not, or if with will
Recreant I falter, I shall follow still.'
                          [Cleanthes]

'Who rightly with necessity complies
In things divine we count him skilled and wise.'
                [Euripides, Fragment 965]

'Well, Crito, if this be the gods' will, so be it.'
[Plato, *Crito*, 43d]

'Anytus and Meletus have power to put me to death, but not to harm me,'
[Plato, *Apology*]

ROYAL

CLASSICS

ROYAL
CLASSICS